The Shell
Easy Bird
Guide

Written by Rob Hume   Illustrated by Peter Hayman

This edition published 2005, by Silverdale Books, on imprint of Bookmart Ltd.
Registered number 2372865, trading as Bookmart Ltd.
Blaby Road, Wigston, Leicester, LE18 4SE.
First published 1997 by Macmillan
an imprint of Macmillan Publishers Ltd.
25 Eccleston Place London SW1W 9NF
and Baslngstoke
Associated companies throughout the world

ISBN 1-84509-310-0

Conceived, edited, designed and produced by
Duncan Petersen Publishing Ltd, 31, Ceylon Road, London W14 OYP

5 7 9 8 6

A CIP catalogue record for this book is available from the British Library.

Typeset by Duncan Petersen Publishing Ltd.
Colour origination by PICA Overseas, Singapore
Printed in Italy by Fotolito Star, Seriate, Italy.

ORDER

In this guide the species follow each other in the usual way for a fieldguide – by general family relationship (taxonomic order). Those that evolved earliest as distinct species come first; those that did so last are at the end.

Generally similar types of birds (ducks, geese, waders and so on) are grouped together.

The best way to find the bird you thought you saw is to browse through pages looking for similar types of bird, then to narrow it down among them.

Contents

About this book

Can a bird guide *really* be easy? And why bother to make an 'easy' bird guide at all?

Let us be honest. Birdwatching is often a difficult craft. Birds themselves can be complicated. Some look very alike. Unusual lighting conditions can make a bird look quite unlike its normal self. Many species have different colours and patterns for males, females or young birds, and at different times of the year. A useful guide has to include at least the common plumage variations. Simplify too much, and you make identification harder than it ought to be.

But, if you can accept this last reservation, we believe that you will find *The Macmillan Guide to Birds* the easiest you've used, and that this will, in turn, make bird recognition easier and more fun than you ever thought possible. Which also answers the question 'Why did we bother?'

How easy?
In making this *the* easy bird guide, we've concentrated on several key points:

➤ **The photos are large and clear, and they work together with the artwork**. The photo is ideal for a lifelike impression; the artwork for feather details. We hope you will find that comparing the two is interesting in its own right, and gives some insights, and perhaps a fresh understanding, of birds that is not possible with other types of guide.

  We've deliberately shared out the important postures of each species between the photograph and the paintings – so if, for example, the photo shows a perched bird, then the paintings concentrate on the bird flight.

➤ **We show prime variations, but keep them as simple as possible** – giving only those likeliest to be seen.

➤ **Simple clear labels.** Where helpful, we've used leader lines to link the artwork labels to the part of the bird being described.

➤ **Simple language.** The text is an 'easy read' for everyone – nine years and upwards. No jargon, and no technical terms unless immediately understandable because they are linked by leader line to an illustration.

➤ **Maps supported by a few simple words of explanation** – always worth reading because birds occur in different places at different times of the year.

■ Purple shading means the bird is resident – stays all year.

■ Red shading shows where a bird is a summer visitor – arriving in the spring to breed, leaving for the south in autumn.

■ Blue shading generally means a winter visitor – visiting the mapped area between autumn and spring, coming from the colder north and east. For a few species (eg melodious warbler) it indicates areas where a bird turns up on migration, and this is explained in the captions next to the maps.

Bear in mind: This is a European guide, featuring some birds present in mainland Europe, but not in the UK.

➤ **A simple, thumbnail sketch of the bird's character and behaviour** under each photo. The way a bird behaves is often as much a clue to identification as its feather markings.

➤ **Lookalikes** are listed and described in a box.

➤ **A simple impression of size** – always an important clue – is given in the silhouette box. The measurement in centimetres is taken from the tip of the bird's beak to the end of the longest tail feather. The weight is given too, in grams or kilograms, to give an idea of the bird's bulk.

We think that birds are among the most compelling and enchanting interests anyone can have. They are everywhere – the most accessible of all wildlife – filling the air with their colour, calls, flight and song. Their extraordinary variety, even in the relatively small part of the globe covered by this book, reminds us every day of the richness of nature. The way they survive by adapting to 'niches', often highly precarious and specialized, opens up endless insights into the workings – and purpose – of nature.

We've spent most of our lives enjoying, and studying, birds for these reasons – and we have much more yet to learn. We hope that this book sets you on that course, too.

Rob Hume
Peter Hayman
2002

Basis for selection
The **main section** of this guide, pages 8 to 371, features more than 220 species which are

- Common
- Reasonably common
- Less common

over the whole of the book's range – Western and Northern Europe – or in *parts* of it. In general, the birds in the main section don't pose a major birdwatching challenge – they are easy to see; and they don't require a special journey.

In the back section, pages 372 to 380, we've included some 30 additional species which we feel readers should know about, but which don't deserve a place in the main section because they are:

- Scarce over the whole of the book's range
- Absent over most of the book's range, but locally common
- Restricted to a rare or specialized habitat
- Hard to see, or
- Require a special journey

Breeding information
Basic information on eggs, incubation and the age which young birds fly is given for interest and for completeness, except in the case of some species which do not nest in the area covered by the guide.

Finding birds

You need to think about three basics in order to find birds:

Distribution Some birds just aren't seen in certain areas. Others are everywhere. The maps in this guide are the quick way to find this out.

Habitat Most birds live in certain types of countryside and are never found elsewhere. Follow the hints in the text under **Places it prefers.**

Time of year It is exceptional to find a bird at completely the wrong time of year. Use the **Where and when** text, and the maps, to find out when you should expect to see it, and when not.

Field craft

Basic birdwatcher's skills:

🏹 **Keep quiet**: not only to prevent the birds from hearing you (in fact, they will probably see you first), but mainly so that you can hear them. You will find more birds by hearing them first – calls, songs, rustles in the undergrowth – than by seeing them first.

🏹 **Look at the *edges* of habitats**: there is most variety where habitats meet. Woodland birds are easier to see at the edges of clearings than inside the wood. Waterbirds, waterside birds and land birds drinking and bathing can all be found at the edges of a pool.

🏹 Remember that **water is a magnet for for many birds.** Visit lakes, reservoirs, flooded gravel pits, marshes or the seaside.

🏹 **Use your binoculars properly.** Learn how to set the adjustable eyepiece. Focus carefully. Raise the binoculars to your eyes while looking at the bird, rather than putting your eyes to the binoculars and swinging them round until you find the right spot – by then, the bird might have flown.

🏹 **Use your field guide.** People who are skilled at finding and identifying birds have all spent a great deal of time looking them up in field guides.

🏹 **Don't jump to conclusions** about what bird you've seen. Don't just find a picture that looks about right, and assume that that is what you saw. First guesses are wrong often enough to make it worth reading the text and thinking about whether *all* the clues add up.

🏹 **Go out with an expert.** It's amazing how much you can learn from someone with experience.

Little grebe

Tachybaptus ruficollis

Call high, short 'tililip' and loud, whinnying trill in summer

Juvenile has striped face, whiter cheeks

Dark all over in summer except for pale bill patch

Narrow, plain brown wings; legs trail in flight

Face dark red (glows chestnut in sun)

Browner, paler in winter, more contrasted dark crown and buffish face

Little grebe

25-29 cm 100-290 g

Sparrow

Blackish body except for puffy buff tail, but flanks show rufous when fluffed out

Little grebes are the smallest, roundest water birds, almost tailless. As buoyant as corks, they dive out of sight when they are disturbed. Underwater feeders, they dive to find small fish, water beetles and insect larvae. They can give their presence away in summer by a high, whinnying trill from some hidden spot on a wide river or from the corner of a reed-fringed lake. They manage to live on the smallest of pools.

The nest is a pad of damp weeds anchored to a drooping branch or stems of waterweed; the female lays four to six dull white eggs and may raise two broods. Like other grebes, they cover their eggs with weed to hide them from passing crows.

In winter, a few move to the sea, but little grebes are most often seen on fresh water all year round.

Smaller than a moorhen. Short-billed. May look slimmer, longer-necked when alert, especially in winter. Chunky head; bill short, straight, pointed. Flies low and fast, skittering over water at first. Rarely on land. Shy; often disappears under water.

WHERE AND WHEN All over Britain and Ireland except in highest areas; also on estuaries in winter.

PLACES IT PREFERS Anywhere from rivers, farm ponds and weedy pools to larger lakes and reservoirs.

LOOKALIKES

Teal, page 52, longer, with longer, broader duck bill.

Coot, page 116, blacker with deeper, paler bill.

Moorhen, page 116, has white patches under more pointed tail.

Black-necked and **Slavonian grebes,** pages 372, 373, more black and white in winter.

Red-necked grebe

Podiceps grisegena

In winter looks dark, drab, brownish-black and dull white. Neck dingy greyish, or tinged brown, breast whiter. Flanks silvery, streaked grey

Crown black to eye level; face dull white or smudged grey with white 'ear' mark in winter

Black cap, dull white face, reddish neck in breeding plumage

Bill yellow with black tip

Foreneck dark, chestnut-red, in summer unlike great crested

Red-necked grebe

40-46 cm 500-1,000 g

Sparrow

Looks dumpier than great crested grebe, with heavy bill and head, thicker neck; darker, heavier, bigger-billed than Slavonian

Call in summer loud, squealing 'ooaa-ek'

Red-necked grebes are extremely handsome birds of reed-fringed lakes in summer, but like other grebes they lose their finery outside the breeding season and become rather dark and dull. Then they can be hard to recognize since they are often at long range, on a large reservoir or out at sea, bobbing about in the waves. They dive much of the time: as soon as the binoculars are focused on them, they disappear. But they have a distinctive appearance and their regular arrival in late summer and autumn (sometimes still with fine red necks) on certain coasts, such as the eastern headlands and estuaries of Scotland and England, gives a clue as to what they are.

The nest, in waterside vegetation, is a typical grebe's heap of waterweed; three to four white eggs are incubated for a month.

Round-backed, tailless, large-headed. Colourful in spring and summer but drab by winter. Flies low, fast, direct, head held out and feet trailing or drooped. Dives underwater for food and to escape disturbance, often reappearing a long way off.

WHEN AND WHERE Breeds in Northern Europe; in winter moves west and south, always scarce in UK.

PLACES IT PREFERS Reedy lakes, open pools, sheltered coasts.

LOOKALIKES

Great crested grebe, page 12, whiter, more slender.
Slavonian grebe, page 372 smarter, smaller, with shorter bill.
Young **coot,** page 116, has thick, blunt bill, short neck.

Great crested grebe

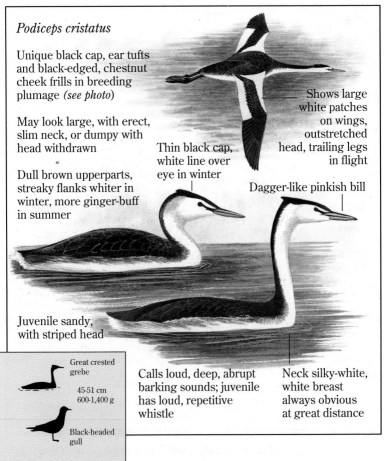

Podiceps cristatus

Unique black cap, ear tufts and black-edged, chestnut cheek frills in breeding plumage *(see photo)*

May look large, with erect, slim neck, or dumpy with head withdrawn

Dull brown upperparts, streaky flanks whiter in winter, more ginger-buff in summer

Juvenile sandy, with striped head

Thin black cap, white line over eye in winter

Shows large white patches on wings, outstretched head, trailing legs in flight

Dagger-like pinkish bill

Great crested grebe

45-51 cm

600-1,400 g

Black-headed gull

Calls loud, deep, abrupt barking sounds; juvenile has loud, repetitive whistle

Neck silky-white, white breast always obvious at great distance

A few decades ago great crested grebes were rare and persecuted for their dense, soft, almost fur-like feathers. Now, thanks to protection and also to the spread of flooded gravel pits, they are widespread waterbirds, typical of larger lakes but at home on slow reaches of big rivers.

They are remarkably elegant, slender creatures, with extraordinary head decorations from around the end of January to mid-autumn, used in displays in early spring.

Like other grebes they make a semi-floating nest of dank weed in waterside vegetation, anchored to reeds or willows. The female lays three to four dull white eggs, which quickly get stained, and hatch after 28 days. The chicks call to be fed with loud, shrill whistles throughout the summer.

Slender, elegant, mallard-sized. Bill held level.
Remarkable displays in spring, pairs face-to-face
with wagging heads, or rising breast-to-breast.
Pairs in summer; in winter, groups or larger flocks.
Dives underwater, reappearing far away.

WHERE AND WHEN Over most of Britain and Ireland except for northern Scotland.

PLACES IT PREFERS Large rivers, open pools and lakes, reservoirs; in winter, larger reservoirs, estuaries, the sea.

LOOKALIKES

Only **pintail**, page 56, is so slim, white-necked – but it has long tail.
   Winter **red-throated diver,** page 372, shorter-necked, bill up-tilted. In winter **black-necked** and **Slavonian grebes**, pages 372, 373, similar but smaller; **red-necked grebe**, page 10, chunkier, thicker-necked.

Fulmar

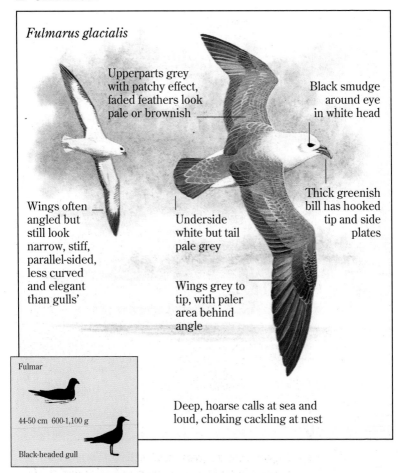

Fulmarus glacialis

Upperparts grey with patchy effect, faded feathers look pale or brownish

Black smudge around eye in white head

Wings often angled but still look narrow, stiff, parallel-sided, less curved and elegant than gulls'

Underside white but tail pale grey

Thick greenish bill has hooked tip and side plates

Wings grey to tip, with paler area behind angle

Fulmar

44-50 cm 600-1,100 g

Black-headed gull

Deep, hoarse calls at sea and loud, choking cackling at nest

From remote northern islands, fulmars have spread around British coasts and on to a few other European cliffs in the past hundred years or so. Some nest on low, earth cliffs in south-east England. On Scottish islands they take to old stone walls, steep grassy banks and even inland crags.

Yet the home of the fulmar is really the open sea and the high, sheer cliffs of the most spectacular coasts. It is a bird adapted to flight in the turbulent air above ocean waves, gliding in steep arcs and long, low swoops which carry it great distances using little energy. On land it can barely stand.

The nest is a simple scrape on a broad ledge or at the foot of an earth bank. A single, big white egg is laid and incubated for eight weeks. The chick flies at eight weeks.

Bigger than a pigeon, with longer wings. Stiff-winged in flight, much dumpier-bodied and thicker-necked than gulls. Squats on belly on cliff ledge, otherwise seen in air or on water. Swims with head erect, tail slightly cocked. Pairs at nest noisy.

WHERE AND WHEN All coasts but commonest in north; any month.

PLACES IT PREFERS Open sea; off headlands and islands; sea cliffs; a few remote inland crags in far north.

LOOKALIKES

Herring gull, page 170, has white tail; black and white wing tips; pale eye; glides on arched wings.

Kittiwake, page 174, has short black legs, black triangle at wing tip, white tail.

Manx shearwater, page 16, much more slender; black and white.

Manx shearwater

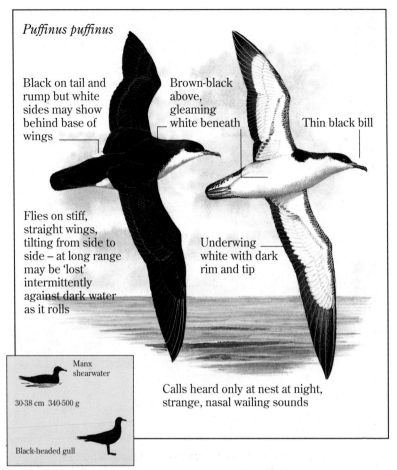

Puffinus puffinus

Black on tail and rump but white sides may show behind base of wings

Brown-black above, gleaming white beneath

Thin black bill

Flies on stiff, straight wings, tilting from side to side – at long range may be 'lost' intermittently against dark water as it rolls

Underwing white with dark rim and tip

Manx shearwater

30-38 cm 340-500 g

Black-headed gull

Calls heard only at nest at night, strange, nasal wailing sounds

Manx shearwaters are made for a life at sea and come to land only to nest and then only at night. They scramble clumsily, using feet, wings and bill, vulnerable to predators such as gulls. Yet they can find their own nest burrow, in the dark, in a colony of tens of thousands of pairs: to our ears the colony is a fantastic cacophony of unearthly calls, but to the shearwaters the call of a mate in a deep tunnel must be unique.

At sea they go far afield to feed, in winter roaming the Mid and South Atlantic. They catch small fish and squid in shallow dives or deeper plunges, often in excited flocks.

The nest is a deep tunnel or rabbit burrow where one white egg is laid in May, hatching in 51 to 54 days. The chick is deserted at 60 days, but does not leave until 72 to 74 days old.

Always over sea unless on breeding islands at night or blown inland by storms. Flies low, gliding with wind, tilting to use air currents. In gales, rises higher in tilting arcs. In calm air, wing beats quick, stiff, laboured, glides shorter.

WHERE AND WHEN Breeds on remote islands in north and west; otherwise around most coasts, spring to autumn.

PLACES IT PREFERS Open sea. Rocky slopes, scree.

LOOKALIKES

Fulmar, page 14, stockier, much paler grey with white head.

Young **gulls** all paler, less contrasted, with broader-based, more angled wings, pale-based tails.

Gannet

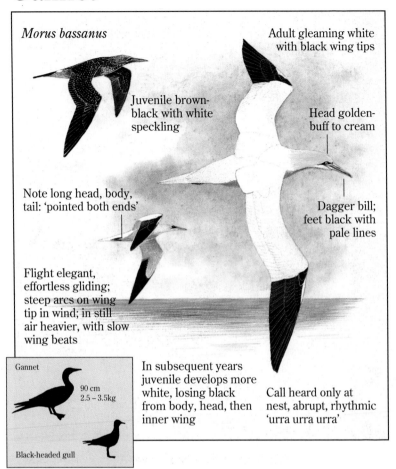

Morus bassanus

Adult gleaming white with black wing tips

Juvenile brown-black with white speckling

Head golden-buff to cream

Note long head, body, tail: 'pointed both ends'

Dagger bill; feet black with pale lines

Flight elegant, effortless gliding; steep arcs on wing tip in wind; in still air heavier, with slow wing beats

Gannet
90 cm
2.5 – 3.5kg

Black-headed gull

In subsequent years juvenile develops more white, losing black from body, head, then inner wing

Call heard only at nest, abrupt, rhythmic 'urra urra urra'

Few birds have the majesty of a gannet. At sea it is the biggest North Atlantic bird, its span close to 2 metres. On its nest ledge it has a presence unmatched by lesser seabirds: it is glorious, gleaming white and warm golden-buff. In a tight-packed colony of thousands, it becomes simply extraordinary, part of a mass of action and noise, thousands of calls mingling into a peculiarly rhythmic, mechanical chorus.

There are few gannet colonies in Britain and Ireland, yet they contain 60 per cent of all gannets; the biggest have 30,000 pairs. Elsewhere in Europe only a handful of sites are occupied, but gannets can often be seen offshore from Norway to Spain.

The nest is a heap of vegetation on a ledge. One egg hatches after 45 days and the chick leaves the ledge after two months.

Much bigger than herring gull. Adult gleams white at sea. Long-winged, with long head and dagger bill, narrow, pointed tail. On land big, goose-like, with unwieldy webbed feet. Plunges into sea with big splash, or in low, angled, headlong dive.

WHERE AND WHEN All coasts, mostly north and west in summer and autumn.

PLACES IT PREFERS Remote rocky islands, some close inshore (Bass Rock) a few mainland cliffs; open sea, larger firths.

LOOKALIKES

Gulls are shorter-tailed, smaller-billed. Young **great black-backed gull,** page 172, square-tailed, less solid brown than young gannet. Piebald immature gannet more patchy than any gull.
   Great northern diver, page 372, far less mobile in flight.

Cormorant

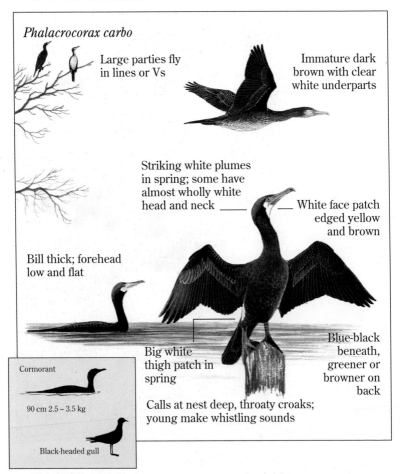

Phalacrocorax carbo

Large parties fly in lines or Vs

Immature dark brown with clear white underparts

Striking white plumes in spring; some have almost wholly white head and neck ____

____ White face patch edged yellow and brown

Bill thick; forehead low and flat

Big white thigh patch in spring

Blue-black beneath, greener or browner on back

Cormorant

90 cm 2.5 – 3.5 kg

Calls at nest deep, throaty croaks; young make whistling sounds

Black-headed gull

A spring cormorant is striking: not quite beautiful but certainly handsome. Some in Britain and most on mainland Europe have a virtually white head, while most briefly get long, wispy white plumes on the back of the head and neck in spring. The square white thigh patch adds more contrast. Most British and Scandinavian cormorants are coastal nesters, but some now breed inland in England and many do so in the Low Countries and along large European rivers, often near heronries. More familiar is the long, low shape of a cormorant swimming on a big lake or a sheltered estuary, typical haunts all year round.

Nests – small platforms or huge piles of sticks – are built on broad ledges of sheer cliffs or in trees. Three to four eggs hatch after 26 to 29 days. The chicks fly after a month or so.

Goose-sized, long-tailed. Thick bill has small hook at tip. Bill angled upwards when swimming. Often stands with wings half spread. Swims low in water, back sometimes awash, tail hidden. Flies high; note long tail, head held forward, angular wings.

WHERE AND WHEN Widespread, especially in winter.

PLACES IT PREFERS Large lakes and reservoirs; estuaries; open coasts.

LOOKALIKES

Shag, page 22, very similar but sleeker, slimmer, with rounder head on thinner neck, thinner bill. Shag never has white thigh patches nor such extensive white on chin.

  Divers sleeker, with pointed bills.

Shag

Phalacrocorax aristotelis

Curly crest for a brief period in spring

Upperwing fades paler in summer

Bill held angled up; forehead steep

Juvenile dull dark brown with pale chin spot

Yellow gape patch

Shag

75 cm 1,500-2,200 g

Black-headed gull

Adult overall oily green-black

Calls at nest deep, throaty and nasal barks

While cormorants like shallow water over tidal mud, sheltered bays and inland waters, shags are birds of the fresh, windblown, open sea and places where surging surf washes the rocks. Usually only after a prolonged gale are they seen inland.

Although a shag is smaller than a cormorant, this is not always at all obvious when the bird stands alone: it looks like the large and impressive bird that it is.

It must have a broad cliff ledge, often beneath a shady overhang, on which to nest. It builds up a huge tangle of seaweed and stems, laying three or more eggs, which hatch after 33 days. The chicks fly when 53 days old. Like the cormorant, it gives away where it has made its nest by producing enormous amounts of white splashings below.

Dark, oily-green adults and brown immatures look sleek, with snaky neck, round head, slim, blob-tipped bill. Flies low, often in ones and twos. May feed in large, close-packed flocks. Often off rocky coasts. Flight fast with quick, deep wing beats.

WHERE AND WHEN All rocky coasts; rare inland.

PLACES IT PREFERS Cliffs, rough seas off rocks, open sea.

LOOKALIKES

Cormorant, page 20, is bigger, flatter-headed, thicker-billed. Shag tends to leap clear of water as it dives; cormorant slides under. Adult shag all dark except yellow chin; adult cormorant has yellow and white face. Juvenile shag is brown with pale chin spot; juvenile cormorant white beneath.

Little egret

Egretta garzetta

Pure white all over

Twin head plumes in summer

Bill grey-black with bluer base

Legs black with yellow feet: sometimes muddy or dull but usually obvious

Straight wispy plumes on back in spring

Flies with head tucked back into shoulders, feet trailing behind

Little egret
53-58 cm
450-600g

Sparrow

The shape of a small heron, but especially slender, very thin in front or rear view

Usually silent

Until the 1980s little egrets were rare in Northern Europe, but they have since increased along the coasts, although not inland. In much of Southern Europe, however, it is more familiar, a typical bird of marshy places, salt pans and sheltered estuaries or rocky coves. Its dazzling white plumage is startling, visible at great range.

A fishing little egret is a joy to watch, as it stands and stares, runs forward, jinks sideways or leaps back, suddenly shooting out its dagger bill on a long, pencil-thin neck. Often it will try to stand on floating weed, flapping its wings to keep balanced and prevent itself from sinking.

Nests are in trees, made of sticks, often in heronries. The three to five eggs hatch after 21 days; the young fly in 45 days.

Size of large gull or mallard on long legs. Bill slim, dagger-shaped. Legs long, slender. Wings rather broad, but quite long, angled in flight. Stands upright; often perches in trees. Active, erratic, jerky feeder, often in shallow water.

WHERE AND WHEN Widespread in Southern Europe; coasts of southern Britain, France.

PLACES IT PREFERS Salt pans, lakes, shallow estuaries, rocky shores.

LOOKALIKES

Grey heron, page 26, much bigger, greyer – looks pale in strong sun but never so white.

Spoonbill, page 30, much bigger, heavier and slower, flies with head outstretched.

Beware gulls in sunshine at long range.

Grey heron

Ardea cinerea

Pale grey above; dark grey in shade, whitish in strong sun

Underside white with black flank marks

Dark flight feathers contrast with pale front of wing in flight

Immature has dull, plainer grey head and neck

Black spots on front of neck; black cap and crest

Bill yellowish, but pink, orange or red in spring

Grey heron

90 cm
1,100-1,750 g

Black-headed gull

Nests in treetops

Typical call loud, explosive, harsh 'frairnk'; bill-rattling at nest

In much of Europe, the grey heron is one of the biggest regular birds, alongside the mute swan or white stork. In flight it is unmistakable, plodding along on its arched wings in a heavy, direct way unlike any other bird. More often, however, it is seen standing by water, or even in a field, sometimes several at a time, looking hunched, grey and dejected. Its long neck is held erect or leaning forwards when it wants to fish. Close views reveal a bright eye, a wispy crest and an intelligent, aware expression. It really is a handsome and charismatic bird.

Herons nest in colonies (heronries) numbering from one or two pairs to more than a hundred. Nests are built in trees (occasionally in reeds); three to five eggs are laid in late winter and hatch after 25 days. The young fly at 50 days or more.

Big, upstanding, but head often hunched into shoulders. Stands stock still or walks slowly, silently forward when fishing. In flight head held back, long legs trailed. When disturbed, launches steeply into air with sudden flurry of broad wings.

WHERE AND WHEN All of Britain and Ireland except highest moors and hills, all year.

PLACES IT PREFERS Riversides, streams, lakes, all kinds of sea shores.

LOOKALIKES

Crane, page 118, more elegant, head and neck outstretched in flight.
  White stork, page 28, white, head and neck outstreched in flight.

White stork

Ciconia ciconia

Enormous; bright to dirty white above and below, white head

In flight shows enormous wings of great length, held flat, fingered at tips

Holds neck and legs outstretched, slightly drooped

Bill red: can look paler with dry mud, or dull and dirty

Legs red, often muddy

Black on wings looks more extensive in flight than at rest

White stork

95-105 cm 3-4 kg

Sparrow

Rattles bill at nest

In recent decades, white storks have faced severe problems in Western Europe as traditional ways of farming have declined in the face of intensive drainage and excessive use of pesticides. Electrocution on overhead wires and droughts in Africa caused many deaths. There has been some recovery in Spain and reintroduction schemes have been successful in the Low Countries and, especially, in France.

The white stork is a well-loved bird, always welcome in a village. Pairs choose prominent positions on buildings for their nests; they will also use tall trees – and poles with cartwheels fixed on top, specially made for them.

Storks migrate to Africa using routes with the shortest possible sea crossings, concentrating at Gibraltar and Istanbul.

Much bigger than heron: swan-sized. Long legs; strides slowly on ground. Often on buildings or tall poles. Nests on chimneys, church towers, building lasting structure of sticks.

WHERE AND WHEN Much of Central and Southern Europe; rare in Britain.

PLACES IT PREFERS Traditional farmland with marshy places, pools, streams; villages.

LOOKALIKES
Black stork, page 376, has black neck and chest.
Grey heron, page 26, has striped head and neck, duller bill and legs, much smaller.

Spoonbill

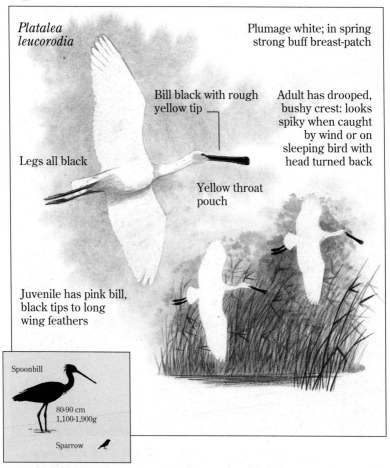

Platalea leucorodia

Plumage white; in spring strong buff breast-patch

Bill black with rough yellow tip

Adult has drooped, bushy crest: looks spiky when caught by wind or on sleeping bird with head turned back

Legs all black

Yellow throat pouch

Juvenile has pink bill, black tips to long wing feathers

Spoonbill

80-90 cm
1,100-1,900g

Sparrow

Walking slowly forwards in shallow water, striding steadily almost in a human manner, the spoonbill sweeps its partly-open bill from side to side under water. It uses the sensitive tip to feel for fish and other small fry which it then snaps up and swallows with a deft backward jerk.

No other bird that wades like this is so large, heavily built and white; a clear view of the unique bill makes identification simple. In the breeding season, spoonbills find shallow lakes surrounded by reeds and dense bushes in which they build bulky nests of sticks and reed stems. In Spain they nest in taller oaks, often mixed with grey and night herons and cattle egrets. The female usually lays four eggs, at four-day intervals, which hatch into chicks with short bills: the special shape develops later.

 Heron-sized, thickset, with sturdy, s-curved neck. Long, thick legs. Bill looks long, slim and down-tilted from side; reveals broad, flat, spoonlike tip from any other angle. In flight, large, heavy, with long, slender neck outstretched and big feet trailed.

WHERE AND WHEN Rare in UK; in Europe mainly in lowland and coastal areas in summer.

PLACES IT PREFERS Reed-fringed lagoons, lakes, muddy estuaries.

LOOKALIKES

Only **egrets** and **swans** are as white; **little egret,** page 24, much smaller.

Mute swan

Cygnus olor

Adult all white

Bill rich orange with black knob, nostrils and tip

Legs grey to black

Juvenile drab brown, soon patched white and pale brown

Juvenile has grey bill with black base and tip; gradually becomes pink, then orange, with age

Mute swan

150 cm 8-14 kg

Sparrow

Mute swans are usually semi-tame and approachable, walking on to shelving shores to beg for bread, but also hissing and snorting in a show of nervy aggression. Although by no means mute - they make a variety of unimpressive, strangled trumpeting sounds - the typical sound of a mute swan is actually the throb of the wings in flight.

Tradition has it that a beat from a swan's wing is enough to break a man's leg: not true, but the bird is nevertheless formidable when something comes near its big, waterside nest, built up high from water level and made from reeds and grass. A male swan in the passion of territorial defence will chase any object which floats by, apparently invading its territory.

Five to seven large white eggs are laid, hatching after 35 days.

Huge; on water often has pointed tail cocked. Wings arched in aggression. Neck may be curved, thick-looking and held back. Also swims straight-necked, but bill angled down. Flies with head and neck stretched out.

WHERE AND WHEN Widespread except in upland regions.

PLACES IT PREFERS Lakes, broad rivers, flooded pits, sheltered estuaries.

LOOKALIKES

Whooper swan, page 34, similar in size, with wedge-shaped head, black and yellow bill held flat, square tail.

Bewick's swan, page 34, like whooper but smaller, head rounder.

Whooper & Bewick's swans

Whooper swan
Cygnus cygnus

Bewick's swan
Cygnus columbianus

A whooper is all white with black legs

Bewick's legs are black, rarely yellow

Bewick's swan is all white

Whooper's bill is long, wedge-shaped, with pointed triangle of yellow each side joined across base

Bewick's bill is black with yellow patches at sides, often separated by black but may be joined across top

Musical honking, babbling calls

Evocative calls: loud, clanging, trumpeting notes

Whooper swan

Bewick's swan

120 cm
5-7 kg

145-160 cm
8-10 kg

Sparrow

Juvenile whoopers are dull brownish-grey; later patchy grey and white, with grey bill marked almost white at side

Juvenile Bewick's is plain greyish, later patchy. Bill grey with whitish sides, often marked with pale pink and crimson

These two swans look alike and are both winter visitors to north-western Europe. After breeding in Iceland and Arctic Eurasia, whoopers move south in winter. They are frequent in parts of Scotland, the Low Countries and a few isolated parts of Wales and eastern England. Here they feed in fields and roost on lakes, estuaries or floods. The nest is huge. Five or six eggs hatch after 35 to 42 days and the young fly at eight weeks.

Bewick's swans are characteristic of lowlands, less often found on the fringes of northern hills than whoopers. In some areas, such as East Anglian floods and parts of the Netherlands, both swans (also mute swan, page 32) feed and roost together in some spectacular gatherings. In the UK Bewick's swans arrive in November and leave in March, truly wild, beautiful swans.

34

A **whooper** *is as large as a mute swan but often straighter-necked, bill held flat, short tail held flat. Musical calls unlike mutes. More agile on land.*

◁ *Whooper swan*

Bewick's *is small, more goose-like but can look slim-necked too. Head round, bill slightly more slender, less flat. Also short- and flat-tailed.*

Bewick's swan ▷

WHERE AND WHEN winters in northern and western Britain, East Anglia. Breeds in Iceland.	**WHERE AND WHEN** North Sea and Baltic Coasts of north-western Europe, including UK and Ireland, April to October.
Whooper swan	Bewick's swan
PLACES IT PREFERS Pastures, stubbles, lakesides.	**PLACES IT PREFERS** Wet pastures and arable land.

Bean & pink-footed geese

Bean goose
Anser fabalis

Bean has big white stern

Bean has a long head and very dark brown neck, breast paler

No dark bars on bean goose's belly

Bill of bean is variably black with orange band or all orange

Bean's legs are yellow-orange

Pink-footed goose
Anser brachyrhynchus

Bill of pink-footed is brown-black with narrow pink band

Pink-footed: round head; short, very dark neck contrasts with creamy-fawn breast

Pink-footed's back is bluer, than bean's, barred whitish

Bean goose
71-89 cm 3-4 kg

Pink-footed goose
75 cm 2-3 kg

Sparrow

Bean has deep, throaty 'ah-unk' or 'kayakak' calls in flight

Legs deep to pale pink

No black on pink-footed's belly

These two geese visit Western Europe in winter and look quite similar. Although still numerous in localized parts of The Netherlands and other lowland areas of Europe, bean geese are rare and very restricted in Britain. They often mix with other geese, notably pink-footed and white-fronted geese, yet special needs limit them to traditionally favoured places.

Pink-feet are among the most numerous of wild geese, forming splendid flocks which fly out to feed in the fields at dawn and return to their lake or estuary roost each evening. Their loud, babbling calls, with high 'wink wink' notes, make the classic goose music loved by many people who enjoy wild and impressive creatures. Both lay three to six eggs which hatch within 26 to 29 days; the goslings fly when about eight weeks old.

Bean goose *is large, long-headed, dark. Upperparts brown, more or less barred with crisp buff lines. Upperwing dark in flight.*

◁ *Bean goose*

Pink-foot *more delicate, round-headed and much smaller-billed. Upper-parts greyer and forewing blue-grey in flight, chest paler buff.*

Pink-footed goose ▷

WHERE AND WHEN in UK, only one regular site in Norfolk; rarely elsewhere; November to February.

Bean goose

WHERE AND WHEN In Low Countries, East Anglia, southern Scotland, Lancashire.

Pink-footed goose

PLACES IT PREFERS Damp meadows, ploughed fields, lakes.

PLACES IT PREFERS Meadows, ploughed fields, marshes, estuaries.

White-fronted goose

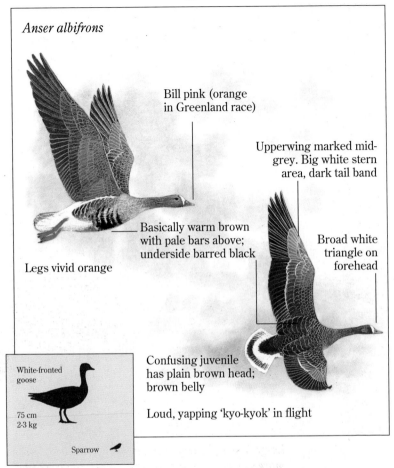

Anser albifrons

Bill pink (orange in Greenland race)

Upperwing marked mid-grey. Big white stern area, dark tail band

Basically warm brown with pale bars above; underside barred black

Broad white triangle on forehead

Legs vivid orange

Confusing juvenile has plain brown head; brown belly

Loud, yapping 'kyo-kyok' in flight

White-fronted goose

75 cm
2-3 kg

Sparrow

White-fronts are abundant in the Netherlands in winter, their increase there probably responsible for the decline in Britain where traditional sites have been deserted and once-large flocks have declined. These are 'Russian' birds which breed in Eastern Europe and Asia. Another form, darker with a deeper orange bill, breeds in Greenland and visits western Scotland, Ireland and one or two places in Wales each winter. Eastern birds tend to be in larger flocks in lower, more open country; Greenland geese feed in smaller groups, in rough fields and marshland, sometimes high on bleak moors.

White-fronts breed in the tundra of the far north, using islands in rivers or raised areas in bogs. The families usually stay together until the following year – just as with other geese.

Large, but agile, angular goose. Bill slimmer, body more slender than a 'farmyard' goose; walks more easily, leaps into flight with ease. Often flies in long lines and V-shapes. Calls sharp, yelping, like pack of small dogs, with yodelling effect.

WHERE AND WHEN Germany and Low Countries have large numbers; in UK in Norfolk, Kent, Gloucestershire; Greenland birds in north and west. October to March.

PLACES IT PREFERS Coastal marshes, pasture; rough grassland, moors.

LOOKALIKES

Young birds without white forehead or black belly like **bean, pink-footed** and **greylag geese,** pages 36 and 40, but bill and leg colours separate them. Greylag has much paler forewing. Pinkfoot has rounder head.

Greylag goose

Anser anser

Forewing (above and below) contrasted very pale grey

Upperparts brown, barred creamy

White stern. Belly pale with, at most, tiny black dots

Bill large, heavy, bright orange

Head and neck pale grey-brown, but can look dark in shadow or turned at angle to sun

Greylag goose

80 cm 3-4 kg

Sparrow

Legs pale pink; occasionally somewhat orange

Hard, rattling 'ang-unk' cackle in flight; calls like farmyard goose

Greylag geese were once common over much of lowland Britain and Europe – our romantic view of wild geese flying down from the north in winter is relatively new. It is odd then that the introduction of greylags into southern Britain has 'spoiled' them for some people. Here is a creature, once revered as a wild bird and a mark of the passing seasons, which now lives beside tame ducks and Canada geese on town lakes and creates something of a nuisance with its boisterous aggression and abundance of droppings. Some of the magic has gone, but it is still pleasant to see them flying wild and free.

The nest, on the ground or on an island, is made of heather and grass stems, lined with down. Four to six eggs hatch after 28 days; the young can fly at eight weeks.

Very big goose, like lighter version of 'farmyard' type. Big head and bill heaviest of all wild geese. Clattering, cackling call notes least musical among geese. Wild birds very wary but increasing numbers of introduced ones are often semi-tame.

WHERE AND WHEN Wild birds breed in far north of Scotland, Iceland; in winter in much of Scotland. Introduced birds in lowland areas almost everywhere, all year.

PLACES IT PREFERS Open pasture, marshes, reservoirs; also now town parks, gravel pits.

LOOKALIKES

Young **white-fronted,** page 38, lighter, more agile.

   Bean goose, page 36, darker, longer in head and bill, with more contrast between neck and chest.

   Canada goose, page 42, always has black neck.

Canada goose

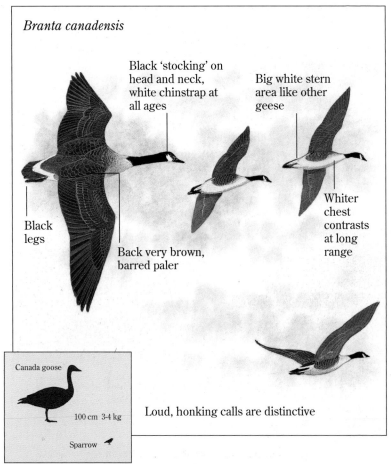

Branta canadensis

Black 'stocking' on head and neck, white chinstrap at all ages

Big white stern area like other geese

Black legs

Back very brown, barred paler

Whiter chest contrasts at long range

Canada goose

100 cm 3-4 kg

Sparrow

Loud, honking calls are distinctive

Originally brought to Britain as an ornamental bird, the Canada goose has become widespread, spreading to adjacent parts of Europe. Because wild geese are linked with folklore and especially the wonders of migration, the presence of semi-tame, resident Canada geese has not always been greeted with pleasure by birdwatchers: some feel that they are a cheat, and view them as little more than farmyard birds. But there is no doubt that they are big, handsome birds and a welcome addition to local birdlife almost everywhere they occur. For many, they are the only wild geese likely to be seen.

The nest is often on an island, close to water, with five to six cream-coloured eggs incubated for 28 days. The goslings can fly when they are six weeks old.

Large, long-necked. Frequently in large flocks, feeding at water's edge, or flying in V shapes and long, ragged lines, neck outstretched. Wings long, broad; action heavy. Form pairs in spring, territory on island or isolated bank of lake.

WHERE AND WHEN All year round; mostly in south and east of UK.

PLACES IT PREFERS Large lowland lakes, grassy meadows, flooded pits.

LOOKALIKES

No other goose has black neck and white chinstrap.

Barnacle goose, page 44, has black chest, grey body.

Brent goose, page 44, much smaller, blacker.

Beware flying cormorants in V formations.

Barnacle & brent geese

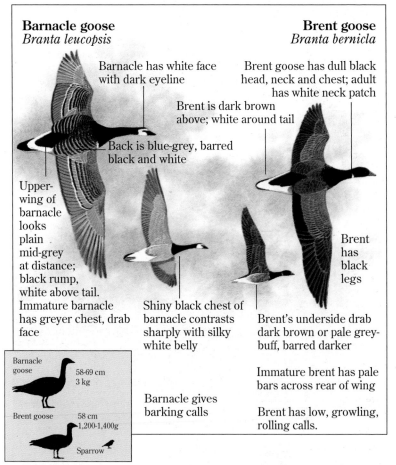

Barnacle goose
Branta leucopsis

Brent goose
Branta bernicla

Barnacle has white face with dark eyeline

Brent goose has dull black head, neck and chest; adult has white neck patch

Brent is dark brown above; white around tail

Back is blue-grey, barred black and white

Upper-wing of barnacle looks plain mid-grey at distance; black rump, white above tail. Immature barnacle has greyer chest, drab face

Brent has black legs

Shiny black chest of barnacle contrasts sharply with silky white belly

Brent's underside drab dark brown or pale grey-buff, barred darker

Immature brent has pale bars across rear of wing

Barnacle gives barking calls

Brent has low, growling, rolling calls.

Barnacle goose   58-69 cm   3 kg

Brent goose   58 cm   1,200-1,400g

Sparrow

Barnacle geese breed in isolated parts of Greenland, Siberia, and Spitsbergen, and birds from these places rcmain separate in winter. Those from Spitsbergen fly to the Solway Firth, Russian ones to the Low Countries and Greenland birds reach western Scotland and filter through into Ireland.

Once regarded as endangered, brent geese have increased with protection and are now familiar on many coasts. Two forms reach Europe in winter, pale ones from Greenland and dark birds from Siberia. The dark-bellied ones are the most abundant, while pale brents are local in Ireland and north-eastern England. Three to five eggs hatch after 24 to 26 days and the young fly about 40 days later.

Barnacle goose *is small-medium, handsome. Thick neck, round head, small, stubby bill. Flies in tight packs.*

◁ *Barnacle goose*

Brent goose *is small, stocky, long-headed; always looks dark with broad white rear end. Feeds and flies in dense flocks with little pattern. Sometimes in long lines when migrating.*

Brent goose ▷

WHERE AND WHEN October to April in Western Isles of Scotland and Ireland, south-western Scotland; rare in East Anglia.

Barnacle goose

Brent goose

WHERE AND WHEN north-western European estuaries, October to May.

PLACES IT PREFERS Remote islands, estuaries, damp pastures, marshes.

PLACES IT PREFERS Mudflats and adjacent salt marsh, pasture, cereal fields.

Shelduck

Tadorna tadorna

At long range looks very white

Black head glossed dark green

Band of orange-brown around front of body is unique

Legs pink

Bill red

Shelduck

60 cm
950-1,400 g

Sparrow

Juvenile drab, dull white with brown-black marks, whitish face

Staccato, deep calls and whistles in spring

Shelducks are generally thought of as seashore ducks, but now many live on flooded gravel pits inland. Others turn up on reservoirs from time to time while on migration.

North-western European shelducks mostly leave for the big estuaries around the eastern North Sea in late summer, to replace their feathers where they are safe and to be sure of ample food during a brief period of flightlessness. This is an example of a 'moult migration', a journey specifically to reach a suitable area for this annual event.

Nests are found in haystacks, under brambles, in ditches and in rabbit burrows. Up to 15 eggs are laid; the young fly at 45 days. A few adults act as 'aunties', looking after young shelducks which gather together in big flocks.

Large, goose-like. Big round head, with 'knob' at base of bill. Long legs, but slow, waddling walk. Heavy, goose-like flight. Frequently in loose flocks or pairs scattered over large area.

WHERE AND WHEN Most British and Western European shores, all year.

PLACES IT PREFERS Muddy bays, estuaries, sandy beaches and dunes.

LOOKALIKES

Nothing else so contrasted. Juvenile lacks bright bill and black head, but resembles no other wild duck or goose.

Shoveler, page 60, much smaller, long and flat instead of upstanding.

Wigeon

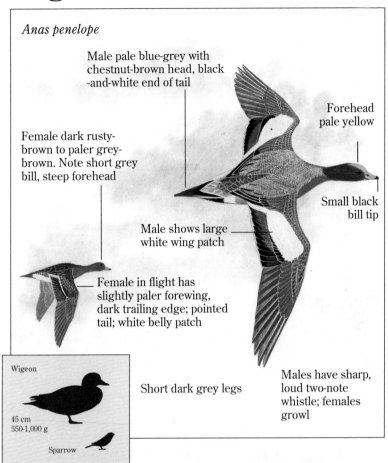

Anas penelope

Male pale blue-grey with chestnut-brown head, black-and-white end of tail

Forehead pale yellow

Female dark rusty-brown to paler grey-brown. Note short grey bill, steep forehead

Small black bill tip

Male shows large white wing patch

Female in flight has slightly paler forewing, dark trailing edge; pointed tail; white belly patch

Wigeon

45 cm
550-1,000 g

Sparrow

Short dark grey legs

Males have sharp, loud two-note whistle; females growl

A few wigeon breed in northern Scotland, in wild, remote places, but the great majority of British and Western European wigeons are visitors from much farther north and east. They arrive in September and leave in March and April.

These visitors come to floods and marshes and often gather in big flocks, frequently feeding much more tightly-packed than most ducks. Huge numbers sometimes carpet the fields and salt marshes beside estuaries, making the air ring with their sharp, high-pitched whistles. They are principally grassland feeders, rather than birds of stubble or ploughed earth, but are equally at home inland and on the coast.

Seven or eight eggs are laid in a downy nest on the ground. They hatch after 24 days and the young fly when six weeks old.

 Medium-sized duck with pointed tail, swept-back wings. Short, stubby bill beneath steep forehead. Short legs but frequently on land. Flocks feed in tight packs, all facing one way, slowly moving forwards.

WHERE AND WHEN Mainly autumn to spring, widespread.

PLACES IT PREFERS Flooded meadows, lakes, rushy pastures, salt marsh, estuaries.

LOOKALIKES

Male **teal,** page 52, darker-bodied, dark head lacks pale forehead. Female teal smaller with bright green on wing.

Female **mallard** and **gadwall,** pages 54 and 50, streaked, sandier-brown, with longer bills.

Gadwall

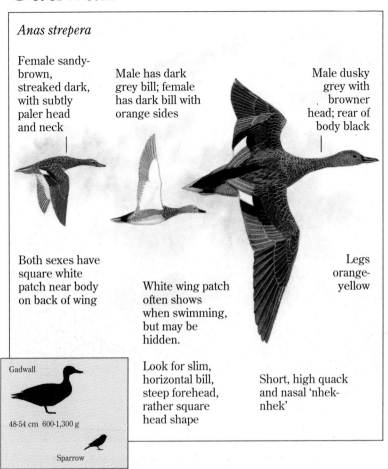

Anas strepera

Female sandy-brown, streaked dark, with subtly paler head and neck

Male has dark grey bill; female has dark bill with orange sides

Male dusky grey with browner head; rear of body black

Both sexes have square white patch near body on back of wing

White wing patch often shows when swimming, but may be hidden.

Legs orange-yellow

Gadwall

48-54 cm 600-1,300 g

Look for slim, horizontal bill, steep forehead, rather square head shape

Short, high quack and nasal 'nhek-nhek'

Sparrow

Gadwalls have been introduced to many areas of Western Europe, so their range has spread; however, they are locally scarce. For example, in England they are numerous in East Anglia and the east Midlands, but rare in the west Midlands.

They are unobtrusive, rather dull-coloured ducks, but close views reveal beautiful patterns; they have a special elegance and poise all of their own. Unlike mallards and wigeon, they are quiet birds, with sharp, rapid quacks and nasal calls.

Of all the ducks, gadwalls seem best at exploiting coots and other birds which dive and bring up waterweed to the surface: the gadwalls pounce upon the weed, eager for the free meal.

The nest, close to water, contains eight to 12 eggs which hatch after 28 days; the ducklings fly at about seven weeks.

A large duck; steep forehead, flat crown, long, slender bill. On water note large, long body; neat, smallish head and neck. Often feeds on water with coots and other wildfowl; not often on land.

WHERE AND WHEN Localised, but widespread, all year round.

PLACES IT PREFERS Lowland lakes, marshes, flooded pits, reedy pools.

Teal

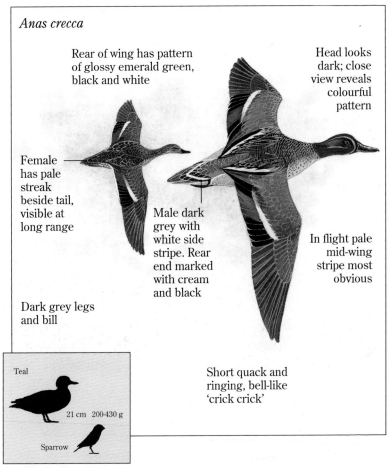

Anas crecca

Rear of wing has pattern of glossy emerald green, black and white

Head looks dark; close view reveals colourful pattern

Female has pale streak beside tail, visible at long range

Male dark grey with white side stripe. Rear end marked with cream and black

In flight pale mid-wing stripe most obvious

Dark grey legs and bill

Teal

21 cm 200-430 g

Sparrow

Short quack and ringing, bell-like 'crick crick'

Teal are small, active ducks: in flight, small parties, with their sudden twists and turns and rolling action, often look more like plovers or other wading birds than ducks. Males have a distinctive sharp, loud, high-pitched whistle, which rings out, often from an unseen bird, over a marsh or lake: a most evocative sound of winter on the wetlands.

Teal are often associated with mud and shallow, muddy water in the waterweed at the edges of lakes. Reservoirs with falling water levels in late summer often attract them. They patter about, feeding in the shallows; there may be scores where only a handful appear to be present at first glance.

Nests are usually near water, in heather or rushes, with eight to ten eggs incubated for 21 days; the ducklings fly at 23 days.

Rather large-headed, with slight bulge on back of head. Slender bill, short legs. Slow, easy walk; swims high in water; takes flight easily. Flies in small groups, rising and falling, alternately showing pale underside and dark upperparts.

WHERE AND WHEN All year, but most are seen August to April.

PLACES IT PREFERS Reservoirs, lakes, marshes, boggy moors and pools.

LOOKALIKES

Male teal is like a tiny **wigeon,** page 48, but head and body much darker; thinner white line along side.

Female duller than most ducks, greyer-brown, with distinct pale streak each side of tail.

Mallard

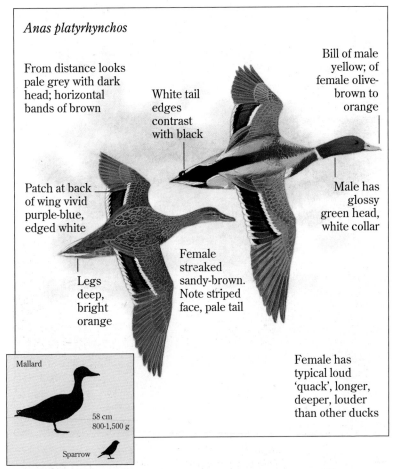

Anas platyrhynchos

From distance looks pale grey with dark head; horizontal bands of brown

White tail edges contrast with black

Bill of male yellow; of female olive-brown to orange

Patch at back of wing vivid purple-blue, edged white

Legs deep, bright orange

Female streaked sandy-brown. Note striped face, pale tail

Male has glossy green head, white collar

Mallard

58 cm
800-1,500 g

Sparrow

Female has typical loud 'quack', longer, deeper, louder than other ducks

Mallards are the most familiar, semi-domestic ducks: they quack, they tip up to show their tails as they feed from the bottom of a pond and they are never shy of coming to take bread in the park. Yet they are true wild ducks and many come to Western Europe from far afield each winter, wild and wary of humans – a result of many being shot every year.

These trusting ducks are among the most attractive of wild-fowl. The male, with his green head and violet-blue wing patch-es is a real dandy. In summer he moults into a browner plumage called the eclipse which lasts until late autumn.

Nests, lined with down from the duck, are usually on the ground near water. Seven to 16 eggs hatch after 28 days, and the ducklings fly when 50 days old.

 Large duck. Heavy body, long wings, long bill. Male has curly tail. In flight shows long head and neck; wings beat below body level. Often upends on water, but also feeds on land, with slow waddle, leaning forward to graze or find seeds.

WHERE AND WHEN Widespread all year around.

PLACES IT PREFERS Any water, from town park lakes to moorland pools, rivers, estuaries, marshes.

LOOKALIKES

Shoveler, page 60, has white breast. Female has bigger bill, shorter tail, is front-heavy.

Gadwall, page 50, has paler legs; female's bill has sharper orange side panels.

Female **wigeon,** page 48, rounder, shorter-billed.

Pintail

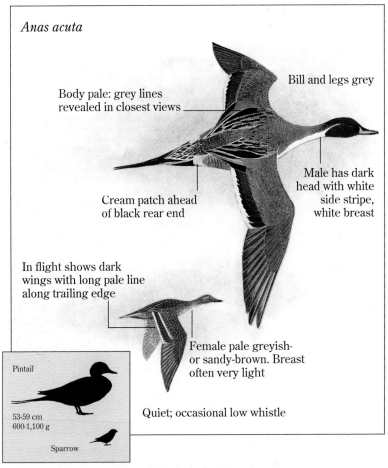

Anas acuta

Bill and legs grey

Body pale: grey lines
revealed in closest views

Male has dark
head with white
side stripe,
white breast

Cream patch ahead
of black rear end

In flight shows dark
wings with long pale line
along trailing edge

Female pale greyish-
or sandy-brown. Breast
often very light

Quiet; occasional low whistle

Pintail

53-59 cm
600-1,100 g

Sparrow

Of the surface-feeding ducks – those which don't usually dive under to feed and have the scientific name *Anas* – the pintail is the most refined. The drake, or male, is particularly long and slender, with a pencil-thin neck and a long tail.

Pintails appear inland on floods and marshy areas, but are usually uncommon: most of the Western European population can be found on a handful of estuaries. They are not like the mallard and teal, which can be seen almost anywhere where there is water. Where they are traditionally common, though, these large ducks gather in hundreds, the white breasts of adult drakes standing out in the grey light of midwinter.

Seven to nine eggs are laid in a nest on a low island; they hatch after 23 days and the young can fly six weeks later.

Long and slim at each end but rather heavy-bodied. Bill slender, parallel-sided. Short legs give awkward walk. In flight very elongated, tapered front and rear. Often feeds on muddy edges of pools or salt marsh. In daytime frequently inactive.

WHERE AND WHEN Mostly winter, on coasts, inland floods and reservoirs.

PLACES IT PREFERS Muddy estuaries, salt marsh, flooded pasture.

LOOKALIKES

Male unlike any other duck: see shoveler, long-tailed duck.

Female like female **mallard** or **gadwall**, pages 54 and 50, but paler, often greyer on head, or more orange-brown, with grey bill. Grey legs unlike mallard's.

Teal, page 52, much smaller.

Garganey

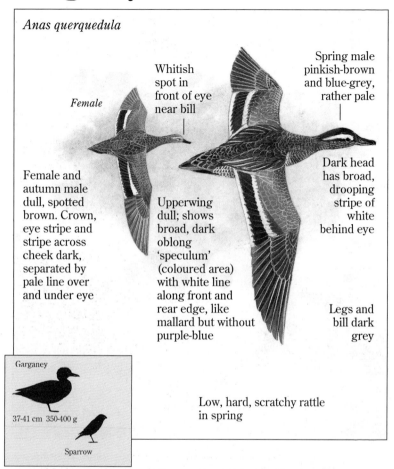

Anas querquedula

Spring male pinkish-brown and blue-grey, rather pale

Whitish spot in front of eye near bill

Female

Dark head has broad, drooping stripe of white behind eye

Female and autumn male dull, spotted brown. Crown, eye stripe and stripe across cheek dark, separated by pale line over and under eye

Upperwing dull; shows broad, dark oblong 'speculum' (coloured area) with white line along front and rear edge, like mallard but without purple-blue

Legs and bill dark grey

Garganey

37-41 cm 350-400 g

Sparrow

Low, hard, scratchy rattle in spring

Garganeys are unusual because they are summer visitors to Europe, unlike most ducks which are more abundant in winter. Garganeys move south to Africa in winter and the protection of African wetlands is essential to safeguard the species.

This is a bird that most people don't know very well, if at all: in Britain and much of Northern Europe it is quite a rarity. Most are seen in spring, when pairs or small groups appear briefly at suitable places, but they often move on before settling down to nest. In autumn they are more difficult to spot, as young birds and males often look like females or other brown ducks. The nest is made in long, coarse grass near reedy lakes or in water meadows and lined with down. Ten to 11 eggs hatch at 22 days. The ducklings leave at five or six weeks.

Small duck, slightly larger than teal. Rather flat, with squarish head, quite long, horizontal bill. Dabbles in shallows and flooded grass. Flight quick, agile, easy, like teal. Flocks in winter but in Europe usually in pairs or small groups.

WHERE AND WHEN March to September, most of Europe, but generally scarce.

PLACES IT PREFERS Shallow fresh water, salt pans, floods.

LOOKALIKES

Female **teal,** page 52, plainer, with duller face lacking white spot near bill and pale band under eye.

Gadwall, page 50, larger with pale legs.

Shoveler, page 60, larger with long bill, orange legs.

Shoveler

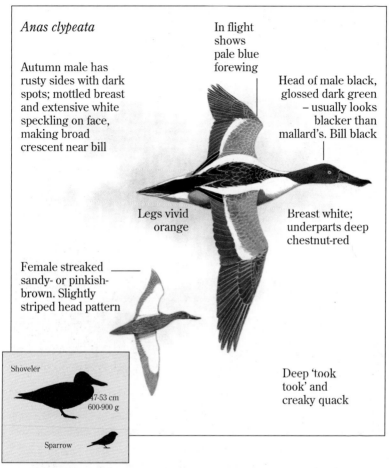

Anas clypeata

In flight shows pale blue forewing

Autumn male has rusty sides with dark spots; mottled breast and extensive white speckling on face, making broad crescent near bill

Head of male black, glossed dark green – usually looks blacker than mallard's. Bill black

Legs vivid orange

Breast white; underparts deep chestnut-red

Female streaked sandy- or pinkish-brown. Slightly striped head pattern

Deep 'took took' and creaky quack

Shoveler

47-53 cm
600-900 g

Sparrow

Shovelers are heavy, lumbering ducks but they have a special appeal. The males are generally easy to tell, but females are much like mallards and can be quite hard to identify on water, on their own. The heavy bill is the best clue. Shovelers are social and sometimes feed in dense flocks, which close up into tight-packed circles, stirring up the water as they move around together or even spin on the surface.

As a shoveler takes flight, the wings create a loud, whoofing noise – a helpful identification feature. Otherwise they are rather quiet and unobtrusive birds, especially compared with the brash, loud-voiced mallards which are invariably not far away. Nests are usually in quite dry places, with eight to 12 eggs hatching after 28 days.

Medium-large duck. Looks front-heavy. Leans forward on water, shoulders often almost awash, bill slopes to water. Long, pointed wing tips above tail. In flight looks stubby at rear, big in front. Photo shows spring/autumn transition.

WHERE AND WHEN Mostly autumn to spring, widespread. Breeds in scattered localities.

PLACES IT PREFERS Lakes, reservoirs, deep floods, estuaries.

LOOKALIKES

Male unlike any other duck. Black head and bill, white breast stand out.

Female like female **mallard**, page 54, but note longer, broader bill; brighter body plumage. In flight shows pale blue-grey forewing.

Pochard

Aythya ferina

Males in summer are a contrasty dark-brown, with a whitish face in similar pattern to female's: often unfamiliar at first glance

In flight, note broad, pale grey wing stripe, but no white

Female drab, grey-brown with echo of male's dark front and rear. Bill has pale central band

Forehead slopes into long bill, which is black with pale band

Adult male has red-brown head, black chest and tail, pale grey body

Face has whitish marks around bill, on chin and in line through eye

On land (only at water's edge) looks very round, short-legged

Deep growling note; nasal 'ah-ahng' when displaying

Pochard

44-48 cm
600-1,200 g

Sparrow

Over much of Western Europe, the pochard is a familiar non-breeding visitor; breeding pochards are scarce. Most come from the east. On many lakes and reservoirs, from early autumn to spring, flocks are to be found mixed with groups of tufted ducks: the two are almost invariably found together.

While tufted ducks are active by day, pochards are frequently night feeders and spend the day simply drifting half-asleep, bills tucked back and eyes opening intermittently to check that all is well. When they do begin to feed, they dive under just as the tufteds do, but they tend to have a more vegetarian diet, eating less animal matter.

The nest of dead reeds is usually built in shallows near the water's edge; the six to 11 eggs hatch after 24 to 28 days.

Medium-sized duck with round head, low, rounded back. Sociable. Swims buoyantly; dives under from surface. Flies fast, direct, changing direction in long, sweeping curves, often in close formation. Often, large flocks will be mostly males.

WHERE AND WHEN Thinly spread over most of Europe; scarce breeder.

PLACES IT PREFERS Reedy pools in summer; any open water, from bleak reservoirs and pits to small lakes, deep floods. Scarce on sea.

LOOKALIKES

Scaup, page 64, has white sides and black head.

Wigeon, page 48, has pale forehead, white wing patch, raised dark tail and white patch on rear flank.

Female pochard paler than female tufted, with pale throat and eye stripe.

Tufted duck & scaup

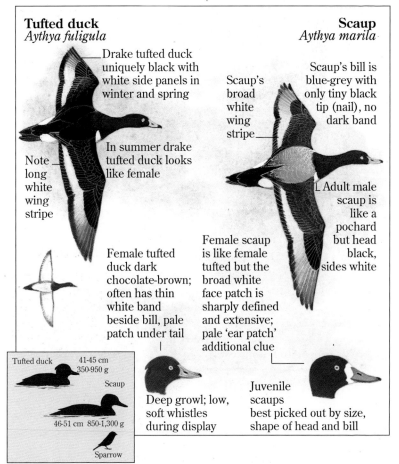

Tufted duck
Aythya fuligula

Scaup
Aythya marila

Drake tufted duck uniquely black with white side panels in winter and spring

Scaup's broad white wing stripe

Scaup's bill is blue-grey with only tiny black tip (nail), no dark band

In summer drake tufted duck looks like female

Note long white wing stripe

Adult male scaup is like a pochard but head black, sides white

Female tufted duck dark chocolate-brown; often has thin white band beside bill, pale patch under tail

Female scaup is like female tufted but the broad white face patch is sharply defined and extensive; pale 'ear patch' additional clue

Tufted duck   41-45 cm
350-950 g
Scaup
46-51 cm 850-1,300 g
Sparrow

Deep growl; low, soft whistles during display

Juvenile scaups best picked out by size, shape of head and bill

Tufted ducks are common except in upland areas: any lake will have some. They often gather in flocks of scores or hundreds together. Inland flocks frequently attract other, rarer, species and searching through the tufteds may reveal a few goldeneyes, even a scaup or smew. The nest is often close to water, in long grass, with six to 14 greenish eggs. They hatch after 23 to 26 days and the ducklings can fly after six weeks.

A scaup compared with a tufted duck looks substantially broader in the body and stands out quite well in a flock. But immature and female plumages are confusing. Most scaup live at sea, riding the waves off the rocks or floating in and out of estuaries with the tide. Eight to 11 eggs take 28 days to hatch and the ducklings fly when 40 to 45 days old.

The **tufted** *is a medium-sized, rounded, active duck. Male has unique drooping 'tassel', female's reduced to small bump or tuft.*

◁ *Tufted duck*

Scaup *is larger, broader-beamed, with rounder head, no tuft. Steep forehead above broad, flat bill. Buoyant; often rests on water, tail cocked. Dives often when feeding. Sociable.*

Scaup ▷

WHERE AND WHEN Almost everywhere with suitable habitat.

Tufted duck

Scaup

WHERE AND WHEN Autumn to spring, mostly around northern coasts. Very rare breeding bird in north.

PLACES IT PREFERS Open water from flooded pits and reservoirs to park lakes, broad rivers, estuaries.

PLACES IT PREFERS Estuaries, sandy bays, shallow sea above mussel scarps.

Eider

Somateria mollissima

Adult male black, white and rich pink, with green head patches visible at close range

Note black cap split by white line

In flight, white front, black underside and rear are distinctive

Female rich brown, barred darker. Speckled brown face, feathers extending down side of wedge-shaped bill in triangle

Eider

58 cm 1,900-2,800 g

Sparrow

Immature males black-brown (often very dark) with irregular white patches, especially on breast; pale stripe over eye

Heavy; often has short tail cocked when swimming. Dives well

Croaking note from female; male has passionate 'ahh-oww' in spring

Eiders are famous for their down, taken from their nests to provide filling for bedspreads and pillows. Like all ducks, the female eider plucks down from her own body to create a soft, warm nest lining. Four to six eggs hatch after 27 to 28 days.

Drake eiders are among the most exotic-looking of Europe's wildfowl, strongly patterned and beautifully coloured, although the delicate detail requires a close view for full appreciation. Females, much drabber than males, reveal marvellously subtle, if far less colourful, plumage patterns when seen close-up: fortunately, they are often approachable.

These are essentially seagoing ducks, rarely seen inland unless sick, or exhausted by storms. Nests are among rocks or vegetation, often in groups.

 Large, heavy duck with wedge-shaped head. Often in shallows near weedy rocks. Large flocks in sheltered bays. Looks bulky but powerful in low-level flight. Young males go through several complicated plumage stages.

WHERE AND WHEN Western and Northern European coasts, all year.

PLACES IT PREFERS Sea coasts, from rocky islands to sandy bays, reefs, sandbanks in estuaries.

LOOKALIKES

No other regular duck has black underside and white upperside of male.

Female **mallard,** page 54, and other duck species, are not barred, as eider, but streaked lengthwise.

Long-tailed duck

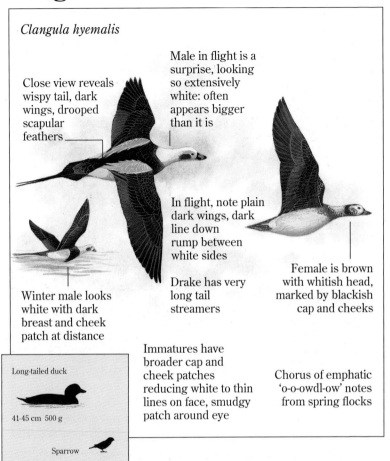

Clangula hyemalis

Close view reveals wispy tail, dark wings, drooped scapular feathers

Male in flight is a surprise, looking so extensively white: often appears bigger than it is

In flight, note plain dark wings, dark line down rump between white sides

Drake has very long tail streamers

Female is brown with whitish head, marked by blackish cap and cheeks

Winter male looks white with dark breast and cheek patch at distance

Immatures have broader cap and cheek patches reducing white to thin lines on face, smudgy patch around eye

Chorus of emphatic 'o-o-owdl-ow' notes from spring flocks

Long-tailed duck

41-45 cm 500 g

Sparrow

Few wildfowl are as lively and attractive as long-tailed ducks: it is sad that so few people see them. It is well worth the trouble of seeking them out on some exciting northern shore, perhaps a large, wild sea loch, where the flocks gather in spring. Here they call loudly and display, the drakes raising their long tails in extravagant gestures to impress the females. All is action and passion, quite unlike the sedate, lazy flocks of pochards on a lowland lake.

In late autumn occasional immature long-tailed ducks appear inland, staying for a week or two. They are unexpected birds which people often find hard to recognize.

They breed in the tundras of the far north. Five to nine eggs are laid which hatch after 23 to 25 days.

Medium-small duck. Chunky, square head with short, deep, stubby bill. Plumage contrasty at most times, but especially male in winter. Young birds in autumn are confusing. Dives often, bobbing back up like a cork; at home on roughest seas.

WHERE AND WHEN Autumn to spring, in northern and western estuaries and firths.

PLACES IT PREFERS Shallow sea over sand, extensive sandy bays, estuaries.

LOOKALIKES

Beware **guillemot,** page 184 especially in flight – longer, pointed bill/head.

   Grebes have dark caps, paler cheeks.

   Pintail, page 56, has tail spike, but otherwise quite different.

Common & velvet scoters

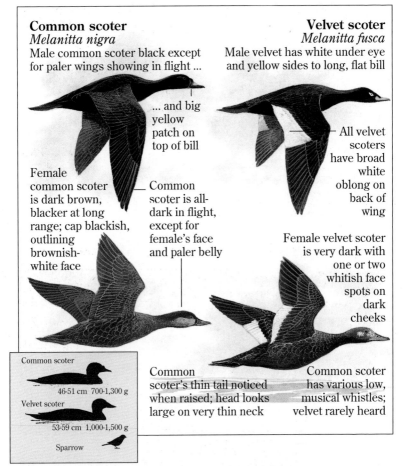

Common scoter
Melanitta nigra
Male common scoter black except
for paler wings showing in flight ...

Velvet scoter
Melanitta fusca
Male velvet has white under eye
and yellow sides to long, flat bill

... and big
yellow
patch on
top of bill

All velvet
scoters
have broad
white
oblong on
back of
wing

Female
common scoter
is dark brown,
blacker at long
range; cap blackish,
outlining
brownish-
white face

Common
scoter is all-
dark in flight,
except for
female's face
and paler belly

Female velvet scoter
is very dark with
one or two
whitish face
spots on
dark
cheeks

Common
scoter's thin tail noticed
when raised; head looks
large on very thin neck

Common scoter
has various low,
musical whistles;
velvet rarely heard

Common scoter
46-51 cm 700-1,300 g
Velvet scoter
53-59 cm 1,000-1,500 g
Sparrow

The open sea is the favoured place for flocks of common and velvet scoters. The best way to see them is to look from a vantage point over a wide bay, or often a featureless stretch of coast, waiting for a distant dark smudge to appear as the swell rises. The scoter flock may get up and fly a few hundred metres, often straggling out into a low, ragged line along the skyline. Just as quickly, the ducks drop back to the water with a clumsy-looking splash. Usually, white wing patches reveal a few velvets.

Should circumstances allow a close approach, on a calm day when sounds travel far over water, their excited, whistling calls can be heard as the males 'sing' to prospective mates.

Both scoters lay five to seven eggs which hatch after 28 days; the young fly after six or seven weeks.

Common scoter *has thin neck, pointed tail. Very sociable, often hundreds together. Fast, low flight. Swims buoyantly. Often raises head and neck, cocking tail.*

◁ *Common scoter*

Velvet scoter *is bigger, heavier, with white wing patch, otherwise similar to common.*

Velvet scoter ▷

WHERE AND WHEN Breeds in north-west (scarce); localized resident off northern and western coasts.

WHERE AND WHEN Northern and Western European coasts, autumn and winter.

Common scoter

Velvet scoter

PLACES IT PREFERS Big, open bays and firths, shallow inshore seas.

PLACES IT PREFERS Large sandy bays.

Goldeneye

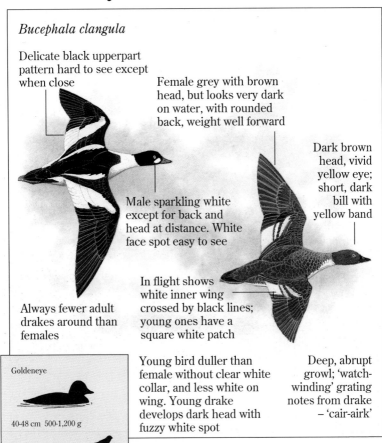

Bucephala clangula

Delicate black upperpart pattern hard to see except when close

Female grey with brown head, but looks very dark on water, with rounded back, weight well forward

Dark brown head, vivid yellow eye; short, dark bill with yellow band

Male sparkling white except for back and head at distance. White face spot easy to see

Always fewer adult drakes around than females

In flight shows white inner wing crossed by black lines; young ones have a square white patch

Goldeneye

40-48 cm 500-1,200 g

Sparrow

Young bird duller than female without clear white collar, and less white on wing. Young drake develops dark head with fuzzy white spot

Deep, abrupt growl; 'watch-winding' grating notes from drake – 'cair-airk'

Goldeneyes are on the increase in Britain, with more spending the winter on a range of inland waters and some now nesting in the Scottish highlands, encouraged by a determined nest box scheme. They remain numerous in Scandinavia.

They are splendid birds, the drakes especially handsome. Like all wildfowl, they look clean-cut and immaculate close-up. You usually see a few of the whiter-than-white males in a group, but the dark grey females and immatures predominate. In many areas, however, there is an upsurge of adult males during early spring, before the flocks head north.

Nests are made in tree holes (or in Scotland in special boxes). The six to 15 eggs hatch in 26 to 30 days. The ducklings fly at 60 days.

Rather large, stocky duck. Male bigger than female.
Big head with steep forehead, round/domed crown,
heavy nape. Back is rounded; tail quite long, often
cocked when asleep. Flies fast and direct, with
whistling wings. Dives constantly when feeding.

WHERE AND WHEN Breeds in northern forest lakes (including north Scotland); widespread in winter.

PLACES IT PREFERS Open water from coasts to reservoirs, pits, even remote upland lakes.

LOOKALIKES

Male **smew,** page 74, has whiter head.

    Goosander, page 78, bigger with long bill.

    Velvet scoter, page 70, has white wing patch but darker body and neck.

Smew

Mergus albellus

Young male develops white forehead and speckled crown in late winter

Male white, more yellow-white than blue-white of goldeneye

Female is grey, with white face surrounded by chestnut cap. Has a blackish eye patch

Flanks pale grey; bold black eye patch. Black on back shows well; marks on nape and sides of breast need close view

Immatures are duller than adults, with less white on wing

In flight, white body recalls shoveler; wings are like goosander's

Smew   36-43 cm 500 g

Sparrow

Thousands of smews visit the Netherlands in winter, gathering on the IJsselmeer in flocks hundreds-strong. At this time they are really exciting birds, always active, a delight to watch. The flock moves around quickly as the front birds dive and those at the back fly forwards, leapfrogging those now searching for food under water.

In the UK, smews are difficult to find except in a few favoured places in the south-east. Those that do visit lakes and reservoirs are often solitary and hard to track down, despite their striking appearance. They are usually found in places that hold the commoner waterfowl, but tend to stay separate from the everyday species such as tufted ducks and pochards. They nest in holes in trees; six to ten eggs are laid, which hatch in 30 days.

Small-medium sized duck, rather barrel-bodied but with small head. Bill small and neat. Swims very buoyantly but can 'sink' low in water. Dives easily from surface. Flight low, straight, fast.

WHERE AND WHEN Winter visitor to coasts and mainly coastal fresh water in Western Europe.

PLACES IT PREFERS Sheltered brackish lagoons, reservoirs, flooded pits.

LOOKALIKES

Male as white as **goldeneye,** page 72, but smaller, with white crown, greyer sides.

Female recalls a small **grebe,** but cap brown, not black.

By far the most likely to be confused with the **ruddy duck**, page 374.

Red-breasted merganser

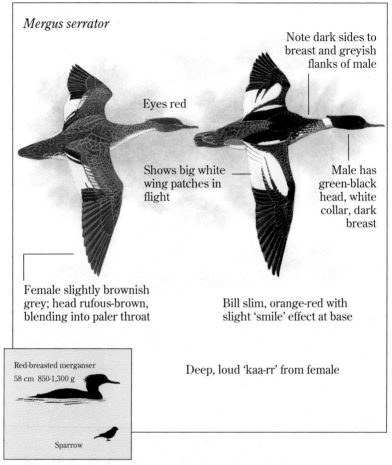

Mergus serrator

Note dark sides to breast and greyish flanks of male

Eyes red

Shows big white wing patches in flight

Male has green-black head, white collar, dark breast

Female slightly brownish grey; head rufous-brown, blending into paler throat

Bill slim, orange-red with slight 'smile' effect at base

Red-breasted merganser
58 cm 850-1,300 g

Sparrow

Deep, loud 'kaa-rr' from female

As this elegant, flamboyant fish-eating bird spreads south, more and more people are able to enjoy the sight of the splendid drake in his spring finery. There are few ducks the equal of a male merganser in breeding plumage, with the wispy crest and red bill adding a dandyish touch to its contrasting deep bottle-green, black, blue-grey and chestnut colours.

Although most abundant along the coasts of the far north, in Scandinavia and Scotland, mergansers have now spread south into Wales and are managing to increase despite persecution by fishermen. In winter, unlike goosanders, they remain mostly coastal ducks, not often seen on large lakes or rivers.

Nests are built in long grass or heather near water. The seven to 12 eggs hatch after 29 days.

Long, low duck of coastal waters. Bill thin, with a hint of an uptilt. Short legs, horizontal stance out of water. Flies with long head straight out, body thin, spindle-like, wings straight, stiff, moving in rapid shallow beats.

WHERE AND WHEN Northern and western coasts all year; more southerly coasts in winter.

PLACES IT PREFERS Sea lochs, estuaries, brackish river mouths.

LOOKALIKES

Female **goosander,** page 78, very like female merganser, but chin and throat more sharply defined; back greyer; bill thicker and deeper red.

Male slimmer than **mallard,** page 54, with fine, spiky bill, wispy crest.

Goosander

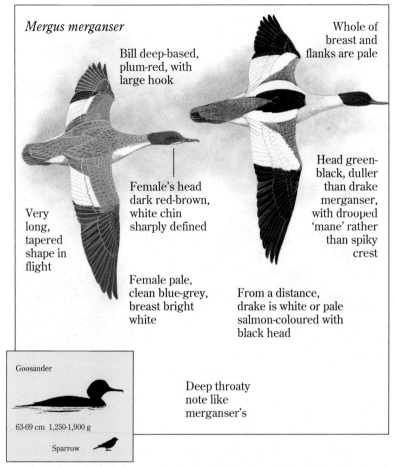

Mergus merganser

Bill deep-based, plum-red, with large hook

Whole of breast and flanks are pale

Female's head dark red-brown, white chin sharply defined

Head green-black, duller than drake merganser, with drooped 'mane' rather than spiky crest

Very long, tapered shape in flight

Female pale, clean blue-grey, breast bright white

From a distance, drake is white or pale salmon-coloured with black head

Goosander

63-69 cm 1,250-1,900 g

Sparrow

Deep throaty note like merganser's

Goosanders are big birds, standing out in mixed flocks of wildfowl on a lake by their size and superior appearance: they sail about like battleships in a flotilla of smaller craft.

Drakes are glorious in pink, white and black. Small groups often visit large gravel-pit complexes, but many spend the winter on rivers. Breeding birds on northern and western streams are a worry to conservationists: despite evidence that they cause no damage, they are vigorously persecuted by fishermen. This is a pity, because most people get much simple pleasure from these impressive birds that bring an exotic touch to a winter's day.

They nest in large holes in trees, or in broken branches. Seven to 13 eggs are laid, which hatch after 34 days.

A large, long-bodied duck. Thick, hooked bill. Short legs. Swims buoyantly; often cocks tail; dives from surface. Flocks usually have larger numbers of the re-headed female than of adult drakes. Mostly on fresh water.

WHERE AND WHEN All year round in the north and west; winter visitor to lowlands.

PLACES IT PREFERS Rushing rivers, large lakes, flooded pits, estuaries.

LOOKALIKES

Drake **merganser,** page 76, more marked on chest and flanks. Female merganser more sullied on foreneck.

Smew, page 74, very much smaller.

Shelduck, page 46, stouter, with chestnut band around body.

Honey buzzard

Pernis apivorus

Wings long and full,
angled back in glide but
broadly spread
in soar.
Active flight is
floppy, elastic,
with steady flaps of
straight-looking wings

Wings held
flat, drooped
at tip

Plumage is
very variable
from bird to
bird, but notice
bands on tail,
one near tip,
two near base

Many birds are dark,
with dark barring on
wings; some very
contrasty with zebra
striping beneath;
others all-dark or
much whiter, white-
headed

Small head,
pale eyes

Honey buzzard

50-58 cm 500-800g

Sparrow

Cuckoo-like head
shape in flight

High, thin 'pihaa'

In much of Europe the honey buzzard is regular and even quite common, although it remains difficult to find on its breeding grounds. In Britain it is an elusive rarity, almost a mythical bird of some larger stretches of forest, or else just a rare and erratic migrant.

It is less aerial than the buzzard and spends more time inside woods and even on the ground, where it raids wasps' and bees' nests for grubs and wax. It spends hours digging out a nest and may return for several days to a productive excavation.

In autumn, they fly south: flocks cross the Mediterranean at narrow points, especially Gibraltar and Istanbul.

The nest is built high in a tall forest tree. Two heavily spotted eggs hatch after 30 to 35 days; the young fly at 45 days.

Large, broad-winged bird of prey. In flight, shows a narrow head and a rather long, narrow, round-cornered tail. Wings long, broad in middle, held flat or drooped.

WHERE AND WHEN Over much of Europe but rare in Britain, May to September.

PLACES IT PREFERS Ancient woodland, mixed forests, parkland.

LOOKALIKES

Buzzard, page 96, is very similar but soars with wings held up in a V; stiffer in active flight.

Soaring **marsh harrier,** page 92, holds wings in V, looks narrow-winged.

Goshawk, page 374, shorter-winged, more massive.

Black & red kites

Black kite
Milvus migrans

Underside of black kite's wing shows dull pale patch with dark bars behind angle

Red kite
Milvus milvus

Underside of red kite's wing shows big white patch behind angle

Black kite's head greyish; upperside of wing has pale band from body to wrist

Black kite dull brown, with rusty tinge to body and tail

Red kite flies beautifully, with long, wheeling glides

Tail of black kite is a sharp-cornered triangle; shallow notch obvious when tail is closed

Red kite rusty-brown, cream and black; top of tail looks reddish

Black kite
53-59 cm
800-1,000g

Red kite
58-64 cm
800-1,000 g

Sparrow

Both have long squealing calls

Head of red kite pale grey to almost white; top of wings have broad cream band from body to wrist

In Southern France and Spain, the black kite is common in areas with traditional farming, although it is now scarce in areas of modern cereal and rape fields with few woods. The red kite is found in similar areas and extends farther north, especially in wilder country with woods and moors intermixed. In the south it is a bird of wooded valleys and mixed farmland. The black kite is also the 'city kite', bold and conspicuous in cities of the Mediterranean and Eastern Europe. Both scavenge on rubbish tips and are often seen around farms, villages and even town centres. Black kites also like rivers where they can snatch sickly fish.

Both build nests in trees; their two or three eggs hatch after 29 to 30 days and the young fly when seven or eight weeks old.

Both kites are slim, elegant birds with long, angled wings, fingered at the tips and usually held arched or flat in flight. The tail is used as a rudder, twisting sideways.

◁ *Black kite*

Red kite has longer tail with deeper fork; black has notched tail, fork not apparent when tail fanned.

Red kite ▷

WHERE AND WHEN Most of Europe except Scandinavia and UK; March to October.

Black kite

WHERE AND WHEN Rare UK; all year in south and west. Leaves north in winter.

Red kite

PLACES IT PREFERS Wooded slopes, riverside fields and trees, refuse tips.

PLACES IT PREFERS Woods, farmland with scattered trees.

Golden eagle

Aquila chrysaetos

Soars in wide circles, very stable

Juvenile blackish with big white patches on under wing and small ones on top. White tail with broad black band

From below, pale patch near bend of wing sometimes obvious, sometimes not

Dark brown; golden-buff tinge on back of head and neck

In flight, upper wing often shows pale buffish across centre; tail pale at base, with dark tip

Wings much longer, tail longer and head narrower than buzzard's; deeply fingered wing tips, longer glides and slower wing beats give eagle more majestic appearance than buzzard

Golden eagle

80 cm 2.8-6.8 kg

Sparrow

Call is a rarely heard, sharp 'kee-ok'

The golden eagle is massive, but often dwarfed by the mountainous landscape it inhabits. Yet the bird has great presence and adds to the drama of such scenery by its occasional appearance high above a peak. Buzzards, often seen much lower down and even perched on telegraph poles, are often mistaken for eagles, but they are much smaller and more lightly built. Eagles are powerful, capable of killing and carrying hares and even young deer, although in winter they eat mostly animals found already dead.

They build a very large nest of sticks on a cliff ledge. The two eggs hatch after six weeks, during which there may be frequent snowfall. The chicks fly after 11 weeks: usually only one survives to leave the nest.

Massive bird of prey; very long wings, longish tail. Narrow head protrudes forwards in flight; wings held in V. Circles slowly in wide, majestic arcs. Sits motionless for long periods. Usually seen high over peaks and ridges, rarely low down or at close range.

WHERE AND WHEN All year, in most wild, mountainous parts of Europe.

PLACES IT PREFERS Mountains, with or without forests, high, remote moors, wild coastal cliffs.

LOOKALIKES

Buzzard, page 96, much smaller, underwing whitish, shorter tail.

White-tailed eagle, page 86, broader wings, shorter wedge-shaped tail.

Griffon vulture, page 88, broader wings, rounded at rear, shorter tail.

White-tailed eagle

Haliaeetus albicilla

Dark brown, usually slightly paler than golden eagle

In flight, wings look long, broad, flat, deeply fingered at tip

Head protrudes in front as far as tail does behind wings

Head is pale, some times cream-white on old birds

Trailing edge has saw-tooth effect, especially on juvenile

Big, pale bill

Immature streaked dark brown; tail dull with dark streaks

White-tailed eagle

90 cm 3-7 k g

Sparrow

Makes a thin, chattering 'krikrikrikri'

Adult has white tail

White-tailed eagles are giant birds of prey, usually heavier and often with a greater wingspan than golden eagles. In flight they look huge and rather heavy, but they are capable of surprising agility: pairs sometimes roll over together, grasping talons in mid air. The white tail of an adult can be seen at very long range.

They are much more often by water than golden eagles, frequently catching ducks and geese or feeding on dead fish. In winter, they may be seen standing on ice, foraging for dead birds, fish and scraps.

White-tailed eagles nest in trees or on cliffs, making a bulky nest. Two eggs hatch after six weeks; the chicks fly 11 weeks later.

Big and bulky. In flight, less elegant than golden eagle, with bigger head, much shorter tail, broader wings held flat, not in a V, when gliding. Sits for hours, hunched on a ledge or even on flat ground. Close views show bare legs (golden's are feathered).

WHERE AND WHEN All year; mostly Northern and Central Europe, rare introduction in Scotland; scarce.

PLACES IT PREFERS Marshes, lakes, coastal cliffs.

LOOKALIKES

Golden eagle, page 84, more shapely, with larger tail; soars on wing in V.

Crane, page 118, and **white stork,** page 28, fly with neck outstretched.

Egyptian & griffon vultures

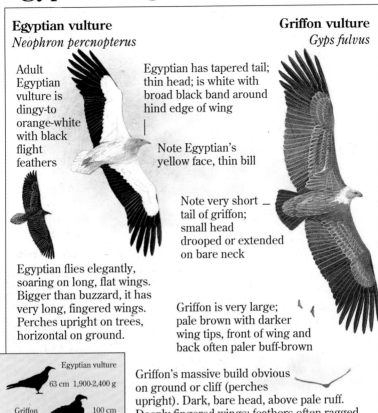

Egyptian vulture
Neophron percnopterus

Griffon vulture
Gyps fulvus

Adult Egyptian vulture is dingy-to orange-white with black flight feathers

Egyptian has tapered tail; thin head; is white with broad black band around hind edge of wing

Note Egyptian's yellow face, thin bill

Note very short tail of griffon; small head drooped or extended on bare neck

Egyptian flies elegantly, soaring on long, flat wings. Bigger than buzzard, it has very long, fingered wings. Perches upright on trees, horizontal on ground.

Griffon is very large; pale brown with darker wing tips, front of wing and back often paler buff-brown

Griffon's massive build obvious on ground or cliff (perches upright). Dark, bare head, above pale ruff. Deeply fingered wings; feathers often ragged

Egyptian vulture
63 cm 1,900-2,400 g

Griffon vulture
100 cm
7.5-11k g

Sparrow

Vast, plank-like wings characterize the griffon vulture. As it turns in the air the subtle curves and warps of its wings create a variety of shapes, first broad and square, then bulging at the rear, then pointed at the tips as the upswept tips curve out of sight. It rarely beats its wings, relying on warm air and upcurrents to stay aloft.

The Egyptian vulture is likewise a bird of Southern and south-western Europe, a scavenger of warm hillsides and hot, sun-washed cliffs. Scruffy and unkempt on the ground, in the air it has a golden glow and a mastery of the elements unrivalled by most predators. Most seen in Europe are adults; young ones spend several years in Africa. Both species nest on bare ledges of cliffs or in small caves, laying one egg.

Vultures fly heavily until well under way, then soar and glide with ease, hardly beating their wings. **Egyptian** *often over wooded hillsides and valleys; Egyptian has thin head, wedge-tail, wings flat.*

◁ *Egyptian vulture*

Griffon *also often high over rocky peaks; has short tail; wings in V.*

Griffon vulture ▷

WHERE AND WHEN Mostly spring to autumn, southern France, Spain.

Egyptian vulture

PLACES IT PREFERS Warm, open hillsides, scrub, towns and villages.

WHERE AND WHEN Mainly spring to autumn, France and Iberia, but some all year round.

Griffon vulture

PLACES IT PREFERS Gorges, cliffs, scrubby hillsides; over open country.

Hen & Montagu's harriers

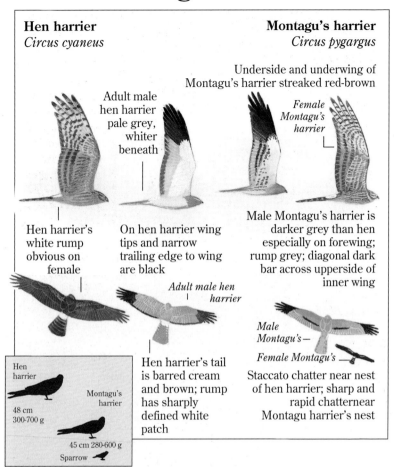

Hen harrier
Circus cyaneus

Montagu's harrier
Circus pygargus

Underside and underwing of Montagu's harrier streaked red-brown

Female Montagu's harrier

Adult male hen harrier pale grey, whiter beneath

Hen harrier's white rump obvious on female

On hen harrier wing tips and narrow trailing edge to wing are black

Male Montagu's harrier is darker grey than hen especially on forewing; rump grey; diagonal dark bar across upperside of inner wing

Adult male hen harrier

Male Montagu's —

Female Montagu's —

Hen harrier
48 cm
300-700 g

Montagu's harrier
45 cm 280-600 g

Sparrow

Hen harrier's tail is barred cream and brown; rump has sharply defined white patch

Staccato chatter near nest of hen harrier; sharp and rapid chatternear Montagu harrier's nest

The hen harrier frequents open hills and northern moors in summer, but spreads out in winter, when it is often on lower, flatter ground. It hunts for small mammals and birds by flying low, often gliding and taking prey by surprise in a sudden dash. Males and females have completely different colouring.

Montagu's harriers are scarcer than hen harriers in most places except southern Europe, where they are characteristic of rolling steppes and cereal-growing areas. Of all the harriers, they are the lightest and most elegant, with the longest, most swept-back wing tips: ideal for riding the warm breezes in Mediterranean summers.

Both hen harrier and Montagu's harrier usually lay four to six eggs; the chicks fly when 35 to 40 days old.

Hen harrier

buzzard-sized but slender; Montagu's even slimmer, male smaller. Long tail, narrow wings. Round, slightly owlish head. Long, slim legs. Both fly with deep flaps and wings held in V in ▶

◁ *Hen harrier*

▶ *wavering glides. Male* **Montagu's** *is lighter in build than hen, with longer, narrower wing tips.*

Montagu's
harrier ▷

Hen harrier

Montagu's harrier

WHERE AND WHEN In Northern and Western Europe; Scotland and Wales; England in winter.

WHERE AND WHEN Southern and Central Europe; April to September.

PLACES IT PREFERS Open heather moors, plantations, marshes, fens.

PLACES IT PREFERS Cereal fields, marshes, steppes.

Marsh harrier

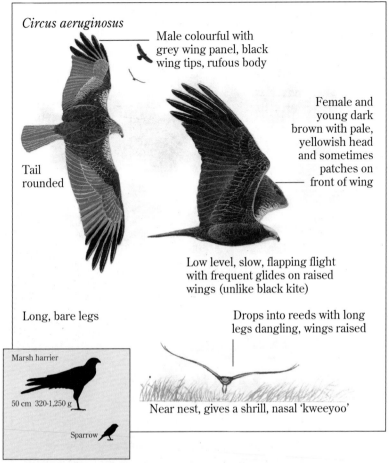

Circus aeruginosus

Male colourful with grey wing panel, black wing tips, rufous body

Female and young dark brown with pale, yellowish head and sometimes patches on front of wing

Tail rounded

Low level, slow, flapping flight with frequent glides on raised wings (unlike black kite)

Long, bare legs

Drops into reeds with long legs dangling, wings raised

Marsh harrier

50 cm 320-1,250 g

Sparrow

Near nest, gives a shrill, nasal 'kweeyoo'

Once so heavily persecuted that it was a great rarity, the marsh harrier is making a comeback restricted only by the scarcity of the reed-beds that it needs for nesting. It is a large, handsome bird which adds a great deal to the lowland scene in areas where it nests or appears while on migration. The reed-beds of the reclaimed polders of the Netherlands are ideal for it, but it can nest in places with much smaller patches of reed beside lakes or even along ditches and rivers.

The marsh harrier eats small ducklings and chicks of water-side birds, water voles and similar small prey; however, it can also catch rabbits and adult birds if it takes them by surprise.

Four or five eggs are laid and incubated for about 36 days. The young leave the nest before they can fly, at 35 to 40 days.

 Buzzard-sized; female much heavier than male, broader-winged. Soars like a buzzard but wings narrower, tail longer; glides with wings in V. Usually low over marshes and adjacent farmland; perches in tops of bushes and trees in reed-beds.

WHERE AND WHEN In summer around coasts of north-western European and inland marshes. In winter most go south.

PLACES IT PREFERS Reed-beds; coastal marshes, floods.

LOOKALIKES

Black kite, page 82, holds wings basically level, rather than in a V.

Sparrowhawk

Accipiter nisus

Male blue-grey above, rusty-orange below; often looks dark in flight

Soars on spread, fingered wings, tail often closed, narrow, long, square-tipped

Flies low, fast, twisting into clearings or dashing over hedges

Female looks paler than male, greyish upperside wearing to brown. Narrow bars on white underside seen at close range

Never hovers like kestrel

Sparrowhawk
27-37 cm
100-335 g

Sparrow

Various shrill screams and chattering calls at nest

Female sparrowhawks are much bigger than males, taking a different range of prey which probably helps the pair to co-exist in a relatively small area. The nippy, lightweight males take sparrows and tits, and the females tackle thrushes and pigeons.

Sparrowhawks suffered enormously in the pesticide era of the 1960s and only now are they back to their usual numbers in the countryside. They still remain elusive and difficult to see properly, except in spring when they rise above their nesting woods in aerial displays; both sexes display in a range of steep dives and 'bouncing' flights above the treetops.

The nest, a flat platform of sticks, is sited near the stem of a tall tree. Four or five eggs hatch after 32 to 35 days; the young fly at 24 to 30 days.

 Long-tailed; wings rather broad, blunt when spread, or angled back to a point. Dashes low through trees, along hedge or into gardens, ambushing prey. Usual flight is fast, stiff flaps between flat glides. Soars in fine weather and dives from a height.

WHERE AND WHEN Almost anywhere except highest moors and mountains, all year.

PLACES IT PREFERS Mixed woods, plantations, farmland with hedges, parks, open ground with finch flocks in winter.

LOOKALIKES

Cuckoo, page 194, has wings tapering to a point, and a broad, floppy tail; head more pointed, and held up in flight.

 Kestrel, page 100, hovers and perches on wires and poles; has longer wings.

Buzzard & rough-legged buzzard

Buzzard
Buteo buteo

Rough-legged buzzard
Buteo lagopus

Buzzard is typically dark brown above, cream below with dark streaks concentrated on chest and lower breast, leaving pale U shape

Upperside of rough-legged's tail white with black tip

Buzzard glides between stiff wing-beats, wings angled; soars with them outstretched and raised. Has bare legs.

Buzzard's tail looks pale, greyish below with fine dark bars

Usually less rich brown than buzzard, with 'frosted' effect on head and underparts. Feathered legs.

Underwing of buzzard is usually cream with dark barring and darker wrist patches. Patterned underside distinctive

Rough legged

Northern buzzards are often paler, creamy overall or underneath

Belly is black, or with blackish patch each side

Buzzard
55 cm 450-1,350 g

Rough-legged buzzard
60 cm 500-1,400 g

Sparrow

Buzzard's call is a powerful, high 'pee-yoo'; rough-legged's is similar but lower pitched

Wishful thinkers may mistake a buzzard for a golden eagle, but there is nothing wrong with a buzzard: it is a splendid bird of prey which bears watching for long periods. In the air, it is buoyant and graceful, sailing to great heights.

In winter, both species are more lethargic, often hunting from perches rather than the air, looking for signs of voles, even worms. Much of their food is dead meat – road-casualty rabbits for example.

Their feet are powerful, but neither the buzzard nor the slightly larger and more elegant rough-legged buzzard is strong enough to cope with prey much bigger than a rabbit.

Buzzards build large nests of sticks and line them with greenery. The young hatch after about a month.

*Both are larger than crow. Wings broad, fingered at tip. They soar with wings in slight V; active flight of **buzzard** stiff, jerky; rough-legged is longer-winged, more flexible and relaxed in flight; often hovers.* ▶

◁ *Buzzard*

▶ **Rough-legged buzzard** *hovers frequently, buzzard occasionally. Both often sit on poles, walls, or on the ground. Buzzard perches upright, hunched head in shoulders. Calls often.*

Rough-legged buzzard ▷

WHERE AND WHEN: Widespread in Europe except for populated lowlands; all year. Low Countries in winter.

Buzzard

Rough-legged buzzard

WHERE AND WHEN Scandinavia; variable numbers move south in winter.

PLACES IT PREFERS Woods; upland valleys with woods, farmland and moors nearby; lowland in winter.

PLACES IT PREFERS Tundra, cliffs; in winter, moors, marshes, farmland.

Osprey

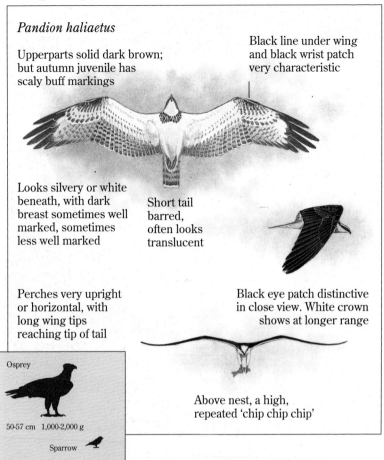

Pandion haliaetus

Upperparts solid dark brown; but autumn juvenile has scaly buff markings

Black line under wing and black wrist patch very characteristic

Looks silvery or white beneath, with dark breast sometimes well marked, sometimes less well marked

Short tail barred, often looks translucent

Perches very upright or horizontal, with long wing tips reaching tip of tail

Black eye patch distinctive in close view. White crown shows at longer range

Osprey

50-57 cm   1,000-2,000 g

Sparrow

Above nest, a high, repeated 'chip chip chip'

Ospreys are rare, but they are big and often obvious, and millions of people have enjoyed watching them at public viewing sites. From a single pair in the 1950s the Scottish population has increased to 100 pairs: thriving, but still not many. Scandinavian ospreys are doing quite well, too.

This is a big bird, a dramatic, powerful fisher that catches its prey in a startling headlong dive which, at the last second, switches to a feet-first plunge into the lake, river or shallow coastal water where it usually hunts.

The huge stick nest is often all-too-easy to see, built in a tall pine tree, on crags or islands. Two or three blotched eggs are laid, which hatch after 35 days and the young leave the nest when eight to ten weeks old.

Much bigger than a buzzard or a crow. Very long wings angled at joint, giving distinctive upward kink in middle when seen from front or rear. Often hovers, like a giant kestrel. Perches quietly on trees for long periods between hunts.

WHERE AND WHEN Mostly Northern Europe in summer; widespread on migration, spring and autumn.

PLACES IT PREFERS Large lakes, forest pools, broad rivers, estuaries.

LOOKALIKES

Buzzard, page 96, not as pure white below and lacks black mask.

Young **great black-backed gull,** page 172, similar in flight but lacks fingered wing tips, doesn't hover or plunge from a height.

Kestrel

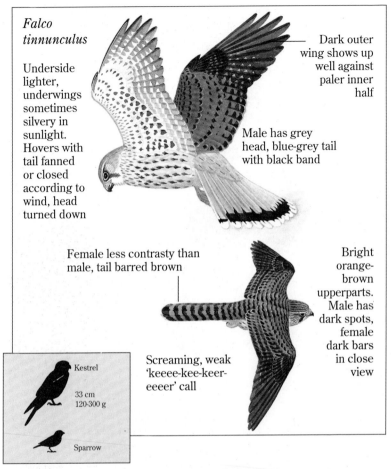

Falco tinnunculus

Dark outer wing shows up well against paler inner half

Underside lighter, underwings sometimes silvery in sunlight. Hovers with tail fanned or closed according to wind, head turned down

Male has grey head, blue-grey tail with black band

Female less contrasty than male, tail barred brown

Bright orange-brown upperparts. Male has dark spots, female dark bars in close view

Kestrel
33 cm
120-300 g

Sparrow

Screaming, weak 'keeee-kee-keer-eeeer' call

Kestrels are the commonest of the European falcons; indeed in most places they are the commonest birds of prey.

Their displays involve fast, dashing chases and special territorial flights with rapid, almost quivering wing-beats; they may also include high soaring and exciting dives. When displaying, they are much more like the dashing falcon of popular imagination than they are in their rather lethargic everyday life spent hunting voles and beetles. Kestrels hunt by sitting and watching as well as by their familiar, and unique, habit of hovering – such a common sight along roadsides.

They nest in hollow trees, barns or on high buildings or cliffs, laying four or five eggs directly on to a bare ledge. These hatch after 28 days and the chicks fly when a month old.

 Pigeon-sized but long-winged, with long, narrow tail. More slender than dove with larger, flatter head. Perches upright on wires or post. Flies purposefully; hovers head to wind as if on invisible string. Usually singly or in pairs.

WHERE AND WHEN Widespread, all year.

PLACES IT PREFERS Anywhere with open ground, from marshes and coastal cliffs to farmland, industrial sites, moors.

LOOKALIKES

Sparrowhawk, page 94, never hovers, rarely perches in open on posts; not spotted or barred above.

Merlin, page 102, smaller, chunkier, more pointed wing tips, more dashing flight.

Merlin

Falco columbarius

Sharp-pointed wings unlike blunter wings of kestrel, but broader-based, quite like sparrowhawk

Flight fast and very low; often perches on ground

Male has grey tail with dark band. Female's tail barred brown and cream

Female dark brown, lacking orange or rufous; creamy beneath with heavy dark streaks, creamy-white cheeks

Nasal, chattering 'ke-ke-ke-kee' and 'wikwikwik'

Male blue-grey above, orange-buff below; can look strongly coloured in sun, but paler in dull light

Merlin
27-32 cm
125-300 g

Sparrow

As with most birds of prey, the female merlin is much larger and heavier than the male. He is a tiny, dashing falcon, while the hen is more compact and heavily built.

Merlins breed on open moors and along the edges of forests but in winter go to coastal marshes and empty farmland, looking for finch and pipit flocks. A merlin hunts pipits, linnets, wheatears and other small moorland birds in summer, also eating many moths. Its pursuit of small birds often becomes a frantic, exhausting chase with many twists and turns.

The nest is a bare scrape in the ground among heather, but in some areas a disused crow's nest in a small tree is used. Four rusty-coloured eggs hatch after 28 to 32 days and the chicks fly at 25 to 27 days old.

Small bird of prey, dove-sized. Square head, chunky bill. Wings broad-based but tapered to short, sharp point. Tail tapered to square tip or broadly fanned. Flies low and fast; hunting flight has rapid, flicking, thrush-like wing-beats.

WHERE AND WHEN In Northern and Western Europe in summer; more widespread in winter.

PLACES IT PREFERS Moors, islands, marshes; in winter, farmland, coasts.

LOOKALIKES

Kestrel, page 100, longer-tailed, with softer, slower wing-beats, more rufous plumage.

Sparrowhawk, page 94, looks longer-tailed and shorter-winged; its wings are broader at tip and look shorter when angled back to point.

Peregrine, page 106, larger.

Hobby

Falco subbuteo

Adult dark slate-grey above with black around eye and black 'moustache'

White cheek and throat obvious

Often flies long distances, turning this way and that, with hardly a wing-beat

Very long, scythe-like wings and short, tapered tail

Dark streaks beneath at close range; at long range looks darker overall

Rusty thighs and vent often hard to see

Lively, shrill 'kew kew kew'

Hobby

32 cm
130-340 g

Sparrow

Juvenile lacks red vent; broad pale edges to browner upperpart feathers. Still has thin black moustache against white cheek

Hobbies are delicate and attractive falcons, living on a mixed diet of large insects – especially dragonflies – and small birds, including martins and swallows.

Insects are caught in beautifully elegant hunting flights, with many sudden accelerations, stalls, turns and dips; birds are chased in much faster, dashing flight with wings almost closed except for bursts of flicking beats of the wing tips.

Hobbies nest late, in early summer, using old crows' and rooks' nests. The chicks hatch when there are many insects about and can be fed a diet of young, easily-caught small birds towards the end of the summer.

Three eggs are incubated for 28 days and the young fly at about 30 days.

Elegant, long-winged, short-tailed falcon; kestrel-sized. Usually looks very dark with white cheek. Flight floating, with shallow, supple flaps between long, turning glides (catching insects), or dashing with deep beats and steep dive after larger prey.

WHERE AND WHEN Much of Europe, April to October.

PLACES IT PREFERS Heathland, edges of woods, farmland with clumps of trees, lakes and flooded pits.

LOOKALIKES

Male **peregrine,** page106, very similar but bigger, broader-winged, barred beneath, no red on vent.

Kestrel, page 100, never so dark or so grey.

Merlin, page 102, smaller, dumpier, doesn't fly high after insects, but similar in chase.

Peregrine

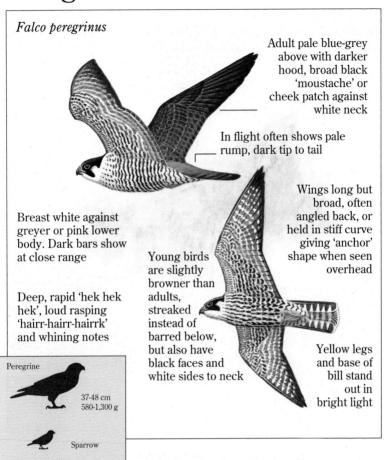

Falco peregrinus

Adult pale blue-grey above with darker hood, broad black 'moustache' or cheek patch against white neck

In flight often shows pale rump, dark tip to tail

Wings long but broad, often angled back, or held in stiff curve giving 'anchor' shape when seen overhead

Breast white against greyer or pink lower body. Dark bars show at close range

Young birds are slightly browner than adults, streaked instead of barred below, but also have black faces and white sides to neck

Deep, rapid 'hek hek hek', loud rasping 'hairr-hairr-hairrk' and whining notes

Yellow legs and base of bill stand out in bright light

Peregrine

37-48 cm
580-1,300 g

Sparrow

The weight difference between male and female peregrines makes them easily distinguishable – females are much heavier. There is also a big difference in size between a large female peregrine and the small, lightweight merlin and hobby.

Peregrines are glorious birds. They hunt pigeons, crows, wading birds, even ducks, which they are capable of knocking out of the sky with a fast power-dive, or stoop.

They nest on cliffs, usually choosing a ledge, often over-looking the sea, that is very difficult for a human or even a fox to reach. Like other falcons, they make no nest but lay their eggs directly on to a simple scrape. Very occasionally, they nest on tall buildings. The two to four eggs hatch after 28 days and the young can fly when they are five or six weeks old.

Large, bigger than a kestrel, more crow-sized. Broad head and shoulders; wings broad at base but taper to long point. Tail wide, tapered to square tip. Flight soaring, often at great height, or direct with fast, deep wing-beats.

WHERE AND WHEN Mainly north-western Europe and Spain, all year.

PLACES IT PREFERS Remote cliffs, moorland, sea coast; in winter almost anywhere, even cities.

LOOKALIKES

Merlin, page 102, much smaller, usually flies very low.

  Hobby, page 104, similar in pattern but has narrower, lighter body, narrower wings.

  Against light, both **fulmar** and **raven**, pages 14 and 332, can look surprisingly similar at some angles.

Red grouse/willow grouse

Lagopus lagopus

Dark, marbled and barred with black, cream and rusty red

Red wattle above eye

In flight, red grouse shows distinctly darker, plain wings and short blacker tail than willow grouse. Willow grouse has white wings

Male redder and darker than female

Small round head, large, bulky body

Red grouse/ willow grouse

38 cm 600-700 g

Sparrow

Typical call a loud cackling or crowing, slowing down to hard 'go-bak, go-bak, go-bak'

Red and willow grouse are the same species. The willow grouse is the mainland European form (or race), which becomes largely white in winter. The red grouse is the Britsh race, usually known just as the grouse, and remains dark red-brown all year.

Few birds are as strictly tied to one location as the grouse, which may hardly move from one area of hill all of its life. Only fierce winter weather pushes it down to sheltered woodland edges and fields. They feed on heather shoots (swallowing grit to help them digest) and they nest in the heather. During spring display flights they rise to a height, then sail down with loud, crowing, challenging calls. Six to nine eggs are laid, which hatch 19 to 25 days later; the chicks fly after 12 days.

Chicken-sized, small-headed, round-bodied bird of heather moors. Flies with stiff, downcurved wings. Often in small parties. Usually hidden in heather until disturbed, but male calls loudly from ridge or hillock.

WHERE AND WHEN In Northern and Western Europe, all year.

PLACES IT PREFERS Open moorland with heather.

LOOKALIKES

Grey partridge, page 110, smaller, paler, with barred sides.
   Female **black grouse,** page 375, bigger, paler, with fine pale line along wing and notch in tail.
   Ptarmigan, page 374, smaller, greyer in summer.

Grey & red-legged partridges

Grey partridge
Perdix perdix

Grey has streaked brown body with brown bars on sides

Orange face

Flies on stiff, arched wings

Grey partridge has grey bill and legs

Dark brown 'horseshoe' on belly of grey

Red-legged partridge
Alectoris rufa

Red-legged partridge has white face outlined in black

Flies on stiff, flat wings with long, low, fast glide before landing

Red bill and legs

Broad bars on sides of red-legged

Red-legged's calls are a short, deep 'chuck-chuck-chuck' and a strange, grating, wheezing

Grey makes creaking, metallic 'ke-eer-ik' and sharp, low 'it it it' calls

Grey partridge
30 cm
320-430 g

Sparrow

Red-legged partridge
34 cm
400-540 g

Grey partridges are declining in the face of modern farming. Their chicks need tiny caterpillars to eat in spring and summer. Pesticides, as well as the loss of hedges and rough grassland, mean few chicks now survive. Grey partridges nest on the ground, often near a hedge, laying as many as 20 eggs. The chicks can fly before they are full grown.

Red-legged partridges are natives of Spain and were brought to England for shooting. Now they are found over most of Britain as well as parts of France and Iberia. They like dry, warm, sandy or stony places and do best in eastern England and, of course, in Spain. Ten to 16 eggs are laid, which hatch after 23 to 24 days; the chicks can fly after just 10 days.

Grey partridge *is pigeon-sized, neat and rounded. Small head, thick neck may be puffed out and held upright.*

◁ *Grey partridge*

Red-legged *is bigger, rounder-backed, slightly longer-legged, with strong face pattern. Both are paler than grouse, usually in different places.*

Red-legged partridge ▷

WHERE AND WHEN
Over most of Europe, all year.

Grey partridge

WHERE AND WHEN
Mainly Spain, France, Britain, all year.

Red-legged partridge

Places it prefers Pastures, hay meadows, cereal fields with hedges and mixed crops.

Places it prefers Dry fields, vineyards, rough grassland and stony hillsides.

Pheasant & quail

Male pheasant mostly dark, rusty-brown with shiny purple, green or lilac and black spots and bars

Pheasant
Phasianus colchicus

Head of male pheasant dark green, red around eye. Many have white ring round neck

Tail of male pheasant long, pointed, stiff, barred dark

Female pheasant pale brown with dark mottles and bars on tail

Female pheasant's tail stiff, pointed, often held up

Quail's flight is low, fast, usually short

Quail
Coturnix coturnix

Call is a liquid 'quick, ik ik'

Top of quail's head is striped; pale throat with black lines on male

Tiny, rounded; buff with dark streaks

Pheasant

53-90 cm
750-1,800 g

Sparrow

Quail
18 cm 80-140 g

Beware young pheasant flying when half-grown, more like partridge

Pheasants are often ignored by birdwatchers as most are reared in captivity and released to be shot. Even those that really are wild are descended from birds originally released by humans. On the other hand, they are truly beautiful birds, worth a close look. Where they are left alone, they become quite tame. They nest on the ground, often in a thicket or in long grass near a hedge or in the edge of a wood. The hen sits tight – difficult to find. In the evening the males roost up in trees, safe from foxes, often making loud crowing calls just as it gets dark.

Quails are rarely seen, being so secretive, but they have a distinctive call which is familiar in Southern Europe. They nest out of sight in dense fields of hay or corn, laying ten to 15 eggs.

Male **pheasant** *unique, long-tailed, cockerel-sized. Female also long-tailed but smaller, duller. Flies up when disturbed, with great clatter; dashes off low and fast, gliding into cover.*

◁ Pheasant

Quail *tiny, like pheasant chick; very hard to see, but calls give it away, especially at dawn and dusk, from cereal fields.*

Quail ▷

WHERE AND WHEN Most of Europe, all year.

WHERE AND WHEN Most of Europe, April to September.

Pheasant

Quail

PLACES IT PREFERS Woods, fields, parks, reed-beds.

PLACES IT PREFERS Large fields of crops.

113

Water rail

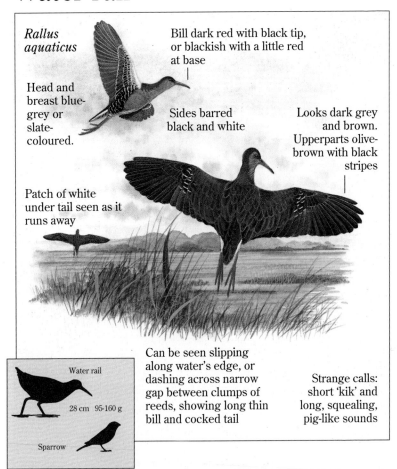

Rallus aquaticus

Bill dark red with black tip, or blackish with a little red at base

Head and breast blue-grey or slate-coloured.

Sides barred black and white

Looks dark grey and brown. Upperparts olive-brown with black stripes

Patch of white under tail seen as it runs away

Water rail

28 cm 95-160 g

Sparrow

Can be seen slipping along water's edge, or dashing across narrow gap between clumps of reeds, showing long thin bill and cocked tail

Strange calls: short 'kik' and long, squealing, pig-like sounds

This is a slender, lightly built bird that seems normal enough in a side view, but from front or back looks amazingly thin. It slips through reeds with hardly a movement to give it away.

Water rails live hidden from human view most of the time, in dense waterside vegetation, but they do sometimes come out on to muddy edges. In winter they may be driven into the open by hard frosts. Occasionally they are quite bold, even stealing maggots and groundbait from fishermen.

The easiest way to tell where they are is to listen for their strange, wailing and squealing calls, almost like noisy piglets.

The main nesting material is dead reeds and the nest is very well hidden in reeds or sedge. Six to 11 eggs are laid; both male and female incubate them for 19 to 20 days.

Small, not much bigger than thrush but longer-billed. Typical deep-bodied shape from side, with short, upturned tail, but very narrow end-on. Flies short distances, low, with legs dangling.

WHERE AND WHEN Most of Europe, all year.

PLACES IT PREFERS Reed-beds, swamps, ditches, dark, overgrown wet places under trees.

LOOKALIKES

Young brown **moorhen,** page 116, much bigger, with short bill. **Snipe,** page 144, has longer bill, probes into mud.

115

Coot & moorhen

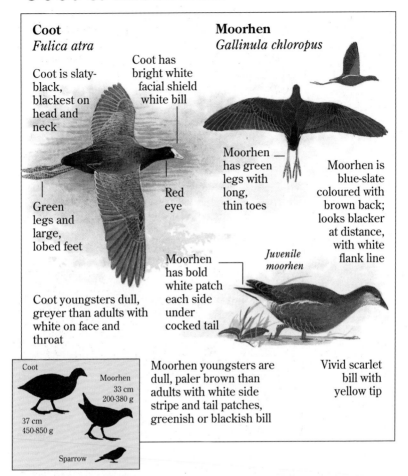

Coot
Fulica atra

Coot is slaty-black, blackest on head and neck

Coot has bright white facial shield white bill

Green legs and large, lobed feet

Red eye

Coot youngsters dull, greyer than adults with white on face and throat

Moorhen
Gallinula chloropus

Moorhen has green legs with long, thin toes

Moorhen is blue-slate coloured with brown back; looks blacker at distance, with white flank line

Juvenile moorhen

Moorhen has bold white patch each side under cocked tail

Moorhen youngsters are dull, paler brown than adults with white side stripe and tail patches, greenish or blackish bill

Vivid scarlet bill with yellow tip

Coot

Moorhen
33 cm
200-380 g

37 cm
450-850 g

Sparrow

Coots are obvious, noisy, active waterbirds which prefer large lakes and reservoirs and frequently come out to feed on nearby grassy banks. Common in most areas where there are suitable places, in winter they sometimes gather in hundreds on big lakes. They are sociable, but quarrelsome in spring when they fight for territories.

Moorhens are quite common but more secretive than coots, often on much smaller pools or even along wet ditches. They feed on land much more often and are less likely to be seen far out on open water. On the water they usually swim one or two together but on land feed in small groups. They can dive under water, but do so much less often than coots.

Coots *are round-backed, low-tailed, smaller than mallard; moorhens are smaller, flatter-backed on water with raised tails. On land coots look very round, standing hunched but* ▶

◁ *Coot*

▶ *upright;* **moorhens** *are more furtive, leaning forwards and moving with a more nervous, springy walk and jerky tail flicks, running into cover if disturbed.*

Moorhen ▷

WHERE AND WHEN Most of Europe except northern Scandinavia; those from Eastern Europe move west in winter.

Coot

PLACES IT PREFERS Large, slow rivers, pools and flooded pits up to large, bare reservoirs and lakes.

WHERE AND WHEN Most of Europe except Scandinavia. Eastern European birds move west in winter.

Moorhen

PLACES IT PREFERS Marshy edges to rivers, ponds and lakes, overgrown wet ditches, nearby damp meadows.

Crane

Grus grus

Black head and neck with broad, curved white stripe; red patch hard to see

Basically grey but upperparts much browner in summer

Long wings pale at front, otherwise smoky-black

Very long dark legs

Head extended in flight; wings broad, fingered, held flat

Drooped black bushy 'tail' visible on ground

Crane

106-118 cm
4,500-6,100 g

Sparrow

Juvenile browner with dull brown head

Loud, clanging, bugling calls

This is a real heavyweight among European birds, standing tall and with a huge wingspan like a stork's or the largest vulture's. It is also famous for its supremely elegant display postures, the wonderful dance of the cranes.

In autumn cranes head south for Spain, where they live among the groves of cork oaks, feeding on acorns. Then in spring they return north to Scandinavia, symbols of the coming spring. They look for remote, wild places in swamps and marshes in which to nest on the ground, unlike herons and storks which find raised nest sites. Two eggs are laid, which hatch after 30 days; the young fly 65 to 70 days later. Elsewhere they are irregular, usually ones and twos as stragglers but occasionally flocks appear briefly in unexpected places.

Huge: swan-sized, but long-legged. Small head but slender neck broadens into thick base and deep chest. Bushy wing feathers hang over tail. Flies high, soaring on long, flat wings or with active wing-beats, head and legs extended.

WHERE AND WHEN Northern Europe in summer, Spain and Eastern Europe in autumn and winter.

PLACES IT PREFERS Marshes, open fields, pastures beneath oaks.

LOOKALIKES

Grey heron, page 26, is smaller, flies on bowed or arched wings, rarely in more than small groups.

White stork, page 28, has greater contrast between black flight feathers and white of rest of wing and body.

Oystercatcher

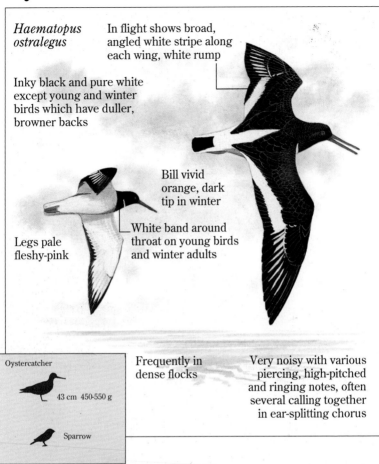

Haematopus ostralegus

In flight shows broad, angled white stripe along each wing, white rump

Inky black and pure white except young and winter birds which have duller, browner backs

Bill vivid orange, dark tip in winter

White band around throat on young birds and winter adults

Legs pale fleshy-pink

Oystercatcher

43 cm   450-550 g

Sparrow

Frequently in dense flocks

Very noisy with various piercing, high-pitched and ringing notes, often several calling together in ear-splitting chorus

Oystercatchers are real characters: when a flock moves to a new sandbank, pushed up by the rising tide, they seem to pour in at a great pace, hitting the ground at a run, almost falling over themselves in a noisy, anxious clamour before they settle down. They while away an hour or two until the mud and sand shows again and then move out to feed on shellfish – but not oysters.

They nest on rocks at the top of a sandy beach, or in a patch of shingle, but many also breed inland in the north, on open grassy fields.

They lay their large, spotted eggs on the ground but sometimes choose odd places, such as the hollow top of a broken log or fence post.

Large, pigeon-sized wading bird. Rather thick bill and legs. Big, domed, angular-looking head. Walks slowly, probing into mud and sand or prising mussels off rocks with beak. Large flocks gather at high tide.

WHERE AND WHEN All year. More seen in west during winter, and in summer over Northern Europe and northern UK.

PLACES IT PREFERS Pastures, coastal pools, beaches, estuaries, sandbanks.

LOOKALIKES

Nothing else of similar shape is so black and white; flocks look mainly black with orange 'slashes', while gulls look more white, avocets much more white, shelducks much heavier, shorter-legged.

Black-winged stilt

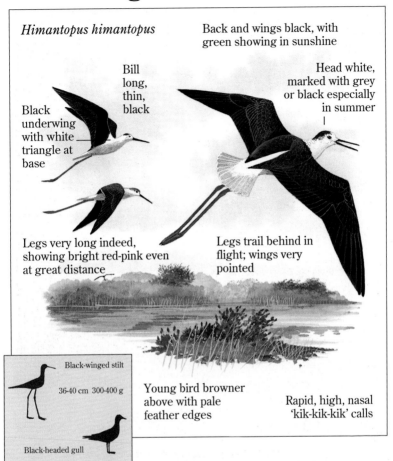

Himantopus himantopus

Back and wings black, with green showing in sunshine

Bill long, thin, black

Head white, marked with grey or black especially in summer

Black underwing with white triangle at base

Legs very long indeed, showing bright red-pink even at great distance

Legs trail behind in flight; wings very pointed

Black-winged stilt

36-40 cm 300-400 g

Black-headed gull

Young bird browner above with pale feather edges

Rapid, high, nasal 'kik-kik-kik' calls

Although photographs give an idea of the strange appearance of a stilt, the bird itself always takes people by surprise, because the legs are so fantastically long. The bill, by contrast, is relatively short – stilts feed by wading in water and picking insects from the surface, rather than by probing into water or mud. In parts of Europe they do quite well in new rice paddies, but traditionally they like marshes with shallow pools and salt pans.

They are ground nesters, often raided by gulls, crows, foxes or other predators. The chicks very quickly learn to walk and feed themselves; like other wader chicks they are born with a warm covering of thick, spotted down. The parents are noisy and aggressive in defence of their family.

Very tall wader, on extraordinarily long legs. Bill very fine, straight or slightly upturned. Spends much time wading in shallow pools. In flight, legs trail out behind, feet often crossed. Makes noisy tern-like calls when breeding.

WHERE AND WHEN Mainly Mediterranean coasts, Spain, western France, rarely farther north.

PLACES IT PREFERS Salty pools, shingly lagoons, sandy coasts.

LOOKALIKES

Avocet, page 124, has more white above, grey legs.

Oystercatcher, page 120, much blacker on head, short-legged, with orange bill.

Can be missed in gull flock on lagoon.

Avocet

Recurvirostra avosetta

Bill black, bent upwards

Gleaming white with black bands. Young birds have browner markings and some brown across back

In flight looks fast, with quite short, blunt-tipped wings, long legs trailing and long head and neck

Black wing tips obvious

Legs very long, blue-grey

Avocet

42 cm 250-350 g

Black-headed gull

Loud, short, liquid whistling calls

The avocet is a symbol of successful bird protection everywhere. The places it needs in order to survive – mostly shallow pools near the coast – are likely to be drained, filled in and built on, or taken over by holidaymakers, unless efforts are made to keep them for birds.

The avocet disappeared from many parts of Europe, including Britain, but has since returned and protection has led to an increase in numbers. In some places several hundreds, even thousands, may be seen together, although most breeding colonies have a few dozen pairs.

Many still do not rear many young, as they are easily taken by foxes. The nest is on dry mud or a stony island, with four eggs which hatch after 22 to 24 days.

Large wader, pigeon- or black-headed gull size, on long legs. Unique upcurved bill. Looks very white, but can be missed among gulls. Walks slowly in water, sweeping bill sideways to find food.

WHERE AND WHEN All year, north-west European coasts, Mediterranean.

PLACES IT PREFERS Shallow muddy pools, salty lagoons, muddy estuaries.

LOOKALIKES

Black-winged stilt, page 122, has black back, red legs.

Gulls short-legged but can look similar at distance when swimming and avocets wading.

Ringed & little ringed plovers

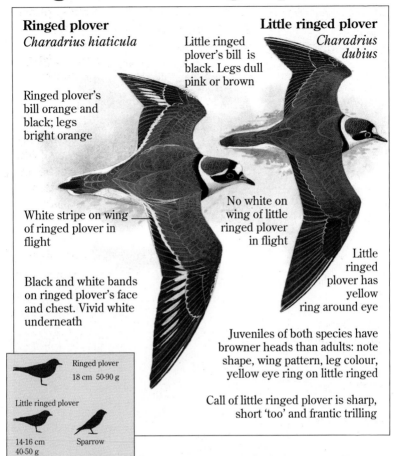

Ringed plover
Charadrius hiaticula

Little ringed plover
Charadrius dubius

Little ringed plover's bill is black. Legs dull pink or brown

Ringed plover's bill orange and black; legs bright orange

White stripe on wing of ringed plover in flight

No white on wing of little ringed plover in flight

Black and white bands on ringed plover's face and chest. Vivid white underneath

Little ringed plover has yellow ring around eye

Ringed plover
18 cm 50-90 g

Little ringed plover

14-16 cm
40-50 g

Sparrow

Juveniles of both species have browner heads than adults: note shape, wing pattern, leg colour, yellow eye ring on little ringed

Call of little ringed plover is sharp, short 'too' and frantic trilling

Ringed plovers are nervous, lively birds of the seashore, nesting on shingle and sand and seeming to be always worried that someone will tread on their eggs, or that a gull might take their chicks. They call constantly and even pretend to be injured in order to draw the intruder away from the nest.

Little ringed plovers nest inland, on stony river banks or beside gravel pits and, unlike ringed plovers, they go south to Africa for the winter. They are rare in Northern Europe, but have become commoner where gravel digging and the spread of spoil heaps from quarries have provided new places for them to nest. Both ringed and little ringed plovers lay four eggs on the ground; they hatch after 24 to 25 days and the chicks can fly when 25 days old.

Ringed plover *is dumpy, stocky, thrush-sized. Brightly coloured bill and legs. Typical call a double, rising 'too-ee'. Usually runs, stops, tilts forward to pick up food, then runs again.*

◁ *Ringed plover*

Little ringed plover *is slender, with dark bill and dull legs. Ringed is often found inland by lakes, but little ringed is rarely found on the seashore.*

Little ringed plover ▷

WHERE AND WHEN All European coast;; inland mainly spring and autumn.

Ringed plover

WHERE AND WHEN March to September; much of Southern and Central Europe.

Little ringed plover

PLACES IT PREFERS Estuaries, sandy and stony beaches, shallow pools.

PLACES IT PREFERS Large rivers, pools, sandbanks.

Golden plover

Pluvialis apricaria

Has round head with big dark eye

Upperparts spotted yellow and black; looks browner in winter except in closest view

Pale line along wing in flight but rump all dark

Underside of wing flashes white

In winter has yellowish chest and clean white belly

Golden plover

27 cm 150-250 g

Sparrow

Underside black in summer, with whiter throat and flanks. Birds seen in the north are blackest and show most white on sides of chest

High, sad 'piooo' calls

In summer the golden plover is a wild and elusive bird – a lonely, penetrating voice in the mist on high ground, well away from people and often heard but not seen.

In winter, though, big flocks live on farmland at lower levels, chased by black-headed gulls trying to steal the worms that golden plovers pick from the damp ground. Like smaller plovers and larger lapwings, they have a characteristic way of moving: they stand still, often tilting their heads, before walking or running a few steps, tilting over to pick at a worm.

In flight, golden plovers quickly separate from lapwings, which are blunt-winged, often forming long lines or Vs. Nests are on the ground, scantily lined; the eggs hatch after 27 to 28 days and the chicks fly when 28 days old.

 Pigeon-sized wader with longish legs, short bill. Round head on slender neck, but usually hunched into shoulders. Flies fast on pointed wings. Often in large flocks during winter, with lapwings. On high moors and rounded hills in summer.

WHERE AND WHEN In Northern and Western Europe in summer; more widespread in winter.

PLACES IT PREFERS Moors; lowland pastures, ploughed fields, marshes.

LOOKALIKES

Grey plover, page 130, similar but bigger, with larger bill; juvenile grey plover is browner than adult, more like golden, but has black patches under wings.

Grey plover

Bill looks short but big and heavy

Pluvialis squatarola

In flight, shows white stripe on wing and white rump patch

In winter pale grey above with dark mottles; juvenile browner

Underside of wing has unique striking black 'armpit' patch

In spring, beautiful pale grey, white and shiny black

Grey plover

28 cm   200-300 g

Sparrow

Slow, hesitant walk, tilts over to feed

Loud whistle, thin 'tee-oo-eeeee' carries great distance

Unlike most estuary birds, whose numbers have declined, grey plovers have been increasing in recent years. It is not clear why: they breed right up in the Arctic, among the most northerly of all birds, and visit Europe outside the breeding season to take advantage of the muddy estuaries which are so full of worms and tiny molluscs.

On the estuaries they tend to occupy small feeding territories, so they spread out; however, at high tide all the birds have to gather to roost at one spot. If the habitat is reduced, by building or drainage, it means that fewer plovers can feed on the small area that is left. Grey plovers may often be seen with redshanks, bar-tailed godwits and knots, but rarely mix with golden plovers.

 Medium-large wader with longish legs, but short, thick bill. Big eye in round head. Feeds in ones and twos but gathers in flocks to sleep. Rare inland. In winter, pale grey but often seems dark at long range on mudflats; head hunched into shoulders.

WHERE AND WHEN Coasts of north-western Europe.

PLACES IT PREFERS Muddy and sandy estuaries, sandbanks, marshes, shallow coastal pools.

LOOKALIKES

Golden plover, page 128, spotted with brighter yellow, has all-white underwing.
  Godwits, page 148, and **redshanks,** page 152, reveal long bills when feeding, but look similar when asleep on beach.

Lapwing

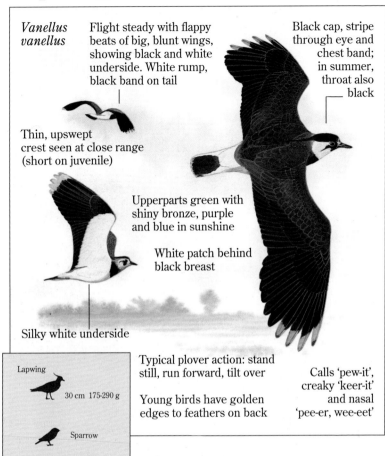

Vanellus vanellus

Flight steady with flappy beats of big, blunt wings, showing black and white underside. White rump, black band on tail

Black cap, stripe through eye and chest band; in summer, throat also black

Thin, upswept crest seen at close range (short on juvenile)

Upperparts green with shiny bronze, purple and blue in sunshine

White patch behind black breast

Silky white underside

Lapwing
30 cm 175-290 g

Sparrow

Typical plover action: stand still, run forward, tilt over

Young birds have golden edges to feathers on back

Calls 'pew-it', creaky 'keer-it' and nasal 'pee-er, wee-eet'

Few birds are so typical of farmland of all kinds – open, grassy pastures, upland sheep paddocks and ploughed fields in winter. Yet it also finds suitable feeding on grassy salt marshes, if not often on muddy estuaries.

It sometimes forms flocks of thousands, more usually a few hundred, often mixed with golden plovers. The same fields frequently have starlings, rooks, black-headed gulls and flocks of skylarks, so a traditional lapwing field is usually a worthwhile place to visit in winter.

In spring, male lapwings perform spectacular tumbling display flights. Females lay four eggs, usually on bare earth, close to short grass where the chicks can easily feed, so areas of mixed farming are preferred.

*Large wading bird, but often on dry ground.
Upswept crest unique in Europe. Shiny colours on
back look green or black at distance, with black
chest, white underside giving flickering contrast in
flight. Broad, round-tipped wings very distinctive.*

WHERE AND WHEN Most of
Europe in summer; moves south
and west in winter.

PLACES IT PREFERS Moors,
marshes, edges of lakes and
muddy reservoirs, lagoons,
farmland.

LOOKALIKES

No other wader is so broad-
winged; **oystercatcher,** page 120,
has jet black back, long
orange bill.

Knot

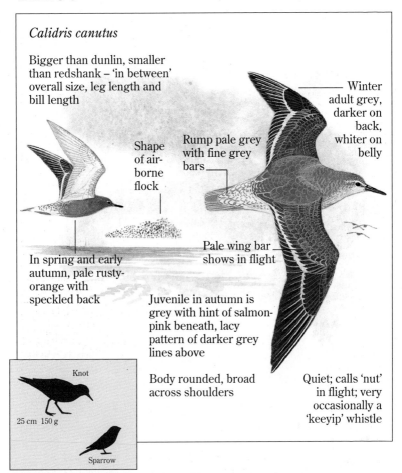

Calidris canutus

Bigger than dunlin, smaller than redshank – 'in between' overall size, leg length and bill length

Shape of air-borne flock

Rump pale grey with fine grey bars

Winter adult grey, darker on back, whiter on belly

In spring and early autumn, pale rusty-orange with speckled back

Pale wing bar shows in flight

Juvenile in autumn is grey with hint of salmon-pink beneath, lacy pattern of darker grey lines above

Body rounded, broad across shoulders

Quiet; calls 'nut' in flight; very occasionally a 'keeyip' whistle

Knot

25 cm 150 g

Sparrow

Of all the waders of European estuaries, the knot is the one most often seen in big, dense flocks, sometimes many thousands together, performing remarkable twists, turns and sudden rises or falls. It is also distinctive in its lack of obvious pattern, or calls: a dumpy, dull bird. Yet a close view shows it to be a beautiful little wader, delicate in all its actions. Juveniles in autumn are especially attractive.

In late spring, now in breeding colours, knots leave for Greenland. On their way there from Western Europe, they call in on Scandinavian coasts to refuel for the long flight over the north Atlantic. They don't have to depart in a hurry: they must wait until the snows clear before they can settle to nest, hurriedly, in the short Arctic summer.

Thrush-sized bird of sea coast. Legs and bill of medium length. Dumpy body, dull in winter. Often feeds in flocks and roosts and flies in huge, dense masses, like twisting smoke. Calls low, unmusical.

WHERE AND WHEN Coasts of north-western Europe, mostly August to April.

PLACES IT PREFERS Mudflats, sandy beaches, marshes.

LOOKALIKES

Dunlin, page 140, smaller, whiter underneath in winter, with short legs but longer bill.

Godwits, page 148, much larger, longer-billed.

Grey plover, page 130, has short bill; not in such dense flocks.

Redshank, page 152, looks darker.

Sanderling

Calidris alba

In winter, pearly-grey above; clean white beneath

Tail and rump dark in middle, white at sides

Bill straight, black; legs black

In flight wings look black with broad white stripe

Young birds in autumn have black specks on back and crown. Some adults are reddish on neck

Sanderling

20 cm 50-70 g

sparrow

Spring adult mottled rusty brown, with reddish breast but pure white underside

Call distinctive very short, hard 'twik'

This is the twinkle-toes of the beach, the small wader that runs in and out with the waves, darting over the wet sand to pick up tiny items of food disturbed by the foaming water. With its legs going like clockwork, it keeps up a continual conversation of short, sharp 'twik' sounds.

In spring, sanderlings can be seen in Europe in rusty-brown and white breeding colours. They are most familiar in their winter grey and snow white. Compared with similar dunlins, they seem brighter, more spick and span. They never have a tapered, drooped bill tip, unlike dunlins which often show this.

They nest in the far north, up into the Arctic Circle, yet some go south in winter as far as the southern tip of South Africa and South America: true globetrotters.

Smaller than a thrush; long, straight bill, slim legs. Looks bright, clean, often very pale. Runs fast, usually in small groups; roosts in flocks with dunlins at high tide. Flight low, fast, on sharp-pointed wings.

WHERE AND WHEN European beaches from August to April or May.

PLACES IT PREFERS Sandy and stony beaches, estuaries. Rare inland (usually spring).

LOOKALIKES

Dunlin, page 140, darker, browner in winter; in autumn young dunlins are yellower, with smudgy marks on belly.

  Knot , page 134, bigger, greyer, far less white in winter.

Purple sandpiper

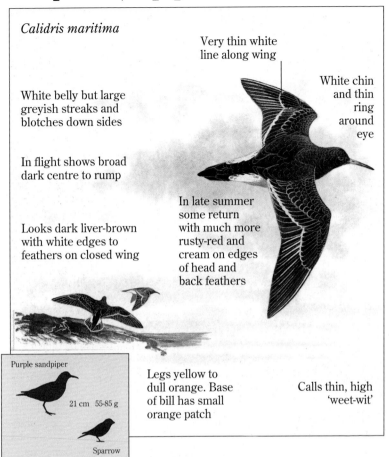

Calidris maritima

Very thin white line along wing

White chin and thin ring around eye

White belly but large greyish streaks and blotches down sides

In flight shows broad dark centre to rump

Looks dark liver-brown with white edges to feathers on closed wing

In late summer some return with much more rusty-red and cream on edges of head and back feathers

Purple sandpiper

21 cm   55-85 g

Sparrow

Legs yellow to dull orange. Base of bill has small orange patch

Calls thin, high 'weet-wit'

Not many wading birds are as fixed to a specialized habitat as the purple sandpiper. It may forage along stony beaches with lines of stranded weed, but not very often: usually it sticks firmly to the rocks and the tangled masses of bladderwrack and other seaweed; also to mussel beds revealed at low tide or old groynes and piers with rusty, weedy piles and pipes.

It is often with turnstones but looks far less patchy in colour. It is hard to spot a purple sandpiper until it moves, but it is worth looking for them along a suitable stretch of coast in autumn and winter. In spring, purple sandpipers fly to the far north, nesting high on Scandinavian hills and in the tundra amongst short shrubs and mosses. Four eggs are laid on the ground; they hatch after 21 to 22 days and the young fly within about three weeks.

Smaller than a thrush. Dumpy, with shortish legs, bill slightly curved down. Feeds on minute creatures amongst seaweed and rocks at edge of sea, often hard to see until disturbed at close range. Darts in and out of rocks with breaking waves.

WHERE AND WHEN Rocky coasts of Western Europe; September to May.

PLACES IT PREFERS Rocky shores with weed, barnacle-encrusted rocks and piers.

LOOKALIKES

Dunlin, page 140, paler, browner, without scaly pattern on wings or orange-yellow legs.

Knot, page 134, bigger, greyer, with dull legs.

Dunlin

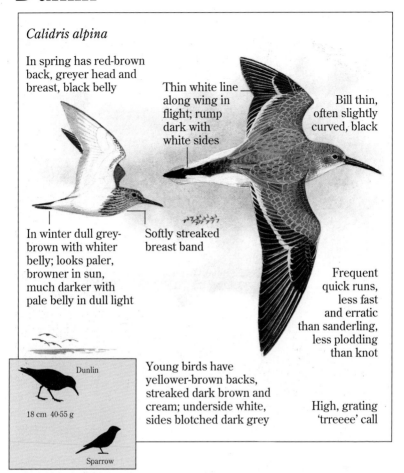

Calidris alpina

In spring has red-brown back, greyer head and breast, black belly

Thin white line along wing in flight; rump dark with white sides

Bill thin, often slightly curved, black

In winter dull grey-brown with whiter belly; looks paler, browner in sun, much darker with pale belly in dull light

Softly streaked breast band

Frequent quick runs, less fast and erratic than sanderling, less plodding than knot

Dunlin

18 cm 40-55 g

Sparrow

Young birds have yellower-brown backs, streaked dark brown and cream; underside white, sides blotched dark grey

High, grating 'trreeee' call

Dunlins are worth studying: they are the commonest and most widespread small wading birds, found at the edges of fresh water and salt water almost all year round. Once you can recognise the dunlin, other small waders are not so difficult.

Dunlins nest on moorland and coastal marshes in the UK and in most of Northern Europe, but some go far north into the Arctic. They have colourful, handsome patterns in spring and summer and many can be seen with these markings before they leave the beaches where they winter. In late summer, bright young dunlins appear, sometimes very tame – perhaps never having seen a human before they migrated south.

Dunlins nest on the ground, laying four eggs in a grass-lined hollow. They hatch after 22 days.

Small wader, not much bigger than a sparrow but long legs and bill give larger appearance. Bill usually slightly curved. Often in flocks, a little scattered, tightening up when flying or coming together to roost at high tide.

WHERE AND WHEN Almost anywhere with water, autumn to spring; Northern and Western Europe in summer.

PLACES IT PREFERS Wet moors, coastal marshes in summer; in winter, mudflats, muddy pools, marshes, seashores.

LOOKALIKES

Knot , page 134, bigger, dumpier, greyer.
Sanderling, page 136, always white underneath, with straight bill, faster run.
  Redshank, page 152, bigger.
  Ringed plover, page 126, has bold black and white pattern on head, not on belly.

Ruff

Philomachus pugnax

In flight shows thin white line along wing and white patch each side of tail ———

Autumn juveniles are deep buff, with sharp pattern of dark brown feathers edged buff all over the back. Face and breast plain buff

Female in summer has black blotches on back

Juveniles have yellow-ochre legs

In winter, legs often orange or yellowish; often shows white on head and neck

Summer male has ruff of black, white or brown, barred or plain

Ruff

Male   Female
22-30 cm 100-250 g
Sparrow

Legs of male often red or orange

Among waders, ruffs are truly extraordinary. Males are much bigger than females and are much more exciting to look at, with remarkable coloured crests, ruffs and facial skin to show off to the hens. In order to make an impression, they get together and fight, but most of it is show. The hens choose the male that looks likely to be the strongest and fittest as a father to their chicks. Females are more camouflaged and altogether less conspicuous than the males. In autumn, ruffs are frequent beside fresh water in all kinds of places. They are taking a rest from migration flights and it is usually the small, very neat juveniles which are seen most often.

Females lay four eggs in long grass; they hatch after 20 to 23 days.

Males pigeon-sized but long-legged. Females and juveniles smaller. Neat, round head on tapered neck, with shortish, slightly curved bill. Walks on mud and wades in shallow water. Flies slowly with rather long, pointed wings. Rarely heard to call.

WHERE AND WHEN Breeds in north-western Europe; elsewhere mostly in autumn, fewer in spring and winter.

PLACES IT PREFERS Shallow pools, rough, wet grassland, sheltered estuaries.

LOOKALIKES

Redshank, page 152, has red on bill as well as legs, broad white band on wing.

Greenshank, page154, has more white on back and longer, slightly upcurved bill.

Knot, page 134, is dumpier; short legs and plainer back.

Snipe & jack snipe

Snipe
Gallinago gallinago

Snipe rich brown with striped head,
long cream stripes on back

Snipe has
very long,
straight bill

Dark cheek stripe
of snipe; cream
centre to crown

In flight, snipe shows pale back
stripes, dark wings with pale line
along the back edge

Jack snipe
Lymnocryptes minimus

Jack snipe small and dark;
centre of crown has
dark stripe

Long cream lines on dark,
glossy back of jack snipe

Snipe   26 cm 100-150 g

Jack snipe

18-20 cm 50-100 g   Sparrow

Snipe has hoarse,
rasping call

Jack snipe flies
off silently

Both these kinds of snipe are birds of wet mud and flooded grassland, where they probe into soft ground for worms. The snipe is far more common than the smaller jack snipe and much easier to see. Snipe often fly up in small groups and dart away with loud calls and sudden zigzags. Jack snipe are quiet, and only fly up at the last moment before being trodden on, going a short distance before dropping down again.

In Western and Southern Europe, although snipe are found all year round, jack snipe only turn up in the winter. They both have narrow heads with large eyes each side, so they can see all round, even behind them, as they bend forwards to feed.

Snipe nest in long grass, laying four eggs which hatch after 22 days.

Snipe *dumpy, blackbird-sized with very long bill. Snipe has spring display flight, diving with tail fanned to create a buzzing noise.*

◁ *Snipe*

Jack snipe *smaller, bill a little shorter in proportion. Short legs. In flight, both have dumpy body, short tail, wings often angled at the wrist.*

Jack snipe ▷

WHERE AND WHEN North and east from central France; moves south and west in winter. Widespread, all year.

Snipe

Jack snipe

WHERE AND WHEN Breeds in extreme north and east of Europe; spreads south and west in winter.

PLACES IT PREFERS Mud, wet grass, in ditches and streams.

PLACES IT PREFERS Wet grass, flooded grassland, sedges, rushes.

145

Woodcock

Scolopax rusticola

Usually seen as silhouette against sky, thickset, short-tailed, with long, straight bill angled downwards

Black bands across back of head; underside all closely barred

Flies with fast, flickering action of wing tips

If disturbed from ground, flies off fast with rushing wings: looks rusty-brown

Call high, sharp 'tswick' and deep growl

Woodcock
34 cm 250-350 g

Sparrow

Woodcocks are special among woodland birds. They choose old conifer plantations and pine forest, damp oak woods with plenty of undergrowth and sycamores with a thick layer of fallen leaves, full of juicy worms. All day they sit still, hard to see because their feathers blend in so well with the leaves and the earth. At dusk, they move out to feed.

In spring they patrol their territories, croaking like frogs and uttering a sharp whistle every few seconds as they fly overhead. In the autumn many Northern European woodcocks leave for Britain and Ireland, crossing the North Sea in search of sheltered places with less likelihood of frost: soft mud is essential for their feeding habits.

They lay four eggs which hatch within 23 days.

 Pigeon-sized. Very long bill, stumpy legs. Long, deep body but very short tail. In flight, wings look broad but taper to short point. Usually impossible to see on ground. Best seen at dusk in summer, flying over trees.

WHERE AND WHEN All year, widespread, but many move south and west in winter.

PLACES IT PREFERS Woodland with boggy clearings, damp ditches.

LOOKALIKES

Snipe, page 144, slimmer, smaller with stripes, not bars, on head.

Owls slower, with broader wings, less likely to fly straight over at treetop height.

Black- & bar-tailed godwits

Black-tailed godwit
Limosa limosa

Bar-tailed godwit
Limosa lapponica

In summer black-tailed has coppery-red head and chest; black bars on sides

In summer bar-tailed is deep rusty-red

In winter, black-tailed is plain, grey on top, pale below

Brown wings; white on rump makes V on back

In winter bar-tailed is grey-brown with brighter chest, streaks on back

Has white band along wing; white patch above black tail

Long, black legs

Black-tailed's long bill is pale orange at base

Tail of bar-tailed is pale, brown and white

Juvenile black-tailed has orange-buff body

Bar-tailed's long bill is slightly curved, pink or orange at base. Legs dark, shorter above joint than black-tailed godwit's

Black-tailed has infrequent, loud 'wicka wicka wicka' call. Bar-tailed's call a low, nasal 'kirruk'

Black-tailed godwit
40 cm
200-400 g

Bar-tailed godwit
37 cm
250-350 g

Sparrow

B lack-tailed godwits nest in the Low Countries and farther north, few in England, more in Iceland. They like wet pastures and low moors. In spring they fly with a rolling, undulating flight, showing off broad white flashes on their wings and tail. In autumn, most move to south-western estuaries in England, Ireland and France, choosing sheltered spots with soft mud. The nest is in short grass; four eggs hatch after 22 to 24 days; the young fly at four weeks.

Bar-tailed godwits are birds of the far north, breeding well inside the Arctic circle. Because the snow there melts so late, many are seen on European estuaries until late May.

Godwits favour the same muddy beaches as knots, redshanks and curlews. At high tide all roost together.

Black-tailed godwit *is tall, upstanding, very striking in flight and colourful in spring. Less streaked than bar-tailed in winter.*

Black-tailed
◁ *godwit*

Bar-tailed godwit *looks shorter-legged, but bill is very long. In winter plumage pattern recalls streaky curlew.*

Bar-tailed godwit ▷

WHERE AND WHEN In summer mostly in far north and west; in winter moves south, more widespread.

Black-tailed godwit

Bar-tailed godwit

WHERE AND WHEN In summer in the Arctic; autumn to spring widespread on Western European coasts.

PLACES IT PREFERS Wet meadows; salt marsh; muddy estuaries and creeks.

PLACES IT PREFERS Muddy estuaries, sandy beaches.

Curlew & whimbrel

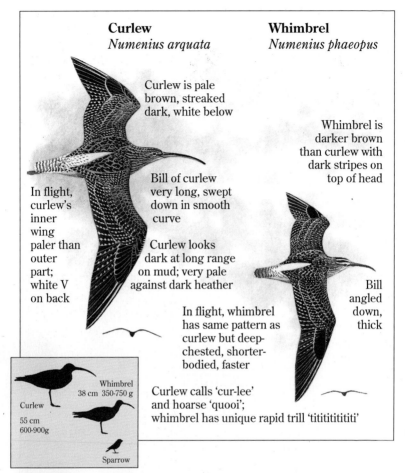

Curlew
Numenius arquata

Whimbrel
Numenius phaeopus

Curlew is pale brown, streaked dark, white below

Whimbrel is darker brown than curlew with dark stripes on top of head

In flight, curlew's inner wing paler than outer part; white V on back

Bill of curlew very long, swept down in smooth curve

Curlew looks dark at long range on mud; very pale against dark heather

Bill angled down, thick

In flight, whimbrel has same pattern as curlew but deep-chested, shorter-bodied, faster

Whimbrel
38 cm 350-750 g

Curlew
55 cm
600-900g

Sparrow

Curlew calls 'cur-lee' and hoarse 'quooi'; whimbrel has unique rapid trill 'titititititititi'

Curlews are found in Europe all year round, while whimbrels visit from spring to autumn. Because they are so much more widespread and common, and have such wonderful calls and songs, curlews are part of folklore and the country scene everywhere. Whimbrels are little-known birds to most people. Both species share long, curved bills, ideal for probing into long, deep tunnels of marine worms and for digging under tussocks of grass or into soft peat to find food. They breed on drier, rank areas of moorland and in rough pastures, but spend much of the year on estuaries where soft mud allows easier feeding. Here they join flocks of other wading birds.

Both species lay four eggs on the ground; these hatch after 27 to 29 days. The young fly after 35 to 40 days.

Curlew *big, with long legs and very long, downcurved bill. Small, round head; long, angled wings. Loud, harsh and clear, liquid calls, and long, excited bubbling song.*

◁ *Curlew*

Whimbrel *smaller, darker, with more 'bent' bill. In flight looks dumpier, with faster wing-beats.*

Whimbrel ▷

WHERE AND WHEN All year, Northern and Western Europe.

Curlew

PLACES IT PREFERS Upland moors, northern pastures, bogs; estuaries, creeks, coastal fields.

WHERE AND WHEN Mostly in north during summer; widespread on coasts in spring and autumn.

Whimbrel

PLACES IT PREFERS Tundra or northern heath in summer; estuaries, beaches in spring and autumn.

151

Redshank & spotted redshank

Redshank
Tringa totanus

Bill of redshank red at base; legs rich orange-red to scarlet. Juvenile has yellow-orange legs at first

Spotted redshank
Tringa erythropus

Spotted redshank is blackish in spring; in autumn some have patches of dull black

Redshank has rich brown, dark streaks. Blacker streaking in summer

In winter, pale grey on top, white below; dark stripe through eye with white line above it

Redshank has white on belly. In flight, reveals big white patch along back and broad white wedge on back of each wing

At all ages spotted redshanks show dark wings in flight and long, narrow patch of white high on back

Juvenile spotted redshank brown with bars on flanks

Legs of spotted redshank very dark red in summer; bright red in winter. Bill very thin; dark red at base

Redshank is noisy with hysterical clamour and loud 'tchyu-u-u'; spotted redshank has clear-cut 'tchew-it'

30 cm
200-250 g

Redshank
27 cm
130-200 g

Spotted
redshank

Sparrow

Redshanks are always jumpy, nervous birds, ready to burst out of a muddy creek at the edge of a marsh or estuary with a sudden explosion of calls at the least disturbance. They feed all over the estuary mud and salt marsh but gather in large, quiet groups at high tide: then they often look very dark compared with the bigger godwits and curlews and much smaller dunlins which may be close by.

Spotted redshanks are much scarcer; they are usually seen in small parties chasing fish fry in shallow pools, sometimes dashing about in short, erratic runs.

Redshanks nest on the ground, laying four eggs; these hatch after 22 to 24 days and the chicks can fly within 28 days. Spotted redshanks breed in the northern coniferous forests.

Both are elegant waders but **redshank** *has slightly shorter legs and bill and dumpier build than spotted redshank. It feeds on mud and at edge of lakes.*

◁ *Redshank*

Spotted redshank *more frequently in water, even swimming, often in small groups. In flight, legs of redshank barely visible, but those of spotted redshank trail well beyond tail.*

Spotted redshank ▷

WHERE AND WHEN All year, Northern and Western Europe; widespread in spring and autumn.

Redshank

PLACES IT PREFERS Wet fields, moors, salt marshes, estuaries, rocky coasts.

WHERE AND WHEN Breeds in extreme north; widespread in spring and autumn, scarce in winter.

Spotted redshank

PLACES IT PREFERS Bogs and northern pools; shallow lakes, estuaries, coastal lagoons.

153

Greenshank

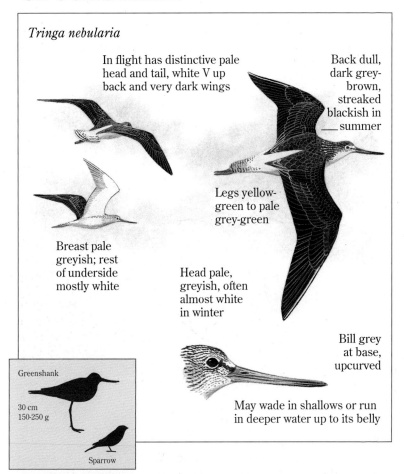

Tringa nebularia

In flight has distinctive pale head and tail, white V up back and very dark wings

Back dull, dark grey-brown, streaked blackish in summer

Legs yellow-green to pale grey-green

Breast pale greyish; rest of underside mostly white

Head pale, greyish, often almost white in winter

Bill grey at base, upcurved

Greenshank

30 cm
150-250 g

Sparrow

May wade in shallows or run in deeper water up to its belly

No wader is more elegant and delicate in appearance than the greenshank. Compared with the dumpy redshank, it looks neater, paler, longer-legged and much more tapered. It is, though, quick and active in its movements, often dashing after tiny fish fry in shallow water with a great deal of splashing as it goes. The green of its legs can be hard to see – they look dull and pale. Greenshanks are wild, elusive birds in summer, when they nest on remote northern moors; in autumn they are more easily found beside lakes and reservoirs and on the shore.

They lay four eggs on the ground; these hatch after 24 days and the young fly at 25 to 31 days old. A few stay all winter in Europe, but most go south to Africa.

Pigeon-sized, but long, slim legs. Bill long, slightly upcurved. In flight looks long-winged and slim-bodied, tail and legs tapered to a point. Wary; easily disturbed, going away with loud, repeated 'tchu tchu tchu' calls.

WHERE AND WHEN Rare in winter; widespread in spring and autumn; in summer in far north-west of Europe.

PLACES IT PREFERS Nests on wet moors, in forest clearings; in autumn beside fresh water and on coastal creeks.

LOOKALIKES

Redshank, page 152, darker, especially on head.

Godwits, page 148, larger, with longer bills and blacker legs.

Ruff in autumn, page 142, much brighter with pale buff feather edges and different rump and tail pattern in flight.

Wood & green sandpipers

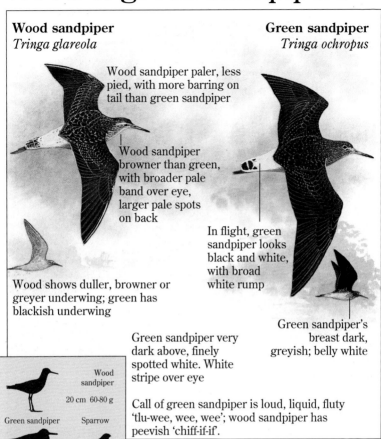

Wood sandpiper
Tringa glareola

Green sandpiper
Tringa ochropus

Wood sandpiper paler, less pied, with more barring on tail than green sandpiper

Wood sandpiper browner than green, with broader pale band over eye, larger pale spots on back

In flight, green sandpiper looks black and white, with broad white rump

Wood shows duller, browner or greyer underwing; green has blackish underwing

Green sandpiper's breast dark, greyish; belly white

Green sandpiper very dark above, finely spotted white. White stripe over eye

Wood sandpiper
20 cm 60-80 g

Green sandpiper   Sparrow

22 cm
70-100 g

Call of green sandpiper is loud, liquid, fluty 'tlu-wee, wee, wee'; wood sandpiper has peevish 'chiff-if-if'.

Green and wood sandpipers are a little larger and much less often seen than common sandpipers. Both nest farther north in Europe and go to Africa in winter, except for a few green sandpipers that stay on tiny inland pools and beside streams all winter through. Like common sandpipers, they have a swinging, bobbing action of the body, especially the green sandpiper, but they are quite different in flight, with a quicker, easier action compared with the common sandpiper's low, jerky flight. Like most waders, they are much commoner in most places in early autumn than at any other time, as young birds move slowly south, resting and feeding for long periods.

Green sandpipers lay in an old thrush or pigeon nest; wood sandpipers nest on the ground. Four eggs hatch after 22 days.

Both are blackbird-sized. **Wood sandpiper** *small-headed, rounder-bodied, longer-legged than green sandpiper.*

◁ *Wood sandpiper*

Green sandpiper *small, tapered at tail; bobs head and swings tail up and down. Flies off fast, zigzagging and gaining height.*

Green sandpiper ▷

WHERE AND WHEN Breeds Scandinavia and east of Baltic. Widespread April to May and August to September.

Wood sandpiper

PLACES IT PREFERS Boggy forest clearings in summer; muddy pools.

WHERE AND WHEN Mostly spring and autumn. Breeds in far north. Scattered during winter.

Green sandpiper

PLACES IT PREFERS Fresh water edges; salt-marsh creeks.

Common sandpiper

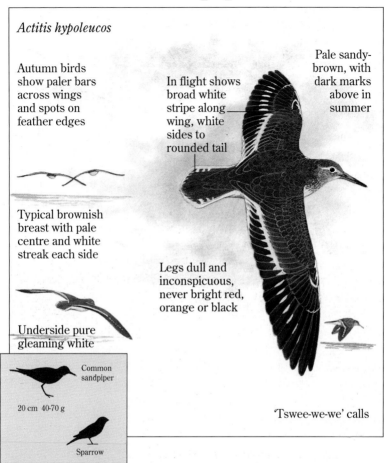

Actitis hypoleucos

Autumn birds show paler bars across wings and spots on feather edges

In flight shows broad white stripe along wing, white sides to rounded tail

Pale sandy-brown, with dark marks above in summer

Typical brownish breast with pale centre and white streak each side

Legs dull and inconspicuous, never bright red, orange or black

Underside pure gleaming white

Common sandpiper

20 cm 40-70 g

Sparrow

'Tswee-we-we' calls

C ommon sandpipers are typical of northern valleys with fast-flowing stony streams, and lakes edged with pebbles and smooth grass. They are noisy, making fast, trilling and ringing 'tswee-we-we' calls which echo around the hills. In autumn they move south, heading for Africa, pausing for a day or two beside all kinds of lakes and pools as they go. Common sandpipers, like many other waders, are seen in this way far from their nesting places. Unlike other small waders, such as dunlins, common sandpipers are unlikely to be seen in groups of more than five or six together: they don't gather in large, dense flocks like many of the true shorebirds.

The nest is on a grassy bank. Four eggs hatch after 22 days; the young fly when four weeks old.

 Thrush-sized. Shortish, straight bill; short pale legs. Long rear body bobs up and down like a wagtail's. Flies with peculiar stiff wings, held in rigid arc or downward curve; wing-beats quick, flicking. Looks pale, with white wing stripes above and below.

WHERE AND WHEN Mostly spring to autumn; few in winter on coasts.

PLACES IT PREFERS Streams, lakes, shallow pools, rocky coasts.

LOOKALIKES
Dunlin, page 140, greyer in winter, with black legs, curved bill, often in flocks.   **Snipe,** page 144, striped, longer-billed.   **Green sandpiper,** page 156, darker, much more black-and-white in flight.

Turnstone

Arenaria interpres

In spring and summer has white head with black on face and breast; bright orange-red on back.

In winter duller, more black on face and breast, back dark oily-brown ——

Complicated white patches on wings and back show in flight.

Legs short, vivid orange

Bill short and stout, black

Turnstone
22-24 cm
80-140 g

Sparrow

Typically low, leaning forward, shuffling on rocks or beach

Abrupt, metallic calls, 'tewk' or 'tikitik'

Turnstones are waders of the high Arctic, rarely breeding in the far north-west of Europe, but they are found on many coasts virtually all year round. There are always a few young birds hanging about in summer, and in winter they are common wherever there are rocks and heaps of washed-up seaweed or shells. Groups are noisy, making quick, bickering calls and sharp rattles as they feed and squabble or fly a few metres if approached too closely. They are usually tame and don't move far unless disturbed from a roost at high tide. Their handsome piebald and tortoiseshell breeding plumage can be seen from about February and again when they return in late summer.

Four eggs are laid which hatch after 22 to 24 days, and the young fly 19 to 21 days later.

Thrush-sized, stocky; short legs and bill. Bill may look upcurved. Loud, sharp, rapid call notes. Often in groups on rocks, or mixed with other waders on pebbly beach. Leans forward and picks about in seaweed or tips up pebbles. Fast, flicking flight.

WHERE AND WHEN Breeds on islands in Arctic; all round coasts most of year.

PLACES IT PREFERS Sandy beaches with strand lines; rocks, seaweed-covered piers, groynes.

LOOKALIKES

Nothing so patterned in summer: **dunlin,** page 140, more streaked, black on belly. In winter, nothing else of same size is so black on breast and white below.

Arctic & great skuas

Arctic skua
Stercorarius parasiticus

Great skua
Stercorarius skua

Arctic skua comes in several forms: dark brown except for white wing flash; paler brown with dark cap and dark above; white below with breast band and black cap

Young great skua can be almost all blackish except for wing patches

Both dive at people who enter their nesting territories

Great Skua is dark brown to rusty with paler neck. Large white wing patch

Arctic chases kittiwakes and terns, often in pairs

Great skua chases gulls and gannets, forcing them into the sea

Arctic skua
38-48 cm 440 g

Great skua
60 cm 1,200 g

Sparrow

Juvenile Arctic skua more barred, paler beneath than dark adult

Great skua has a low, quiet 'tuktuk' call; Arctic's is a loud, wild, nasal 'yahh-ow'

Skuas are exciting birds of the north, breeding on remote, wild islands and passing south in the autumn along Western European coasts. They can catch fish and often kill smaller birds, but they also specialize in chasing gulls and terns in order to make them drop the fish they have caught: they are the pirates of the oceans. Arctic skuas are elegant and beautiful; great skuas can be just as quick but look heavier and bulky. The best way to see them is to watch from a headland in autumn, especially if there is a strong wind blowing onshore which brings them closer to land. They stand out from gulls, looking much darker, with a flash of white in each wing.

Both nest on the ground; two eggs hatch after 25 to 29 days. The young fly when a month old.

Both are gull-like. **Arctic skua** *is tapered, with long tail ending in narrow point. It has long, narrow wings, angled and pointed*

◁ *Arctic skua*

Great skua
bulky, with short, almost square tail. It has broad wings with short, sharp point.

Great skua ▷

Arctic skua

Great skua

WHERE AND WHEN
Breeds Iceland, Scandinavian coasts, Scotland: widespread off coasts, April to October.

PLACES IT PREFERS Bleak coastal heath, peat bogs; at sea except when nesting.

WHERE AND WHEN
Breeds Iceland, Faroes and Scotland: widespread off Western European coasts, April to October.

PLACES IT PREFERS Bleak coastal heaths and moors; at sea when not nesting.

Black-headed gull

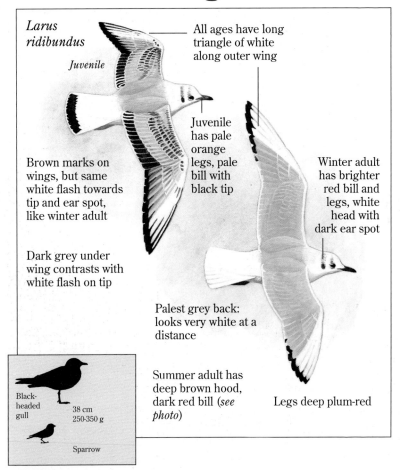

Larus ridibundus

Juvenile

All ages have long triangle of white along outer wing

Brown marks on wings, but same white flash towards tip and ear spot, like winter adult

Dark grey under wing contrasts with white flash on tip

Juvenile has pale orange legs, pale bill with black tip

Winter adult has brighter red bill and legs, white head with dark ear spot

Palest grey back: looks very white at a distance

Black-headed gull 38 cm 250-350 g

Sparrow

Summer adult has deep brown hood, dark red bill (*see photo*)

Legs deep plum-red

Black-headed gulls are everywhere. They have always nested inland and foraged on moors and farmland, but in recent decades they have become more frequent at refuse tips, in gardens and parks and anywhere where people leave scraps. Because of this they are the easiest gulls to see and to recognize – the pattern of white on the wing is especially striking.

They follow the plough and dive for worms, or chase lapwings and other birds to steal worms from them, keeping up a babble of chuckling and squealing calls. From a colony in early spring the noise of several hundred black-headed gulls is a deafening chorus of chattering noises and harsh screams.

They nest on the ground or in rushes, laying two or three eggs which hatch after 23 to 26 days; chicks fly at 35 days old.

 Larger, longer-winged than pigeon. Slim and tapered. Thin bill. Short, square tail, wings long, angled, tapered to long point. Noisy, quarrelsome, often bold around park lakes, car parks and the beach. May come into gardens or stand on roofs.

WHERE AND WHEN All year; widespread in Europe.

PLACES IT PREFERS Upland lakes, pools, reservoirs, coasts, wet fields, rubbish tips.

LOOKALIKES

Most **gulls** have white head in summer.

Terns have jet-black caps, rather than brown hood.

Common gull

Larus canus

Immature has pale orange legs, bill with sharp black tip

Immature has brown back; tail pure white except for broad, neat black band

Wing tips blunt, black with large white spots; more black beneath than on herring gull

Head grey, streaked, in winter

Darker grey back than black-headed gull; prominent white patch between grey back and black wing tips

Round head with dark eye; small bill is greenish, with no red

Legs grey to yellow-green

Common gull

40 cm
370-450 g

Sparrow

Calls squeaky 'yip' and loud, squealing wail thinner and higher than herring gull's

In much of Northern Europe and parts of northern Britain this is a familiar gull in summer, but it is scarce farther south. In winter it is found far more widely than in summer, yet there are still large areas where it is scarce for no obvious reason.

It is a gull of open, smooth grassland, including playing fields, where it spends much time walking about in search of worms. It will join in the scramble of gulls at a refuse tip, or on the beach, but is usually a little more shy and quiet than the black-headed or much bigger herring gulls. In summer, it prefers sheltered bays and rocky outcrops, or open moorland not far from the sea, rather than exposed sea-cliffs and islands.

Nests are on rocky islets or in boggy areas. Three eggs hatch after 24 to 27 days; young fly at 35 days old.

Bigger than a pigeon; short legs and bill; long, tapered wings. Elegant shape. Rounded head with small bill, round dark eye. Flies easily and well, with easy, relaxed action but less soaring than bigger species.

WHERE AND WHEN Northern and Western Europe in summer; widespread in winter.

PLACES IT PREFERS Rocky inlets, stony shores, moors, beaches, lakes.

LOOKALIKES

Herring gull, page 170, has a similar pattern but is much bigger, with pale eye, red spot on bill.

   Black-headed gull, page 164, smaller, paler, with white triangle along wing and red legs.

Lesser black-backed gull

Larus fuscus

Gradually gets dark grey on back and wings as it gets older

Legs yellow, brightest in summer

Dark grey above (blacker in north); black wing tips have white spots

Juvenile dark with black bill, dark wings with double dark band across inner wing, solidly black-brown outer wing

Bill yellow with red spot

Head pure white in summer, streaked grey-brown in winter

Call deep 'uh-uh' and deep, throaty laughing wail, deeper than herring gull's

Lesser black-backed gull   52 cm   600-1,000 g

Sparrow

The lesser black-backed gull is a large, elegant and attractive gull, especially handsome in summer when its plumage is immaculate and its legs are vivid yellow. At this time they congregate on islands and clifftops, often on flatter ground than the herring gulls which breed nearby. It is an aggressive bird and, despite being smaller than a herring gull, can chase them away when feeding at sea. It seems to go farther from land more often than herring gulls. A blacker-backed subspecies in Scandinavia feeds much more at sea, and dives for fish. The lesser black-backed also migrates to Africa for the winter, travelling much farther than most herring gulls.

Nests are on rocks or in grass or heather; the three eggs hatch after 24 to 27 days and the young fly at 30 to 40 days.

Larger than mallard; long wings. Long, tapered shape when standing, legs short. Big yellow bill with red spot. Swims well; walks easily; flies with long glides; can soar high in the air. Often follows ships.

WHERE AND WHEN Mainly in Northern and Western Europe in summer; some spend winter in Iberia and Britain.

PLACES IT PREFERS Islands, rocky coasts, moors, beaches, lakes.

LOOKALIKES

Herring gull, page 170, is much paler grey above.

   Great black-backed gull, page 172, blacker (except in Scandinavia, where lessers are also very black) and much bigger.

Herring & yellow-legged gulls

Herring gull
Larus argentatus

Northern herring gulls are darker than in UK

Herring gull in winter has brown streaks on head

Both species pale silvery-grey and white, wing tips black with white spots

Herring gull's legs usually pale pink. Bill yellow with red spot

Juvenile mottled brown; base of bill pale; wing has one dark band along rear edge and pale patch behind angle

Gradually gets pale grey on back as it gets older

Yellow-legged gull
Larus cachinnans
Yellow-legged has smooth, mid-grey back; head mostly white in winter

Yellow-legged's legs are bright yellow. Bill often brightly coloured

Immature yellow-legged more contrasted, with blacker tail band, than young herring gull

Herring gull
Yellow-legged gull
55 cm 750-1,200 g

Sparrow

These are both the 'typical' seagull, the silver-grey and white bird with black wing tips that steals food from rubbish bins, snatches sandwiches from holidaymakers and makes loud, squealing calls from rooftops at any seaside town. In the north, herring gulls are bigger and darker grey; in Britain they are relatively smaller and paler, with more black on the wing tip. In France and Spain the bird is darker again, has yellow legs and is treated by some people as a different species altogether, the yellow-legged gull. In summer both species are bold and approachable, but in winter, especially inland, they frequently become shy and difficult to approach.

Nests are on rocks or cliff ledges; three eggs hatch after 28 to 30 days.

Both are large, long-winged, with heavy, hook-tipped bill. Fierce pale eye. Long, broad wings taper to point; flies brilliantly, soaring and gliding along cliffs or behind ships.

◁ *Herring gull*

Both swim well. Often in large flocks, sitting around for hours on fields or quiet beaches, mixed with other gulls. Noisy and aggressive.

Yellow-legged gull ▷

WHERE AND WHEN Widespread especially on coasts, all year; many move inland in winter.

Herring gull

PLACES IT PREFERS Islands, cliffs, beaches, tips, open fields, lakes.

WHERE AND WHEN Mediterranean, Iberia and western France; in autumn some move to south-east England, Netherlands.

Yellow-legged gull

PLACES IT PREFERS Beaches, islands, refuse tips.

Great black-backed gull

Larus marinus

Wing tips black with large white patches

Very big; upperparts deep black, slightly browner in summer

Juvenile ——— brown above with big black spots, much paler on head. Bill very big, black

Bill yellow with red spot

Gets black patches on back as it gets older

Head stays white, even in winter

Legs very pale whitish-pink

Great black-backed gull

65 cm
1,400-1,800 g

Sparrow

Next to lesser black-backed gull, can look 'twice as big' - twice as heavy, but not much longer overall

Call short, very deep 'aowk' and 'uh-uh-uh'

O f all the gulls, this is the biggest, meanest and most impressive. Its great bulk makes it obvious in a mixed flock in winter. On the coast, where it nests, it chooses the highest rocks and makes itself look extra important: it also has the deepest, hoarsest, least musical calls.

In winter, most great black-backs stay on the coast but increasing numbers move inland to feed on tips and join the big gull roosts on some lakes and reservoirs, gathering at dusk in their hundreds. At this time they feed on all sorts of scraps and refuse, but in summer they are capable of killing birds as big as puffins and eating them in one gulp.

Nests in isolation on clifftops, laying two or three eggs which hatch at 27 to 28 days; young fly when two months old.

 Goose-sized. Long wings; very thick, hooked bill. Big white head; pale eye. Looks heavy and fierce, bad-tempered. Flies well but lumbering low over water. Often on highest crag of sea cliff or island.

WHERE AND WHEN All year in Northern and Western Europe; spreads to eastern England and Low Countries in winter.

PLACES IT PREFERS Cliffs, islands, all kinds of beaches, refuse tips inland.

LOOKALIKES

Lesser black-backed gull, page 168, is smaller, slimmer, with yellow legs; paler on back; much more streaked on head in winter.

Young **herring gull,** page 170, has smaller, paler bill.

Kittiwake

Rissa tridactyla

Juvenile has black band on neck and black W mark across wings

In winter head is grey with dark smudge behind eye

Large white head; short white tail

Beware faded immatures in summer, with the W on the wing dull and patchy

Pale grey above, palest just before wing tip

Bill greenish-yellow; legs black or dark brown

Wing tips 'dipped in ink' – black with no large white spots

Kittiwake

40 cm   350-425 g

Sparrow

At colonies, calls constant loud, nasal 'kitt-i-a-wake' and high sighing notes

One of the most handsome and attractive gulls, the kittiwake is a true sea gull, spending most of its life out over the ocean. It is thoroughly at home at sea, even in a gale, when it flies in long, rising and falling arcs, using the strength of the wind to move long distances with little effort. It is rare inland, although some seem deliberately to cross land in the early spring; in late autumn some appear inland after prolonged storms. It comes to breed on sheer cliffs, making precarious nests of seaweed and grass on the tiniest ledges and bumps. The two eggs hatch after 27 days and the young fly after 42 days. On some northern cliffs, kittiwakes nest in tens or hundreds of thousands, a wonderful sight – and sound.

Pigeon-sized. Very short legs; long wings; weak bill, round head with gentle dark eye. Flies well with bounding action, relaxed wing-beats. Very noisy at large colonies. Not usually mixed with gull flocks on beaches or tips.

WHERE AND WHEN Cliffs and oceans of north and west.

PLACES IT PREFERS Coasts and open sea, sometimes on buildings and piers.

LOOKALIKES

Common gull, page 166, has pale legs, white spots on wing tips and walks about in fields.

Herring gull, page 170, is much bigger.

Sandwich tern

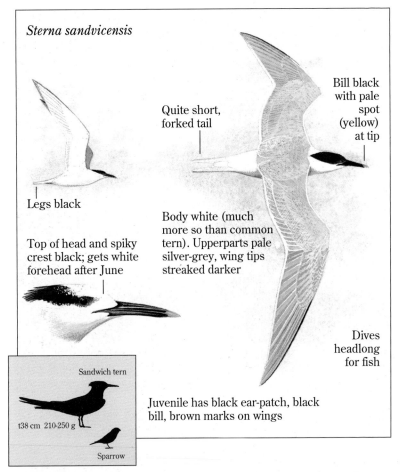

Sterna sandvicensis

Quite short, forked tail

Bill black with pale spot (yellow) at tip

Legs black

Body white (much more so than common tern). Upperparts pale silver-grey, wing tips streaked darker

Top of head and spiky crest black; gets white forehead after June

Dives headlong for fish

Sandwich tern

t38 cm 210-250 g

Sparrow

Juvenile has black ear-patch, black bill, brown marks on wings

All terns are nervous and highly-strung, but the Sandwich is the most erratic of all. One year there may be a big colony in some sand dunes or on a shingle spit, the next there are none. A fox can make a colony desert; and a high tide or a wind blowing sand over their eggs can ruin the nesting season of hundreds of pairs.

Sandwich terns spend the winter in West Africa and return to Europe at the end of March or in April, earlier than other terns; they stand out because they are a little larger and much whiter. As they fly over the sea they give loud, harsh, slightly squeaky 'kirrick' calls.

The one or two eggs are laid on sand or shingle and hatch after 25 days; the young fly at 28 to 30 days.

Pigeon-sized but very long and slim, especially in the wing. Long, spiky bill. Very short legs, hardly walks. Flight elegant, bouncy; dives into water with loud splash. Very noisy at nesting colonies.

WHERE AND WHEN Northern and western coasts in summer; more widespread in autumn.

PLACES IT PREFERS Dunes, shingle and sand beaches, the sea.

LOOKALIKES
Black-headed gull, page 164, has brown hood.   **Common** and **Arctic terns,** page 178, have red legs and bill, darker grey back.

Common & Arctic terns

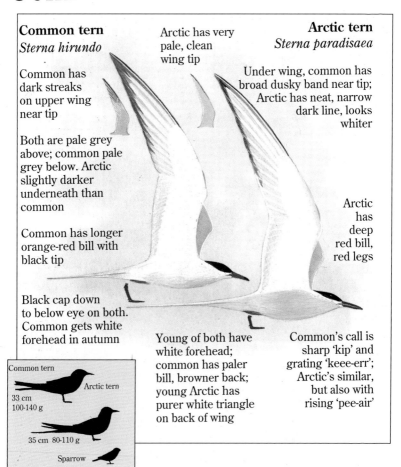

Common tern
Sterna hirundo

Arctic has very pale, clean wing tip

Arctic tern
Sterna paradisaea

Common has dark streaks on upper wing near tip

Under wing, common has broad dusky band near tip; Arctic has neat, narrow dark line, looks whiter

Both are pale grey above; common pale grey below. Arctic slightly darker underneath than common

Arctic has deep red bill, red legs

Common has longer orange-red bill with black tip

Black cap down to below eye on both. Common gets white forehead in autumn

Young of both have white forehead; common has paler bill, browner back; young Arctic has purer white triangle on back of wing

Common's call is sharp 'kip' and grating 'keee-err'; Arctic's similar, but also with rising 'pee-air'

Common tern
Arctic tern
33 cm
100-140 g
35 cm 80-110 g
Sparrow

These are two very similar terns, often confused. Both are lovely, elegant birds with long wings and very long, deeply forked tails like a swallow's. They fish offshore, diving from the air head first to catch a fish in the bill. They are noisy and may be aggressive at the nest, even diving down to hit people on the head if they come too close. They move south in autumn, the common tern going to the seas off West Africa, the Arctic tern going right down into Antarctica beyond South Africa. It is often said that the Arctic tern spends most of its life in daylight, going from the Arctic summer to the Antarctic summer where the sun hardly sets. Common terns are much more likely to be seen on lakes inland. Both nest on the ground, laying one to three eggs which hatch after 21 to 22 days.

Both are pigeon-sized but slim and lightly built. Very short legs. Pointed bill slimmer, sharper than gulls'. Long, angled, pointed wings. Very long tail with pointed streamers each side.

◁ *Common tern*

Arctic *has longer tail than common; shorter bill and legs; rounder head; dumpier neck.*

Arctic tern ▷

WHERE AND WHEN Coasts and large river systems of Europe; April to October.

Common tern

PLACES IT PREFERS Inshore waters, sandy beaches, lakes, reservoirs.

WHERE AND WHEN Coasts of Northern Europe, inland in Iceland and northern Scandinavia, April to October.

Arctic tern

PLACES IT PREFERS Bleak heathland, tundra, rocky islets; open sea on migration.

179

Little tern

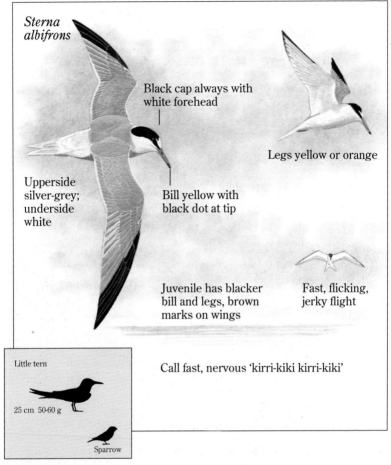

Sterna albifrons

Black cap always with white forehead

Legs yellow or orange

Upperside silver-grey; underside white

Bill yellow with black dot at tip

Juvenile has blacker bill and legs, brown marks on wings

Fast, flicking, jerky flight

Little tern

25 cm   50-60 g

Sparrow

Call fast, nervous 'kirri-kiki kirri-kiki'

Little terns are indeed the smallest terns, fast and furious rather than elegant and graceful like their larger cousins. By comparison, they look like clockwork toys; when they dive for fish they hit the water with a smack, throwing up a small splash of spray, but hardly with enough force to go right under.

Little terns nest right at the edge of the waves on a beach, so their eggs are often washed away by high tides or when a gale blows up. Also, they are especially likely to be disturbed by humans, because they prefer the sandy or pebble beaches where people gather on summer weekends. In autumn they move south, going to Africa for the winter.

One to three eggs hatch after 18 to 22 days and the young fly 19 to 20 days later.

Thrush-sized; very slim. Short legs; spiky, pointed bill. Long, narrow, pointed wings held angled in flight. Tail quite short, forked. Stands on beach but barely walks except for shuffling waddle. Noisy. Splashes into water after fish.

WHERE AND WHEN Spring to autumn, beaches and islands.

PLACES IT PREFERS Sand and shingle; estuaries.

LOOKALIKES

Other terns much bigger, slower, with red or black bill and legs.

Black tern

Chidlonias niger

Juvenile paler, browner above but still has same pattern as autumn adult and dark breast spots. Head has distinctive black cap with 'ear flaps'

Bill blackish; legs dark reddish

In summer, sooty black except for white under tail, pale grey underwing

Wings broader than little tern's; tail broader, squarer, pale grey

In autumn, dusky grey above, white below; distinct grey smudge each side of chest

Call short, squeaky 'kik'

Black tern

25 cm
60-80 g

Sparrow

Black terns are 'marsh terns', birds of fresh water and sheltered coasts, which dip to the surface to pick up insects and tiny fish fry. They behave differently from the 'sea terns' which dive right in to catch fish; they look different too – their summer plumage is much blacker and their tails are less deeply forked.

In many areas of Western Europe they are migrants in spring and autumn and have the habit of turning up, every few years, in unexpected numbers for a day or two. Sometimes 'black tern days' involve several hundred birds where normally there might be ten or a dozen. Such influxes, dependent on the weather, are unpredictable and therefore all the more exciting.

Nests are in floating waterweed; two to four eggs hatch after 21 to 22 days; chicks fly at 19 to 25 days.

 Smaller than a pigeon, long-winged, very short-legged. Dainty, buoyant flight, often swooping down to water but rarely diving in. Usually flies low, slowly, head to wind. Often stands on buoy, post, pier or boat.

WHERE AND WHEN Spring to autumn, most of Europe.

PLACES IT PREFERS Marshes, freshwater lakes, shallow pools, coasts.

LOOKALIKES

Young **common tern,** page 178, in autumn is similar but paler, with pale-based bill and longer, paler tail.

Arctic tern, page 178, in summer has pale cheeks, paler grey underside.

Guillemot & razorbill

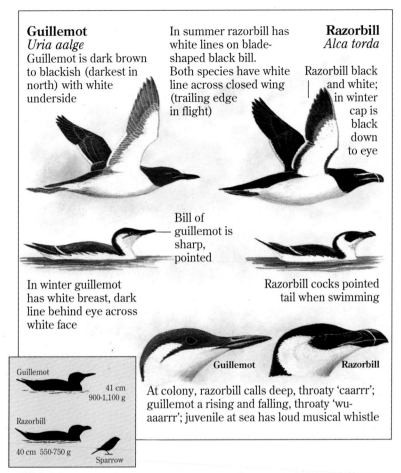

Guillemot
Uria aalge
Guillemot is dark brown to blackish (darkest in north) with white underside

In summer razorbill has white lines on blade-shaped black bill.
Both species have white line across closed wing (trailing edge in flight)

Razorbill
Alca torda

Razorbill black and white; in winter cap is black down to eye

Bill of guillemot is sharp, pointed

In winter guillemot has white breast, dark line behind eye across white face

Razorbill cocks pointed tail when swimming

Guillemot

Razorbill

Guillemot
41 cm
900-1,100 g

Razorbill
40 cm 550-750 g
Sparrow

At colony, razorbill calls deep, throaty 'caarrr'; guillemot a rising and falling, throaty 'wu-aaarrr'; juvenile at sea has loud musical whistle

Both these species are seabirds which come to land only to nest on sheer cliffs above the ceaselessly moving sea. Razorbills choose cavities and deep ledges, while guillemots line up in rows along the most open, exposed ledges where they lay their large, pear-shaped eggs directly on to bare rock. The rocks quickly become white with droppings, the whole place smelling of fish, but the lively scene and constant sound of calling birds makes their nesting colonies some of the finest sights of the bird world. At sea, both razorbills and guillemots swim like corks, diving under to catch fish. They use their wings under water rather than their feet, 'flying' after their prey.

Both lay a single egg which hatches after 28 to 37 days; chicks leave the cliffs long before they can fly.

Both are pigeon-sized but squat; very short-legged. **Guillemot** *has pointed bill, square tail.*

◁ *Guillemot*

Razorbill *has deep, blunt bill, pointed tail often cocked. Fast flight with whirring wings, low and straight. Both swim very well, often diving; stand upright on cliff ledges.*

Razorbill ▷

WHERE AND WHEN Cliffs and oceans of north-western Europe.

WHERE AND WHEN Coasts from north-western France to Iceland and Scandinavia.

Guillemot

Razorbill

PLACES IT PREFERS Sea and sea cliffs; open sea except when nesting.

PLACES IT PREFERS Cliffs in summer; otherwise at sea.

Puffin

Fratercula arctica

Upperside
shiny black

Bill big in summer,
mainly red with
yellow lines

Underside white

Face grey,
surrounded by
black. In winter,
face darker, smudgy

Legs bright orange

Puffin
30 cm 350-450 g

Sparrow

Deep, slow
'arr-ooarr' at
burrow

In winter and
juvenile, bill
smaller, darker
and harder to
see at distance

Puffins are everyone's favourites: but to see them you have to travel to the coast and usually to the north. They breed in very small colonies in northern France but in Ireland, Scotland and a few places in Norway they are found in many thousands at traditional sites. After breeding, they go out to sea and are rarely seen from land unless driven in by a storm. Next spring, they suddenly appear in flocks offshore, waiting a few days before they come to land again for the first time. Then they clear out old burrows or dig new tunnels in which to nest. Some very large colonies have been abandoned after all the loose soil had been worn away by tunnelling puffins. The single egg hatches after 39 days and the chick leaves its nest after 38 to 65 days.

Pigeon-sized; upright, waddles easily on short legs. Swims very well; dives often. Flies low, fast and straight with rapid wing-beats. Takes off from cliff with steep dive. Can float in rising air currents.

WHERE AND WHEN Islands and cliffs from north-west France northwards, all year.

PLACES IT PREFERS Grassy slopes above cliffs, broken rock on cliff faces; at sea when not nesting.

LOOKALIKES

Little auk, page 376, smaller, with small bill, longer wings in flight.

Guillemot and **razorbill,** page 184, bigger, with longer head and neck shapes.

Rock dove

Columba livia

Blue-grey, with white blob above bill, two large black bars across wing

Underside of wing white

Lower back has big, square white patch

Town pigeons can be similar, or spotted darker; white; red-brown; or various mixtures of colours

Shiny purple and green on sides of neck

Rock dove

34 cm   250-300 g

Sparrow

Fleshy patch on bill small (larger on domestic pigeons)

Typical crooning, like domestic pigeon

True rock doves are now rare. Thousands of years ago, they were domesticated; their descendants, racing and dovecot pigeons of all colours, have gone wild again and taken over from the original type except in the far north and west.

The real rock dove is a handsome bird, fast-flying and wild, ideally suited to a life on and around the cliffs from deserts in Africa to the wild Atlantic coast. Groups dash by, sweep down with stiff wings held up in a V, and turn out of sight into a hidden cave. They fly to fields to feed, often taking advantage of cereal crops where they can find fallen grain, but they also like areas of short grass where they eat succulent shoots and roots.

Two eggs are laid on a ledge in a cave and hatch after 16 to 19 days; chicks fly 35 days later.

 Same size and shape as racing pigeon, but neater bill. Short legs – walks with typical pigeon waddle. Rarely perches on trees. Flight fast, wings long and pointed, tail short and square.

WHERE AND WHEN Coasts of far Northern and Western Europe; some inland cliffs.

PLACES IT PREFERS Rocks of all kinds, caves, nearby pasture and cereal fields.

LOOKALIKES

Easily confused with **domestic pigeons**.

Stock dove, page 190, rounder, has grey rump and smaller wing bars.

Stock dove & wood pigeon

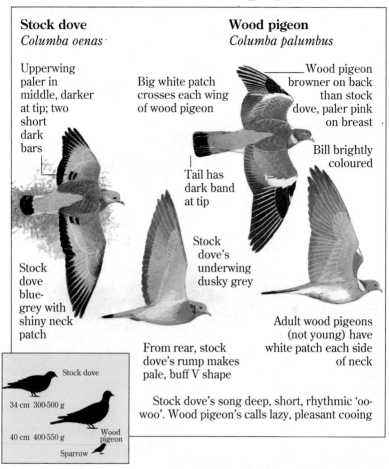

Stock dove
Columba oenas

Wood pigeon
Columba palumbus

Upperwing paler in middle, darker at tip; two short dark bars

Big white patch crosses each wing of wood pigeon

Wood pigeon browner on back than stock dove, paler pink on breast

Bill brightly coloured

Tail has dark band at tip

Stock dove blue-grey with shiny neck patch

Stock dove's underwing dusky grey

Adult wood pigeons (not young) have white patch each side of neck

From rear, stock dove's rump makes pale, buff V shape

Stock dove's song deep, short, rhythmic 'oo-woo'. Wood pigeon's calls lazy, pleasant cooing

Stock dove

34 cm 300-500 g

40 cm 400-550 g Wood pigeon

Sparrow

Stock doves are widespread but rarely abundant, while wood pigeons can be seen in flocks of hundreds, especially in winter. Both are handsome pigeons, the stock dove bluer, the wood pigeon more contrasted and bright. Sometimes wood pigeons are tame and easily seen in town parks and gardens, but in farmland, where they are shot as pests, they are usually much more shy. They make their nests of twigs in trees and thickets, and usually lay two white eggs which hatch after 17 to 19 days; the young fly at 16 to 35 days. Stock doves like to nest in barns or old trees with holes; but they also nest on cliff ledges under overhangs and can be seen far up on remote hillsides or on wild, windswept shores. The two eggs hatch in 16 to 18 days, and the young fly after 27 days.

Stock dove
*size and shape
of domestic
pigeon, but
rounder head
and wing.*

◁ *Stock dove*

Wood pigeon
*bigger, longer
wings and tail,
longer neck,
looking less
rounded in
flight. Both
perch on trees,
wires, buildings.
They walk easily
and fly fast,
noisily with
clattering wings.*

Wood pigeon ▷

WHERE AND WHEN
Not northern
Scandinavia;
those from north
and east of
Germany move
south and west
in winter.

Stock dove

Wood pigeon

WHERE AND WHEN
All except
extreme north of
Europe; eastern
populations
move west in
winter.

PLACES IT PREFERS Farmland, woods,
cliffs, quarries.

PLACES IT PREFERS Farmland, woods.

Collared & turtle doves

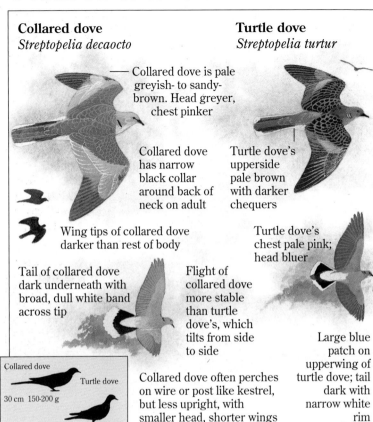

Collared dove
Streptopelia decaocto

Turtle dove
Streptopelia turtur

— Collared dove is pale greyish- to sandy-brown. Head greyer, chest pinker

Collared dove has narrow black collar around back of neck on adult

Turtle dove's upperside pale brown with darker chequers

Wing tips of collared dove darker than rest of body

Turtle dove's chest pale pink; head bluer

Tail of collared dove dark underneath with broad, dull white band across tip

Flight of collared dove more stable than turtle dove's, which tilts from side to side

Large blue patch on upperwing of turtle dove; tail dark with narrow white rim

Collared dove often perches on wire or post like kestrel, but less upright, with smaller head, shorter wings

Collared dove

Turtle dove

30 cm 150-200 g

28 cm 130-180 g

Sparrow

Collared doves are now found over most of Europe, but a few decades ago they were rare in the north and west. Their spread in the Twentieth Century is one of the most remarkable natural changes in the bird world. They still nest in dry pine woods of south-eastern Europe, but are also at home in moist, cold gardens and farmland of the north. They feed on grain around warehouses and chicken runs. Their monotonous but pleasant 'cu-coo-cuk' calls are well-known. Turtle doves have a softer, purring call, a sound of high summer. In winter they go to Africa. In recent years they have become scarcer in much of Europe, perhaps because of changes in farmland habitat.

Both species lay two eggs which hatch after 14 to 18 days, and the chicks fly at 18 days old.

Both are smaller than town pigeon, but longer-tailed, slimmer; both have small, round heads, and both walk on tiny legs, with head bobbing. Flight quite quick. On **collared dove**, *tail looks long.*

◁ *Collared dove*

Turtle dove
has shorter, more pointed tail and angled, pointed wings, with backward wing flicks and sideways rolls. Display flight with fanned tail, spread wings, glides in wide circle.

Turtle dove ▷

WHERE AND WHEN
Most of Europe; all year.

Collared dove

Turtle dove

WHERE AND WHEN
All Europe except Ireland, Scotland, Iceland, Scandinavia; April to September.

PLACES IT PREFERS Gardens, woodland edges, town parks with evergreens.

PLACES IT PREFERS Farmland and heaths with hedges, patches of woodland.

193

Cuckoo

Cuculus canorus

Underside pale, closely barred

Dark grey, wing tips darker

Head soft grey; yellow eye easily seen at close range

Young ones red-brown with dark bars and cream spots; pale spot on back of head

In flight, head held high, wings beat below body level

Tip of tail blackish with white spots

Whitish stripe underneath wing obvious in flight

Juvenile has rounder wings at first, heavy, floppy flight

Cuckoo

33 cm 100-140 g

Sparrow

When perched, tail often raised between drooped wing tips

Loud, soft 'cuckoo' note; hoarse cackle and liquid bubbling call from female

To most people the cuckoo is just a welcome, wandering voice, the bird itself unknown and unrecognized. It is, in fact, quite large and not difficult to see. Follow the 'cuckoo' call and there will be a long, slim, rather odd-looking bird on a wire (or, far less obvious, perched in the middle of a tree), or flying low and fast across a clearing.

Cuckoos like moorland and reed-beds, where they watch meadow pipits and reed warblers nesting. Once the hen cuckoo finds a nest she can steal an egg and replace it with one of her own. When the egg hatches, after just 12 days, the young cuckoo pushes out the other eggs or chicks and claims all the food from its foster parents. It flies at 19 days old. Amazingly, the baby cuckoo can find its way to Africa and back all alone.

Pigeon-sized; long-winged and long-tailed. Flies with small head held high, wings broad-based but tapered to point. Tail often fanned. Perches with drooped wings, tail sways from side to side. Easily heard, but elusive.

WHERE AND WHEN Throughout Europe; April to September.

PLACES IT PREFERS Bushy moors, marshes, woodland edge, farmland.

LOOKALIKES

Sparrowhawk, page 94, has narrower tail without spots, blunter wing tips.

Kestrel, page 100, slim-tailed, longer wings, blunt head.

Barn owl

Tyto alba

Upperparts golden-buff, mixed with grey. Continental mainland birds darker, greyer than British

Underside streaky buff (mainland Northern Europe) or white

Wings buff to whitish with dark bars across wing-tip feathers

Wings look slightly short and body too small for large head

Eyes black

Barn owl

36 cm 250-350 g

Sparrow

Heart-shaped, white face

Various harsh hissing and snoring calls from nest; shrill shriek

Few birds are so hugely popular as the barn owl, even though most of us hardly ever see a wild one in real life. It is one of the larger owls; in Britain they look mainly white, especially if seen in the brightness of car headlamps, but in much of Europe they are darker, more grey and buff. They like places with rough grass where voles and mice live and where they can easily catch them. They fly low, looking intently at the ground until they see or hear a movement, diving down to seize the prey in their sharp claws. In darkness they rely on their ears for finding prey: one of the reasons why the feathers of an owl are so soft and its flight so silent.

Nests in holes in trees or old buildings. Four to seven white eggs hatch after 30 to 31 days; the young fly at 50 to 55 days.

Broad-winged; big, rounded head; skinny body and thin, knock-kneed legs. In flight, wings broad-based, quite narrow at tip. Flight low, quick, with frequent turns and pauses. Hovers before short headlong dive. Often perches on post or building.

WHERE AND WHEN All year, most of Europe except Scandinavia.

PLACES IT PREFERS Farmland with grass, meadows, marshes, rough ground near coasts, moors.

LOOKALIKES

Other owls may also look white in car headlights at night. **Short-eared owl,** page 202, is more streaked, with dark 'wrist' marks.

Little owl

Athene noctua

At dusk

Wings short, rounded; flies with bursts of wing-beats between switch-back swoops

Top of head has small pale spots. White 'eyebrows' give fierce frown

Eyes cold yellow, ringed with black

Tail very short, barred

Dark brown with whitish spots above. Streaked dark brown and cream underneath

Little owl

23 cm 150-200 g

Sparrow

Calls include loud, clear whistles and a sharp 'kip kip kip'

Little owls are widespread in Southern and Central Europe and North Africa; in England and Wales they were introduced by humans and have become well established. Nevertheless, they have recently declined over much of their range. They eat worms, beetles, grasshoppers, crickets, and a few small birds, mostly after dark although they are often seen by day. They live in traditional sites for years, often to be seen on a favourite perch in the sunshine, lazing away the hours until it is dark enough to hunt. If disturbed, a little owl will try to size up the intruder, bobbing and twisting its head to get a good look from all angles.

Two to five white eggs are laid in deep, narrow holes; they hatch after 27 to 28 days. The chicks fly when 30 to 35 days old.

 Thrush-sized but stocky. Very short legs. Broad, flat-topped head. In flight, wings broad and rounded; action fast, swooping. Perches on trees, barns, telegraph poles. Often on ground. Often mobbed by smaller birds.

WHERE AND WHEN All year, most of Europe except Scandinavia, Scotland, Ireland.

PLACES IT PREFERS Farmland; dry, stony hillsides; edge of moors.

LOOKALIKES

Other common owls are larger. **Tawny owl,** page 200, much bigger, dark-eyed.
Short-eared owl, page 202, much longer-winged.

Tawny owl

Strix aluco

Most are red-brown, some grey-brown

In flight, wings all dark, barred; held slightly curved down in glide

Underside streaked and barred

Face large, round, with big dark eyes. Whitish line each side of bill

Line of white spots down each side of back

Wing tips short of tail, blunt

Usually seen in dark, perched on tree, pole or chimney, looking upright, rounded, broad

Loud, clear or hoarse hoots; frequent loud, sharp, nasal 'ke-wick' or 'too-wit'

Tawny owl

37 cm 400-650 g

Sparrow

Although not one of the giant owls, such as an eagle owl or snowy owl, the tawny is big, stocky and heavily-built. It is a woodland owl and remains in its small territory all year.

Some owls, such as the short-eared and the barn owl, eat just one or two kinds of voles or mice and rear many young in some years and none in others, depending on numbers of prey. The tawny owl tends to eat a variety of foods and has a more stable lifestyle, rearing a few young each year without dramatic fluctuations. At the nest, tawny owls can be aggressive, their attacks on humans so silent that they are occasionally dangerous, but generally they are harmless and beautiful birds.

Two to five white eggs hatch after 28 to 30 days; the young fly 32 to 37 days later.

Bigger than a pigeon. Heavily-built with large, round head and broad body. Perches upright in tree or ivy. Moves to open perches after dark. Flies with fast beats of broad, blunt wings. Loud song and calls give them away at night.

WHERE AND WHEN All year, all Europe except far north and Ireland.

PLACES IT PREFERS Woodland of all kinds, big gardens, parks.

LOOKALIKES

Short-eared owl, page 202, long-winged, paler, with pale eyes.

Long-eared owl, page 202, longer-winged, pale-eyed, but silhouette when perched not always easy to tell from tawny unless 'ears' are raised.

Long-eared & short-eared owls

Long-eared owl
Asio otus

Rich brown, paler below, with fine streaks and bars

Short-eared owl
Asio flammeus

In flight, long-eared shows dark underside, wings with orange-buff patch near tip

Short-eared owl is pale, buffish with cream spots; underside streaked but belly white

Ear tufts of long-eared are long, and may be held flat or raised parallel or in V; whitish V on face beside dark bill

Long, pale wings, with dark wrist patch and buff patch near tip

Eyes of short-eared fierce yellow, set in black. Eyes of long-eared deep orange

Long-eared owl

Short-eared owl

36 cm
300-400 g   37 cm 270-350 g

Sparrow

Long-eared has deep, moaning hoot; young's calls are like a squeaky hinge; short-eared has short, deep 'boo-boo-boo'

These two magnificent owls are very alike. The short-eared is the most easily seen, hunting at dusk, or even during the day, flying low over open ground in a lovely soft, gliding, wavering flight. Long-eared owls prefer to sit deep inside thickets or dense treetops by day, coming out to hunt at night. They sometimes roost in groups of five or ten, even 20 or more together in one tree, although often only one or two can be seen from below. For prey, both rely on small voles, which vary in number year by year, so the owl numbers also vary from one year to the next in most places. They wander far and wide, settling wherever the food supply is most abundant.

Long-eared owls lay three to five eggs in old nests of other birds in trees. Short-eared lay four to eight on the ground.

Both are long-winged, short-tailed, big-headed owls. **Long-eared** *can stretch itself upright, but looks dumpy when relaxed; short-eared perches more at angle.*

◁ *Long-eared owl*

In flight **short-eared** *slightly longer-winged. Ear tufts (feathers, not ears) long, obvious if raised on long-eared; short and rarely seen on short-eared.*

Short-eared owl ▷

WHERE AND WHEN Sparse throughout Europe; not in northern Scandinavia; all year.

Long-eared owl

PLACES IT PREFERS Woods, shelter belts, thickets near marshes.

Short-eared owl

WHERE AND WHEN Northern Britain; scatted in Scandinavia and Low Countries; more widespread October to March.

PLACES IT PREFERS Moorland, marshes, flat agricultural land.

Nightjar

Caprimulgus europaeus

Big dark eyes closed to slits in daylight

Male has large white spots on wings and corners of tail, sometimes obvious even after dark

Wings look long, slim, often held up in V; tail narrow, or a broad fan-shape

Whole plumage rich brown, cream and grey, spotted and barred like a piece of bark or dead leaves

Nightjar

27 cm 65-100 g

Sparrow

Usually flies quite low or around treetop height, not high in sky

Deep, nasal 'goo-ik' call and prolonged, wooden, throbbing churr

Of all European birds, the nightjar is one of the most remarkable and peculiar. It looks owl-like, but as soon as it takes flight it reveals long wings and tail quite unlike any owl and a wonderful light, airy, bounding, erratic flight. It appears at dusk, flying over heaths and woodland clearings, catching moths in mid-air with its huge mouth. The male also has a fantastic song, a deep, throbbing, churring sound, something like a distant motorbike, which goes on and on for minutes on end, sometimes with abrupt changes of pitch. At the end the bird often flies away with several loud claps of its wings. It is an eerie, fascinating and beautiful creature.

Two eggs are laid on bare ground; they hatch after 17 to 18 days and the chicks fly when 16 to 17 days old.

Solitary. Flat, broad head, tiny bill (but wide mouth). Tiny legs. Long wings narrow for whole length; tail often looks broader, fanned at tip. Sits on ground or along dead branch by day; later across branch in normal way.

WHERE AND WHEN Most of Europe except much of Scandinavia; May to August.

PLACES IT PREFERS Heaths, woods with rough clearings, moors.

LOOKALIKES
Owls all have shorter tails, dumpier bodies.   **Swift,** page 206, much thinner, sharper-winged, flies higher.

Swift

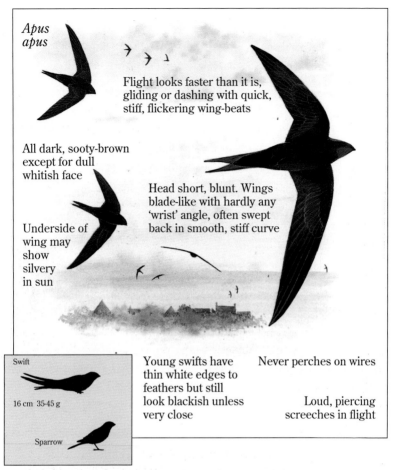

Apus apus

Flight looks faster than it is, gliding or dashing with quick, stiff, flickering wing-beats

All dark, sooty-brown except for dull whitish face

Head short, blunt. Wings blade-like with hardly any 'wrist' angle, often swept back in smooth, stiff curve

Underside of wing may show silvery in sun

Swift

16 cm 35-45 g

Sparrow

Young swifts have thin white edges to feathers but still look blackish unless very close

Never perches on wires

Loud, piercing screeches in flight

Swifts are fabulous birds, leaving the nest at just a few weeks old, then spending a few days wheeling high over the nesting colony, before heading south to Africa. There they remain, all day and every day, high in the sky, probably sleeping on the wing at night. Not until they are three years old do they return to Europe, and it may be only then that they come back to solid ground for the first time. They nest inside deep, dark holes in buildings or cliffs. Two or three eggs hatch after 20 days; the young fly 37 to 56 days later. Swifts are often confused with swallows and house martins, but are really very different, much stiffer-looking, more dashing and never seen sitting still. They also arrive in Europe later in spring and leave early, at the end of the summer.

 Small but very long-winged. Head short, blunt, bill tiny. Tiny legs, cannot perch or walk. Wings long, scythe-shaped. Tail deeply-notched. Seen in air, often in noisy flocks circling at great height or in dashing, screaming parties around rooftops.

WHERE AND WHEN Whole of Europe; late April to August.

PLACES IT PREFERS Open air; above villages, towns, marshes, lakes.

LOOKALIKES
Swallow, page 236, much longer-tailed, broader-winged, slower in flight, less stiff.
House martin, page 234, fluttering, short-winged, white underneath.
Alpine swift, page 208, bigger, white underneath.

Alpine swift

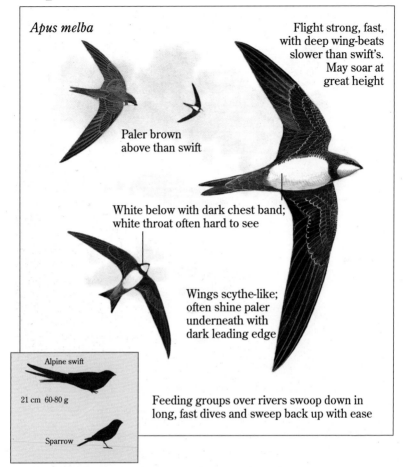

Apus melba

Flight strong, fast, with deep wing-beats slower than swift's. May soar at great height

Paler brown above than swift

White below with dark chest band; white throat often hard to see

Wings scythe-like; often shine paler underneath with dark leading edge

Alpine swift

21 cm   60-80 g

Sparrow

Feeding groups over rivers swoop down in long, fast dives and sweep back up with ease

Although every inch a swift, this bird is bigger, heavier and much more powerful than the swift (page 206). It is found over mountains and cliffs: look for it wheeling high over peaks or dashing through dramatic gorges – just what you might expect for such a fast-flying, powerful bird. At home in the air in everything it does, it catches insects on the wing and probably sleeps as it flies, snatching brief catnaps.

Like the swift, it migrates south to Africa each autumn, crossing the Mediterranean and the Sahara Desert. Parties can be seen over towns in Southern Europe, sometimes mixed with other swifts, when the size is more obvious than if seen alone.

Three eggs are laid inside a cavity in a cliff or building. They hatch after 20 days and the young fly 45 to 55 days later.

Thrush-sized but slim, very long-winged. Head short; tiny bill and legs. Wings long, slender but broader-based, powerful. Tail notched. Never seen perched except to cling outside cliff crevice or hole in wall.

WHERE AND WHEN Southern Europe north to Alps; April to September.

PLACES IT PREFERS Cliffs, gorges, old towns and castles.

LOOKALIKES

Swift, page 206, smaller, slimmer; very rarely shows white on body.

Hobby, page 104, broader, darker.

Kingfisher

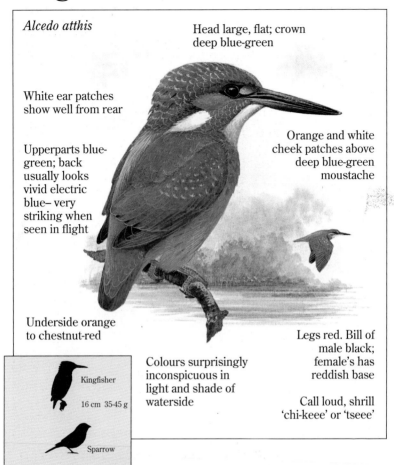

Alcedo atthis

Head large, flat; crown deep blue-green

White ear patches show well from rear

Orange and white cheek patches above deep blue-green moustache

Upperparts blue-green; back usually looks vivid electric blue– very striking when seen in flight

Underside orange to chestnut-red

Kingfisher

16 cm 35-45 g

Sparrow

Colours surprisingly inconspicuous in light and shade of waterside

Legs red. Bill of male black; female's has reddish base

Call loud, shrill 'chi-keee' or 'tseee'

Seeing a kingfisher for the first time, many people are surprised by its size: it is not much bigger than a sparrow. They may also be surprised at how difficult it is to see: it may be colourful, but it does not necessarily stand out.

The best way to spot a kingfisher is to listen for its high whistles as it flies across the water. The vivid pale blue streak on the back is the most striking part when seen in flight.

Kingfishers nest in tunnels a metre long, dug into earth banks above water. Six or seven eggs hatch after 19 to 21 days and the young fly after 23 to 27 days. Young ones learn to fish for themselves as their parents may be busy rearing a second brood. Many become waterlogged in their efforts to catch fish, or are driven away by adults that claim the river as their own.

Smaller than a thrush; about the size and shape of a starling but tiny legs, very short tail, long, thick bill. Perches upright, or leaning forward. Hovers over water; flight fast, low, heavy, straight. Often heard before it is seen, flying off with shrill whistle.

WHERE AND WHEN All year, all Europe except Scandinavia.

PLACES IT PREFERS Shallow rivers, lakes, flooded pits, salt-marsh creeks.

LOOKALIKES

Nothing else looks so stocky and big-headed, nor so colourful except the much larger **bee-eater,** page 212.

Bee-eater

Merops apiaster

In flight, wings show chestnut and blue; underneath silvery with black rear edge

Upperside red-brown with large areas of golden-yellow

Large yellow throat patch

Underside turquoise-blue, looks bright in sun

A young bee-eater is greener above than an adult, duller on head, tail square

Bee-eater

28 cm 48-78 g

Sparrow

Holds wings out straight and flat in flight. Soars and circles, speeding up in chase after insect

Loud, quite deep, ringing 'prrrup'

Nothing fits the Mediterranean summer better than the fine colours and elegant form of a bee-eater, or better still, a group of bee-eaters. As often as not there are ten or 20 of them, perching on wires or dead branches and flying out over open ground to catch large insects in flight. They constantly call with liquid, rippling notes which carry far over the parched landscape. They make their nest holes in sandy ground, tunnelling into flat soil or steep banks. Six or seven eggs hatch after 20 days; the young fly when 20 to 25 days old.

Bee-eaters really do eat bees and wasps and may be immune to their stings to some degree: but they do wipe the tail of a wasp against a branch before swallowing it, to remove the sting and venom.

 Thrush-sized but long and slim. Long tail, with thin central spike on adult. Wings straight, pointed. Flight easy, swooping, with quick beats between long glides on flat, outstretched wings. Bill quite large, pointed, slightly curved; legs very short.

WHERE AND WHEN Iberia, southern coast of France, Italy; April to September.

PLACES IT PREFERS Open countryside with bushes, wires, scattered trees.

LOOKALIKES

Swallow, page 236, small, dark, far less brightly coloured.

Hoopoe

Upupa epops

Tail black with white band

Pale sandy-pink or buff body

Crest fan-like or held flat, pointing backwards; feathers orange-buff, tipped black

Slender black bill

Back and wings broadly barred black and white

Often hard to see in sun and shade until it flies up and away. Soft, far-carrying, quick 'poo-poo-poo' call

Hoopoe

27 cm 55-80 g

Sparrow

Named after its three-note call, the hoopoe is a bird characteristic of Mediterranean lands, but it extends north to the Baltic in summer. A few find their way to Britain in spring but rarely stay to breed. Despite the sharp contrast of black, white and sandy-pink, the hoopoe is not easy to pick out as it waddles about, especially in sandy places with summer flowers and stones breaking up the colour of the ground. On open grass, which it likes, the hoopoe is a little more visible.

It has nasty feeding habits, probing beneath cowpats and other dung and rubbish, and it is famous for its filthy nest in a tree hole or old building in which it lays seven to eight eggs. They hatch after just 15 to 16 days and the young fly when 26 to 29 days old.

Bigger than a thrush, slim, with big head and fan-like crest which can be raised or held flat. Bill long, slim, slightly curved. Legs short but walks well and quickly. Probes into soil with bill. Flies fast, low, with rhythmic, flicking beats of broad wings.

WHERE AND WHEN Southern and Central Europe, mostly spring to autumn.

PLACES IT PREFERS Edges of woods, dry fields, sandy places near walls and hedges, heathland.

LOOKALIKES

Nothing else is so boldly barred or extravagantly crested.

Jay, page 322, has black and white on wings and tail but no crest, heavier body and bill.

Wryneck

Jynx torquilla

Wings brown, spotted; rump looks paler, greyer

Tail pale grey with fine dark bars

In flight, wings look round, tail long, broad, pale

Round head has dark band through eye

Long, wavy blackish stripe down back of neck and middle of back

Chin and throat yellowish with fine dark bars

Wryneck

17 cm 30-45 g

Sparrow

Loud, nasal 'quee-quee-quee-quee'

One of the woodpecker family, the wryneck looks and behaves more like some odd kind of warbler or small thrush. A close view reveals an intricate and attractive pattern of greys, browns and buff, with streaks and bars of dull black. At a distance it looks pale, and is hard to pick out against a dead branch or beside a stone wall, where it might be searching for ants. It is easily missed and would rarely be seen were it not for its loud, nasal calls which draw attention to it in spring.

Although this is a bird of continental forests, it is quite often seen on coasts far from its nesting areas in autumn, when wrynecks join the great migration south into Africa.

Seven to ten eggs, laid in a hole in a tree or wall, hatch after 12 to 14 days; the young fly at 18 to 22 days.

Smaller than a thrush. Short, slim bill. Large head, feathers sometimes raised; head often twists curiously. Tail long, broad, extending well beyond short wings. Short, stout legs and strong feet give firm grip on bark; hops about on ground.

WHERE AND WHEN Most of mainland Europe, spring to autumn; on coasts when migrating.

PLACES IT PREFERS Old woods, coniferous forest, farmland with scattered trees.

LOOKALIKES

Nightjar, page 204, has tiny feet, hardly moves on ground.

No **warblers** have such a complicated plumage pattern.

Green woodpecker

Picus viridis

Vivid greenish-yellow rump shows best in flight

Crimson top of head; black moustache, male's with red streak in centre

Looks big, pale. Back apple-green

Under-side pale greenish white

Head held up in flight, neck looks thin, body too heavy. Flaps in quick bursts between swoops with wings closed

Green wood-pecker

32 cm
170-200 g

Sparrow

Young bird has dark bars over neck and chest

Loud, yelping 'kwee-kwee-kee-keekee'

Most woodpeckers eat ants at times, but the green wood-pecker is a real ant specialist, eating ants and ant larvae all year round. It even digs them out from under the snow. It also picks at bark and dead wood to find beetle larvae. Often seen hundreds of metres from trees, it flies up at the least disturbance, usually with a loud, squealing call, and dashes off to the nearest tree. There it perches up against a thick branch or the trunk, peering round from the other side: getting a close view can be quite difficult.

Spring 'song' is similar to the call, but more musical, powerful and clear. Unlike other woodpeckers, the green rarely drums.

Five to seven eggs are laid inside a hole bored into a tree. They hatch after 17 to 19 days; the young fly 23 to 27 days later.

Bigger than thrush, slender. Large head on thin neck. Short, stiff tail. Short legs, but hops on ground and trees. Wings short, round; flight fast with long, deep switchbacks. Often feeds on ground, flies up into trees if disturbed. Noisy.

WHERE AND WHEN All Europe except northern Scandinavia, Ireland; all year.

PLACES IT PREFERS Mixed and broadleaved woods, heaths, dry waste ground.

LOOKALIKES

Female **golden oriole,** page 380, similar but has short bill, squarer tail, longer wings and thrush-like flight.

Black woodpecker

Dryocopus martius

All black
except for
head

Male has
fiery red cap

Typical
woodpecker
shape

Female red
on back of
head only

Black woodpecker

45 cm 270-360 g

Sparrow

Loud, hysterical
rattle and long, sad
'pse-eeee' note

Eye almost white

This is the biggest and finest of the mainland European woodpeckers, unknown in the British Isles. It is crow-sized and all black except for some vivid red on the head. In flight it manages to combine the appearance of a crow, a cormorant and the true woodpecker that it really is: altogether an odd-looking creature. When pecking at wood to get at insects, it has great power and persistence.

The nest hole of a black woodpecker, with a smooth patch beneath worn away by its tail, is a useful clue that it is around in summer. In winter, it is harder to find, often drifting away from the woods into gardens and smallish thickets. The four to six eggs hatch after 12 days; the youngsters fly at 24 to 28 days old.

 Crow-sized. Large, angular head and chisel-bill on thin neck. Pale eye distinctive. Usually seen upright on tree trunk, but also often on ground. Uses tail as prop. Flies strongly, with little undulation. Noisy.

WHERE AND WHEN Most of mainland Europe, all year.

PLACES IT PREFERS Large forests of conifers in mountains; lowland woods, mixed, conifer or beech.

LOOKALIKES

Beware **carrion crow**, page 330, **rook,** page 328, **jackdaw,** page 328: none has red on head, but jackdaw enters tree holes.

Great spotted woodpecker

Dendrocopos major

Long, broad white patch each side of back

Wings barred with white

Black cap and moustache. Male has red patch on back of head

Black and white above, buff below

Large, vivid red patch under tail very eye-catching

Great spotted woodpecker

23 cm 75-83 g

Sparrow

Young bird has red cap edged black

Loud, sharp, abrupt 'tchik'

There are six black and white woodpeckers in Europe, of which this is by far the most widespread and commonly seen. It is a striking bird, extremely handsome, but often overlooked and rather secretive. Its call is a useful clue, and in spring it drums loudly, rattling its bill against a dead branch in a sudden, short, resounding burst. It is stiff-tailed and creeps upwards on trees supported by the tail and its stout legs, but has to come down backwards.

It can also hang beneath branches. A regular visitor to bird tables, it hangs on to baskets of peanuts or lumps of cheese or fat. Like other woodpeckers, the great spotted chips out a round hole, deep into solid wood, for a nest. Four to seven eggs hatch after 10 to 13 days; the young fly at 20 to 24 days.

Stout bill; short legs. Moves in jerky hops and shuffles. Flight strong, fast, often quite high, bursts of wing-beats between deep undulations. Loud call attracts attention. Taps noisily on wood when looking for food. Hangs on to cones to extract seed.

WHERE AND WHEN All year, widespread except in Ireland.

PLACES IT PREFERS Many kinds of woodland, from scrub to ancient forest; gardens.

LOOKALIKES

Lesser spotted woodpecker, page 224, much smaller, more barred.

Lesser spotted woodpecker

Dendrocopos minor

Black and white above, dingy white underneath

No clear white shoulder patch

Head buff or whitish with black moustache. Female has black and white cap, male's red

Back barred with white, often square white patch in centre

Tiny; usually high up but sometimes in tall, woody stems near ground

Lesser spotted woodpecker

14 cm 20-25 g

Sparrow

No red under tail

High, nasal, quick 'pee-pee-pee-pee' call, especially in spring

This is a true woodpecker, coloured black, white and red like several other woodpecker species worldwide, but it is very much smaller than other woodpeckers and, unlike them, it usually flutters among the highest twigs of trees. It is elusive and often missed, although its high, weak call gives it away. Usually it is heard calling once or twice from one tree, then again from a tree some way off, without being seen as it slips from one to the other. Catch a decent glimpse of the male and you will see a vivid red cap.

Lesser spotted woodpeckers chisel out distinctively small nesting holes, often in soft trees, frequently in swampy ground or near water. Four to six eggs hatch after 11 to 12 days; the young fly 18 to 20 days later.

 Tail slightly spiky at tip. Bill pointed. Very short legs. Hops and flutters among twigs. Taps on wood and drums with longer, weaker drum than great spotted woodpecker. Flight bounding, up-and-down in typical woodpecker style.

WHERE AND WHEN All year, most of Europe except Ireland, southern Spain.

PLACES IT PREFERS Old woods, hedgerows with tall trees, parks.

LOOKALIKES

Great spotted woodpecker, page 222, is much bigger, with white patches each side of back.

Crested lark

Galerida cristata

Underwing shows brighter, pale orange in sunshine

No white on wing or tail

Tail edged orange or rusty-red, paler in centre

Underside mostly pale with smudgy breast streaks

Greyish to sandy brown, streaked darker above

Crested lark

17 cm 30-40 g

Sparrow

Soft, floppy flight, often low over ground to next look-out perch

Frequent loud, fluty calls

Now scarce in parts of north-western Europe where once it was more frequent, the crested lark is still characteristic of much of the southern coastal areas and all of Spain. It sits on walls and old barns, trots along roadsides, or scuttles about on dry, sandy ground, frequently pausing to give a loud, fluty whistle. Often it will raise its short, spiky crest before flying off with curiously floppy beats of its broad, round wings. In spring it flies up high, singing a longer and more elaborate version of its call notes, less of a continuous outpouring than the skylark's song. Crested larks don't move far, as a rule, and remain extremely rare away from the areas where they breed. They lay three to five eggs in a nest on the ground; they hatch after 11 to 13 days and the young fly at 15 days.

Small; stocky, with short tail, short, rounded wings. Crest can be upright or laid back, pointed. Stout bill. Walks well and runs quickly. Feeds on ground, often on roadsides, rarely perches in tree or bush, but often on buildings.

WHERE AND WHEN Scattered in France and Low Countries, across Central Europe, Iberia. Not UK.

PLACES IT PREFERS Sandy ground, cereal fields, warm, dry hillsides.

LOOKALIKES

Skylark, page 228, usually browner, with breast band of finer dark streaks; crest blunt, trailing edge of wing white.

Woodlark, page 377, has bolder wing and tail pattern.

Skylark

Alauda arvensis

Warm buff-brown, streaked dark above

Wings reveal whitish line along rear in flight

Underside silvery-white with buff breast finely streaked in distinct bib

Tail dark with white edges

May drop like a stone from high point of song flight

Often in flocks during winter

Short, blunt crest often flat, can be raised

Skylark

18 cm 30-50 g

Sparrow

Short 'chirrup'; song may be unbroken for minutes; fast, flowing warble, usually in flight

Skylarks are pretty little birds, seen up close, but still mainly streaky brown: it's not their looks that make them so well-loved, but their unique, silvery warbling song that carries miles across fields and moors in summer.

Skylarks are declining almost everywhere, but still remain among the most widespread and numerous of small European birds. They so dislike bushes and trees that they are hardly ever seen close to a field edge or underneath a wall or hedgerow, keeping well out in the open. They nest on the ground and sing, not from a perch, but in a unique hovering song flight, when they look as if they are being raised on an invisible string.

They nest on the ground, laying three to five eggs which hatch after 11 days; young fly when 18 days old.

Larger than a sparrow, smaller than a thrush. Stocky; short, angular tail; rather long, straight-edged wings. Walks and runs well on ground; perches on walls, rarely on trees or bushes. Flight direct, or undulating.

WHERE AND WHEN Throughout Europe; all year.

PLACES IT PREFERS Open ground of all kinds, farmland, moors, heaths.

LOOKALIKES

Crested lark, page 226, has spiky crest.

Woodlark, page 377, has rounder wings, shorter tail, less white shows in flight.

Pipits are slimmer.

Sand martin

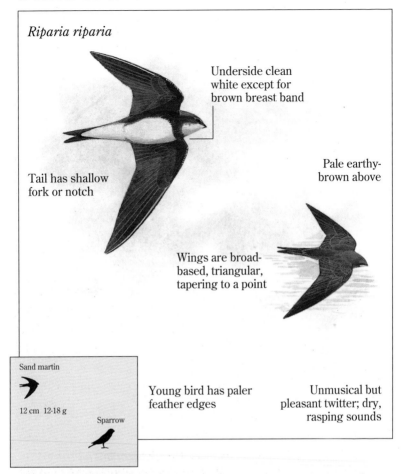

Riparia riparia

Underside clean white except for brown breast band

Pale earthy-brown above

Tail has shallow fork or notch

Wings are broad-based, triangular, tapering to a point

Sand martin

12 cm 12-18 g

Sparrow

Young bird has paler feather edges

Unmusical but pleasant twitter; dry, rasping sounds

In the 1970s droughts in Africa posed a very serious threat to the survival of sand martins. Weakened through lack of food, they were finding it difficult to cross the Sahara on their way north in spring. Now, however, numbers have recovered in Northern Europe. The weather in Africa may have improved, but also it seems that today's sand martins are smaller, perhaps tougher, than they once were. The differences are very small, but show evolution in action at a rapid rate.

These are aerial birds, nesting in holes in earth cliffs but feeding in the air on flying insects. They often gather over water where insects are abundant, especially early in spring. They lay four to six eggs which hatch after 14 to 15 days; chicks fly at 22 days old.

Smaller than a sparrow; long-winged, notch-tailed. Tiny legs: they perch well but cannot walk properly. Often on wires or dead trees. Flight quick and fluttering with wings angled back, flicked in and out. Usually in small flocks. Constant twittering.

WHERE AND WHEN Throughout Europe, March to September.

PLACES IT PREFERS Earth banks, sand quarries, riversides, lakes.

LOOKALIKES

Swift, page 206, much bigger, darker; **Alpine swift,** page 208, much bigger, more powerful and longer-winged.

    Crag martin, page 232, bigger, darker, more confident flight.

Crag martin

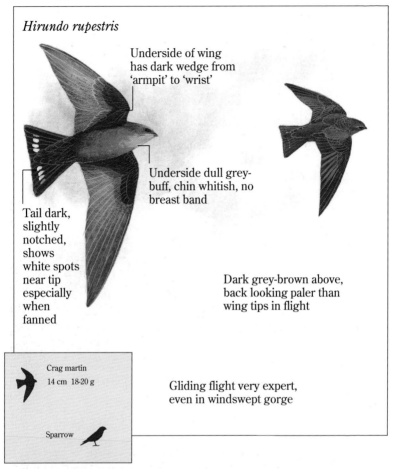

Hirundo rupestris

Underside of wing has dark wedge from 'armpit' to 'wrist'

Underside dull grey-buff, chin whitish, no breast band

Tail dark, slightly notched, shows white spots near tip especially when fanned

Dark grey-brown above, back looking paler than wing tips in flight

Crag martin
14 cm 18-20 g

Sparrow

Gliding flight very expert, even in windswept gorge

All the swallows and martins are fine fliers, but the crag martin is perhaps the best of them. It is not as well-known as the swallow or the house martin, living as it does in much more remote places, but it is very skilled on the wing. It is mostly a quiet bird, not very conspicuous, but sometimes a pair or two may be seen sitting on a rocky ledge, giving out short, sharp twittering notes. Their nests are made of mud, like house martins', but in more of an open cup shape. Three to five eggs hatch within 13 to 17 days; the young fly at 24 to 27 days old. Unlike the other martins, crag martins stay in Southern Europe in winter, moving from high summer haunts down to sheltered river valleys.

Swallow-sized; tail short. Wings long, pointed, broad, held rather straight. Flight wonderfully light and acrobatic, swooping in switchback fashion across face of cliff, sometimes high up. Perches on rocks. Frequent in mountain areas, gorges.

WHERE AND WHEN Most of year in southern Europe, in summer north to Alps.

PLACES IT PREFERS Mountains, cliffs, rivers.

LOOKALIKES

Sand martin, page 230, smaller, paler, more of a flutterer.

Alpine swift, page 208, much bigger, longer-winged.

House martin

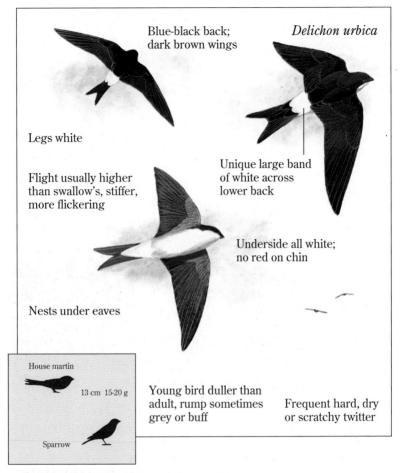

Blue-black back; dark brown wings

Delichon urbica

Legs white

Flight usually higher than swallow's, stiffer, more flickering

Unique large band of white across lower back

Underside all white; no red on chin

Nests under eaves

House martin

13 cm 15-20 g

Sparrow

Young bird duller than adult, rump sometimes grey or buff

Frequent hard, dry or scratchy twitter

Few birds are as well known and popular as the house martin – after all, it nests on our homes. However, they can make a mess underneath their nests, which sometimes makes them less welcome than they might be.

People always confuse swifts, swallows and house martins, but they are very different. The house martin is the one with the mud nest and the big white patch on its back. In Southern Europe, though, many nest not on buildings but in the more traditional site: a cliff, alongside crag martins. They still nest on cliffs, but much more rarely, in parts of Britain.

Occasionally house martins are forced by bad weather to fly south even when they have young in the nest. Three to five eggs hatch in 14 to 16 days and the young fly at 22 to 32 days.

Smaller than a swallow; wings triangular, quite broad. Tail slightly forked. Tiny legs covered with white feathers. Tiny bill. Perches on wires, roofs, but not trees. Comes to ground to collect mud for nest. Feeds in flight, usually above rooftop height.

WHERE AND WHEN All Europe, March to October.

PLACES IT PREFERS Small towns, villages, new housing, lakes.

LOOKALIKES

Swallow, page 236, has all-blue back, red throat.

Swift, page 206, all blackish, no white.

Swallow

Hirundo rustica

Forehead and throat deep red, edged dark blue

Tail shows row of large white spots near tip when spread

Short black legs and feet not feathered

Nests in outhouses, barns

Flight low, elegant, swerving, with wings gently flicked back

Outer tail feathers long and thin; shorter on juveniles

Upper-parts steely-blue, wings browner

Swallow
18 cm 16-25 g

Sparrow

Under-side white, cream or orange-buff

Soft, gentle chirruping sounds, song with purring trill in middle

Swallows are symbols of summer. While house martins and swifts feed high in the air, swallows skim over open meadows, weaving from side to side while chasing big, juicy flies. Sadly, because insecticides have reduced the number of flies, especially around cattle, the swallow has declined.

In autumn they start gathering in flocks – small family groups at first, but then large ones, in readiness for the flight south. Groups may be seen on overhead wires, but the biggest flocks will be over reed-beds, where they roost.

Swallows nest on beams or other narrow supports, under some sort of roof: not under eaves, like house martins, but anywhere with an open door or window. The four or five eggs hatch within 15 to 16 days and the chicks fly 18 to 23 days later.

Sparrow-sized, but long, slender wings and tail. Tiny legs and bill. Tail forked, long streamers in adults, longest on old males. Wings long, angled, blunt at tip. Perches on wires, roofs, sometimes trees. Feeds in low flight over open ground.

WHERE AND WHEN All over Europe, April to October.

PLACES IT PREFERS Farmland with scattered trees; villages; farmyards.

LOOKALIKES

House martin, page 234, has white rump.
   Swift, page 206, all black.

Meadow & tree pipits

Meadow pipit
Anthus pratensis

Underside of meadow pipit is cream to pale orange-buff, with long dark-brown streaks. Streaks on flanks, as on chest

Meadow pipit is pale greyish-olive to warm brown above, streaked darker

Tree pipit
Anthus trivialis

Tree pipit like meadow, but slightly more yellow below; strongly striped breast, clearer flanks with thinner streaks; thicker bill; shorter hind claw

White sides to tail

Legs pale orange

Meadow pipit
15 cm 18-22 g

Tree pipit
15 cm 20-25 g

Sparrow

Meadow calls thin 'pee pee pee' or 'seep seep' and sharp 'pit'; tree pipit calls short, buzzy 'teees' or 'tease'

Smaller than sparrows or larks, pipits are more dainty, spindly-legged and wag-tailed. They walk rather than hop, slipping through tall grasses with ease. In flight, the meadow pipit is a flutterer, skipping along in little jerky bounds; the tree pipit is more direct and fast. Meadow pipits seem nervous and highly-strung by comparison, making little, squeaky chirps as they go; tree pipits walk more confidently and fly up to go far away in a straight line, calling with louder, firmer, buzzing notes. Tree pipits are summer visitors, but meadow pipits gather into small flocks and roam open ground all winter through, before returning to open hills and moors in spring.

Both species lay two to six eggs on the ground; they hatch after 12 to 14 days and the chicks fly at 12 days old.

Both are small, thin-legged, with thin, sharp bills. **Meadow pipit** *has very long hind claw; its song flight begins and ends on the ground.*

◁ *Meadow pipit*

Tree pipit *usually starts to sing from treetop perch. Both walk with slightly bobbing, to-and-fro action of head. Usually hard to tell apart unless by call or song.*

Tree pipit ▷

Meadow pipit

Tree pipit

WHERE AND WHEN Northern and Central Europe; all year.

WHERE AND WHEN All Europe but rare Spain and Ireland. April to October.

PLACES IT PREFERS Open moors, marshes; farmland in winter.

PLACES IT PREFERS Plantations, edges of woods, heaths.

Rock pipit

Anthus petrosus

In Scandinavia, spring birds have less streaking on orange-pinkish breast, paler lines above eye and below cheeks

Dull, grey-brown, softly streaked

Legs dark red-brown to black

Underside yellowish-buff, with blurred olive streaks

Calls like 'feest', fuller than meadow pipit's; song similar, in parachuting flight

Tail edged palest grey rather than white, separates rock from meadow pipit

Rock pipit

17 cm 22-26 g

Sparrow

Until recently, the rock and water pipit (which is featured in the back section on page 377) were thought to be varieties of the same species, but now they have been separated. The rock pipit is a bird of coastal districts, appearing inland occasionally on migration in spring and autumn. It can often be seen close up, showing its subtle but distinctive colours. Water pipits are usually much more wary and fly off long before you can get a close view. Both are difficult to tell from the meadow pipit (page 238) – but with experience you may notice that the meadow pipit is smaller, and that its call is slightly different.

Rock pipits nest amongst rocks and grassy tussocks on the coast, laying four to six eggs which hatch in 14 to 15 days; the chicks fly after 16 days.

Smaller than sparrow; slim. Dark legs unlike meadow pipit. Rather stoutly built; longer bill than meadow pipit. Walks well, flirts tail. Flight fast, low, flitting. Song flight ends in parachute to ground like meadow pipit's.

WHERE AND WHEN Northern and western coasts of Europe.

PLACES IT PREFERS Rocky shores, also salt marsh and sandy beaches in winter.

LOOKALIKES

Meadow pipit, page 238, very similar, but smaller; different call and white, rather than dusky grey outer tail feathers. See also **tree pipit**, page 238.

Water pipit, page 377, very similar, but much more wary.

Yellow/blue-headed wagtail

Motacilla flava

Juvenile duller, browner, with dark bib effect; white wing bars

Black legs and bill

Female paler, more olive or browner on back, whiter on throat

Yellow wagtail

In the UK, male has yellow and green head. In France, head is pale blue with white stripe over eye; in Spain, darker with less white; in Scandinavia, darker still with no white over eye

Broad white sides to long black tail

Blue-headed wagtail

Male green on back, bright yellow beneath

Yellow/blue-headed wagtail

17 cm 16-20 g

Sparrow

Loud, sweet 'tsweeep' or 'tsrreee' mostly in flight

Yellow wagtails have confusing variations which are grouped into several subspecies, or races, in Europe. Generally, the blue-headed is found in mainland Europe, the yellow-headed in the UK. Usually it is best to ignore variations and concentrate on the type that appears in your own area, but sometimes, especially in spring, individuals of different races may appear together on migration: interesting but difficult to identify.

They are all lively, pretty wagtails of grassy places, but decreasing in number where damp fields have been drained and insecticides have removed their food. They are ground-loving birds, perching only briefly in trees or bushes. Four to six eggs are laid on the ground, hatching within 11 to 13 days. The young fly after 16 days.

Slimmer than sparrow. Slender, long-tailed. Slim bill, spindly legs. Bobs tail when walking. Flies with up-and-down swoops. Leaps forward or flies up to catch flies. Often around cattle or sheep catching disturbed insects.

◁ *Yellow wagtail*

Blue-headed wagtail ▷

WHERE AND WHEN Summer, all of Europe; yellow in UK, blue-headed and grey-headed races on European mainland.

PLACES IT PREFERS Wet meadows, grassy places, marshes, mud.

LOOKALIKES

Grey wagtail, page 244, has yellow under tail but greyer back, tail longer, legs shorter.
    Pipits are more streaked.

Grey wagtail

Motacilla cinerea

_____ Winter male and female paler, duller, whiter on belly, most yellow under tail

Juvenile more buff below, yellow only under tail and at rear edge of rump

In flight shows long white stripe along wing, both above and below

Upperparts grey or blue-grey, not green. Rump yellow-green, shows best in flight

Long black tail broadly edged with white

Underside of male vivid yellow in spring

Male has black chin in summer

Loud call, penetrating, explosive 'chikzit' or 'stit'

Grey wagtail

18 cm 17-23 g

Sparrow

Few small birds are as tied to the waterside as the grey wagtail. In winter it appears in strange places, beside park ponds and shallow streams, even around large puddles on car parks or flat roofs. In summer, it prefers tumbling streams and clean, tree-lined rivers; here it feeds on insects and larvae washed up on shingle and around rocks in mid-stream, or rises to catch flies in mid-air. The grey wagtail is the longest-tailed of all wagtails, with an exaggerated up-and-down 'wag', or bob, of the tail whenever it is on the ground. Its calls and song are thin but penetrating, heard above the noise of rushing water in rugged woodland and rocky gorges.

Nests are in steep riverside banks; four to six eggs hatch in 11 to 14 days and the chicks fly 13 to 14 days later.

Slimmer than a sparrow. Very long, slender shape. The long tail and whole rear of body sways up and down. Short legs and short, thin bill. Flight quick, darting, long narrow tail obvious. Sharp, intense call. Always near water. Usually ones and twos.

WHERE AND WHEN Most of Europe except Scandinavia, all year.

PLACES IT PREFERS Upland streams, gorges; lower down in winter.

LOOKALIKES

Yellow wagtail, page 242, has greener back and rump, shorter tail.

   Pied wagtail, page 246, not yellow under tail.

Pied/white wagtail

Motacilla alba

UK male is black on top, white below, with big black bib, sooty flanks

Male pied, summer

Male on European mainland is pale grey above, with whiter underside, smaller cap and bib, wings often browner with broad white bars

Juveniles lack black throat, may lack black cap; look greyer above, tinged yellow or buff below with thin black bar across chest

Juvenile pied wagtail

Many confusing plumages in autumn, but all have long black tail with white sides, greyish back, white bars across dark wings

[C]

Female in UK dark grey on back; on European mainland paler, especially on rump

Female white wagtail, winter plumage

Pied/white wagtail

18 cm 20-25 g

Sparrow

Loud, cheerful 'swurree' and hard 'tissik'

Pied wagtails are waterside birds for most of their lives, but less dependent on water than grey wagtails (page 244). They are at home feeding on tarmac and concrete, familiar birds in towns. In some places hundreds gather to roost each night inside glasshouses or factory buildings. More often, small parties can be watched around gravel pits or lakesides, or individuals picking food from the water's edge where titbits are blown up by the wind. They have feeding territories and each one may defend a stretch of shoreline in winter. In most of mainland Europe, the grey-backed 'white wagtail' is normal, but in the UK the black-backed 'pied' is the typical variety.

Nests are made in cavities, rubble or woodpiles; the five or six eggs hatch after 11 to 16 days. The young fly in 11 to 15 days.

Long, slim shape. Round head, fine bill. Spindly legs. Long narrow tail, swung up and down when on ground. Walks and runs on open ground. Flies with short up-and-down swoops. ▶

◁ *Pied wagtail*

▶ *Usually in pairs or small groups; roosts in large flocks.*

White wagtail ▷

WHERE AND WHEN All year in Southern Europe and UK, summer in north.

PLACES IT PREFERS Any open space from roads or car parks to riversides, marshes and farmyards.

LOOKALIKES

Grey wagtail, page 244, has yellow under tail.

Palest **yellow wagtails,** page 242, may be greyish above, but usually greener and more yellow below.

Dipper

Cinclus cinclus

Juvenile greyer, bib duller with dark scaly feather edges, belly grey

In UK head and back browner, band of chestnut beneath white bib. Mainland Europe birds blacker

Blackish except for big white bib, or with browner head

Dipper   18 cm   60-70 g

Sparrow

Bobs or bounces body up and down without tilting forward

Loud, hard 'zik' or 'strit' call

The dipper lives exclusively around running fresh water, just as a treecreeper is found nowhere but on trees; it is even more closely married to water than the grey wagtail, page 244. No bird has so little variety in its choice of habitat. Only when the weather is hard and rivers freeze do dippers move down to large lakes and even the seashore for a while.

Dippers are the only small songbirds – unless you count the kingfisher – which feed underwater, not only diving in but actually walking in and holding on to the bottom with their strong toes, picking about for insects with their bills. And they nest over running water, or even behind waterfalls, flying through the cascade of spray to get to their brood. The four to five eggs hatch in 16 days; the young fly 20 to 24 days later.

Smaller than a thrush. Rounded, dumpy, short-tailed. Tail held flat. Short, thin but strong bill. Legs quite long, stout, toes and claws long. Bobs and dips as if on a spring. Swims well; dives under from surface. Flies low, fast, following stream.

WHERE AND WHEN All year, most of Europe except south-eastern England, north-western France, Low Countries.

PLACES IT PREFERS Clean rivers with tree-lined banks, boulders, shingle.

LOOKALIKES

Nothing else is as dumpy, or has such a white breast against a dark body.

Wren

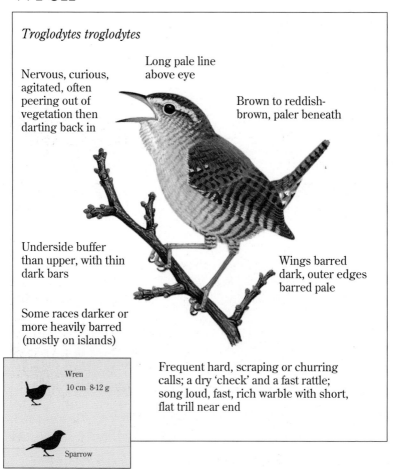

Troglodytes troglodytes

Nervous, curious, agitated, often peering out of vegetation then darting back in

Long pale line above eye

Brown to reddish-brown, paler beneath

Underside buffer than upper, with thin dark bars

Some races darker or more heavily barred (mostly on islands)

Wings barred dark, outer edges barred pale

Wren
10 cm 8-12 g

Sparrow

Frequent hard, scraping or churring calls; a dry 'check' and a fast rattle; song loud, fast, rich warble with short, flat trill near end

Wrens are well-loved and well-known, tiny birds which survive in the darkest, dankest places underneath brambles and fallen logs, amongst piles of flowerpots and old gardening equipment: anywhere where the tangle of leaves, roots and cobwebs might hide a spider or two. Even in the hardest winter weather, wrens search the same old places, not bothering with food put out for birds by humans. The occasional really bad winter kills thousands of them and, for a while, their numbers can plummet. Given a few good years, though, they quickly bounce back, to bring the garden or wood alive again with their resounding songs.

The domed nest is made in a bank or roots; five or six eggs hatch within 14 to 15 days and the young fly 16 to 17 days later.

Tiny: smaller than a blue tit. Rusty brown, with darker and paler bars. Tail short, often cocked upwards. Bill quite long, fine. Legs thin but strong, feet large. Short wings whirr in low, quick flight. Loud outbursts of calls and song.

WHERE AND WHEN All Europe; all year except in north, where in summer only.

PLACES IT PREFERS Anywhere from woods and parks to cliffs, moors and heaths.

LOOKALIKES

Cetti's warbler, page 378, bigger, broader-tailed, loud song more abrupt, lacks trills.

Dunnock

Prunella modularis

Bill thin, dark (unlike sparrow, finch or bunting)

Most of head grey except for streaked, browner cheeks

Underside grey, with sides of breast and flanks tinged bright brown and streaked darker

Eye pale

Upperside rich brown with thick dark streaks

Both birds are shown in wing-waving display

Dunnock

15 cm 20-24 g

Sparrow

Legs thin, pale orange

Tail plain dark brown

Loud, thin 'seee'; song a short, fast, slightly flat warble

Dunnocks live complicated lives. Not content with a single mate, both male and female may have two or more; there are the most bizarre triangles and even larger groups in any area that holds a number of breeding dunnocks. In spring they display, singing loudly and waving their wings in an odd, unco-ordinated way. This is illustrated in the painting above. More usually, they are quiet and shuffle about on the ground, creeping under shrubberies and across flower beds, always jerking their wings and giving tiny, lightning-quick flicks of their tail feathers. They seem dull and inconspicuous but are common, easy to see and distinctive.

The nest is in a hedge or bush; four to five eggs hatch in 12 to 13 days and the young fly when 12 days old.

Smaller than a sparrow. Slender bill. Dumpy, with slim tail. Often crouched, head down or foward-leaning. Short, round wings, often raised or waved one at a time. Jerks forward on ground in short, shuffling hops. Sings from top of bush or hedge.

WHERE AND WHEN All year, whole of Europe.

PLACES IT PREFERS Thickets, woods, gardens, cliffs, moors, heaths.

LOOKALIKES

Buntings have thicker bills, mostly blacker tails with white sides.

Sparrows, page 338, are plain below, thick-billed.

Wren, page 250, smaller, less grey.

Robin

Erithacus rubecula

Forehead, face and breast orange-red, edged blue-grey

Adult pale olive-brown to sandy-brown above

Underside dull white, with brownish flanks

Can look round and dumpy (often in cold) or sleek (especially in hot weather)

Juvenile pale, ginger-brown with pale spots above, dark scales below. Lacks red at first; then gets red spots on breast

Juveniles

Thin dark bill; very spindly legs

Loud 'tik' and thin, high 'seeeh'

Song prolonged, flowing, but hesitant and sad or wistful warble, stronger in spring

Robin

15 cm 18-20 g

Sparrow

Robins have always been popular: alert, nervous yet bold and often ready to be tamed (especially if tempted by food). Though familiar garden birds in most areas, in parts of mainland Europe robins are shyer, woodland birds. They sing in autumn, on through the winter and especially in spring, but it is the late autumn song that has the most impact, coming as it does when most species are silent. In spring, two males will fight for a territory with such passion that one bird is sometimes killed. Robins are famous for nesting in odd places, anywhere from old letter boxes to discarded pots and pans in ditches: usually, they like a bushy bank with a hidden cavity where they can nest in great secrecy. The four to six eggs hatch in 13 to 14 days; the young fly within two weeks.

Smaller than a sparrow. Cocky, flat-headed, broad-shouldered. Flirts short, narrow tail, flicks rounded wings. Hops, pausing in upright or forward-leaning stance. Often in trees, feeds mostly on ground. Flight low, flitting. Sings most of year. Solitary.

WHERE AND WHEN Throughout Europe; all year except in north, where summer only.

PLACES IT PREFERS Woods with dense undergrowth, thickets, gardens, parks.

LOOKALIKES

Nightingale, page 256, and **redstart** lack red breast; juvenile similar to young nightingale, but duller on tail.

Nightingale & thrush nightingale

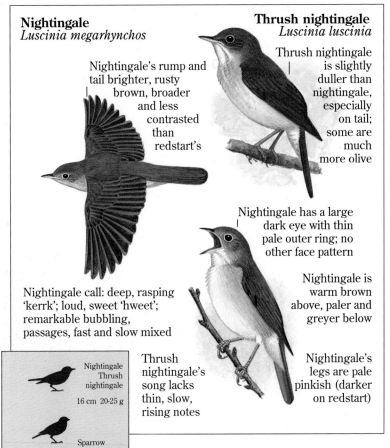

Nightingale
Luscinia megarhynchos

Thrush nightingale
Luscinia luscinia

Nightingale's rump and tail brighter, rusty brown, broader and less contrasted than redstart's

Thrush nightingale is slightly duller than nightingale, especially on tail; some are much more olive

Nightingale has a large dark eye with thin pale outer ring; no other face pattern

Nightingale call: deep, rasping 'kerrk'; loud, sweet 'hweet'; remarkable bubbling, passages, fast and slow mixed

Nightingale is warm brown above, paler and greyer below

Nightingale
Thrush
nightingale

16 cm   20-25 g

Sparrow

Thrush nightingale's song lacks thin, slow, rising notes

Nightingale's legs are pale pinkish (darker on redstart)

Many people have never heard a nightingale and yet it is popularly regarded as the finest of all European song-sters. Perhaps it is: certainly nothing equals the deep, throb-bing, passionate notes for power, richness and variety. The thrush nightingale has equally rich notes and great power, but lacks the long, thin, rising notes so typical of the nightingale. These suddenly tumble into phrases of full-throated, bubbling warbles at great speed. Both are usually heard from the depths of a thicket, but sometimes one will sing from a more open perch. Many people hear 'nightingales' singing at night, often under street lights, but these suburban singers are invariably robins. Both species lay four or five eggs which hatch in 13 to 14 days; the young fly 11 to 12 days later.

Rather dumpy. Small but stout bill, strong legs. Tail quite broad, often cocked between drooped wing tips. Both perch on twigs, hop and run on ground. Flight low, quick, flitting into cover. ▶

◁ *Nightingale*

▶ *Calls distinctive but song most obvious feature in spring.*

Thrush nightingale ▷

WHERE AND WHEN Central and Western Europe, not northern UK, Ireland or Scandinavia; April to September.

Nightingale

PLACES IT PREFERS Blackthorn and other thickets, damp hedges, dense undergrowth in woods.

WHERE AND WHEN Mainland Europe only; April to September.

Thrush nightingale

PLACES IT PREFERS Leafy woods and thickets, often on lake shores.

Black redstart

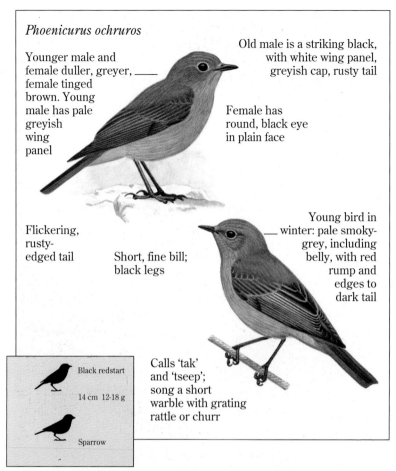

Phoenicurus ochruros

Younger male and female duller, greyer, ——— female tinged brown. Young male has pale greyish wing panel

Old male is a striking black, with white wing panel, greyish cap, rusty tail

Female has round, black eye in plain face

Flickering, rusty-edged tail

Short, fine bill; black legs

Young bird in — winter: pale smoky-grey, including belly, with red rump and edges to dark tail

Black redstart

14 cm 12-18 g

Sparrow

Calls 'tak' and 'tseep'; song a short warble with grating rattle or churr

Black redstarts in Britain and Ireland are chiefly autumn and winter migrants, in very small numbers, mostly on the coast, although a few pairs breed. In Spain they are birds of wild cliffs and rocky hillsides, sharing their home with Alpine choughs, Alpine accentors and chamois. Yet they also breed commonly in old villages with big tiled roofs and ancient chimneys, around stone barns and farmhouses and on giant factory buildings and power stations. It seems that anything hard, bare and angular will do. The black redstart brings welcome life to a village, singing from the rooftops, flitting along the streets, always diving out of sight just as you catch sight of it.

The four to six eggs hatch in 12 to 13 days; the young fly after 16 to 18 days.

Smaller than a sparrow. Robin-like shape but longer, square tail. May be very upright or dumpy. Tail constantly flickers. Flight low, fluttering, sweeping up on to roof or wall; may 'tumble' along roof chasing flies.

WHERE AND WHEN Central and Southern Europe, rarer in UK and north. All year.

PLACES IT PREFERS Towns, factories, remote cliffs, mountains, rubble near coast.

LOOKALIKES

Redstart, page 260, similar in autumn; female more buff-coloured, less smoky-grey, with whiter belly.

Redstart

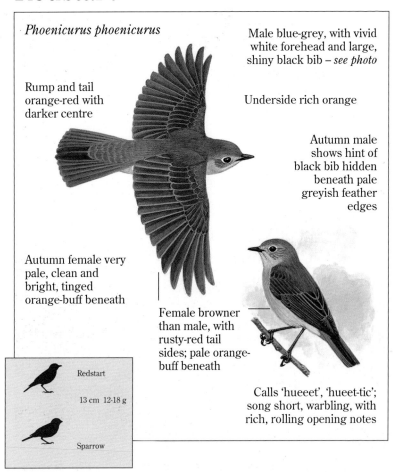

Phoenicurus phoenicurus

Male blue-grey, with vivid white forehead and large, shiny black bib – *see photo*

Rump and tail orange-red with darker centre

Underside rich orange

Autumn male shows hint of black bib hidden beneath pale greyish feather edges

Autumn female very pale, clean and bright, tinged orange-buff beneath

Female browner than male, with rusty-red tail sides; pale orange-buff beneath

Redstart

13 cm 12-18 g

Sparrow

Calls 'hueeet', 'hueet-tic'; song short, warbling, with rich, rolling opening notes

Redstarts are woodland birds, but they can, on migration, turn up in coastal scrub, dunes and on rubble, when you may see them in company with black redstarts (page 258). In summer, they share their woods with wood warblers and pied flycatchers, also spilling out on to bushy hillsides. Males sing from the very tops of tall trees, or down in the thick foliage of a big oak, usually elusive despite their bright colours. Otherwise they are always on the move, flitting about and settling briefly with their tails constantly vibrating up and down, flashing rusty-red. They are hole-nesters, just as ready to use a wooden nest box as an old woodpecker hole or a cavity in a rotting tree trunk. The six eggs hatch in 12 to 14 days and the chicks fly two weeks later.

 Smaller than a sparrow. Slim, with long, narrow, square-tipped tail. Tail flickered non-stop. Thin, shortish legs; fine bill. Round head with beady dark eye. Flight low, showing colour of tail in upward swoop to perch. Hops on ground.

WHERE AND WHEN Almost whole of Europe (not Ireland), April to October.

PLACES IT PREFERS Oak and other old woodland, edges of moors with scrub and scattered trees.

LOOKALIKES

Black redstart, page 258, darker, greyer especially underneath.

Young **robin,** page 254, is shorter-tailed, and lacks red tail sides.

Whinchat

Saxicola rubetra

Breast bright buff fading to white below

Autumn birds are like pale, drab females with paler feather edges on wings, and still duller head pattern

Spring male is a contrasty black-brown, white and peach-buff

Bold white stripes above and below black cheeks; dark cap, orange chin

Female paler, browner on head with cream stripe over eye. Back pale brown with darkish streaks

Tail dark with white patch each side; small white mark in wing

Summer male

Whinchat

13 cm 17-20 g

Sparrow

Perches upright in obvious places, but not in trees

Calls 'hyu tak tak'; song robin-like with churrs and grating sounds

Whinchats have declined in many areas as rough grassland with scattered thistles, teasels and other tall-stemmed plants have disappeared. They also like very young conifer plantations, but these soon become too tall and dense: slopes of heather and bracken with scattered thorn bushes are the most likely places to find them. Whinchats are typical chats, like stonechats and wheatears and their near-relations, robins and redstarts. They are smart, lively birds, usually perching with head up, wings flicked, looking about for food or danger from predators. If disturbed they call frequently, especially if they have young nearby when they always seem to be on edge.

Their five or six eggs, in a nest on the ground, hatch in 13 days; the young fly 13 days later.

Smaller than a sparrow. Upright, short-tailed. Short bill; strong, slim legs. Perches at top of stems or bushes, on posts or fences. Flits from perch to perch; catches insects in air or on ground. Usually in ones and twos. Curious, watchful; calls often.

WHERE AND WHEN All of Europe except Spain (where a migrant), April to September.

PLACES IT PREFERS Grassy areas with bushes, heaths, clifftops.

LOOKALIKES

Stonechat, page 264, has blacker or browner head with less pale colour over eye and on chin.

Stonechat

Saxicola torquata

Flicks all-black tail when perched

Female browner, with hint of neck patch beside dark brown head; underside a rich rusty-buff

Spring male boldly patterned, with very dark head, broad white splash on each side of neck

Underside reddish to bright orange, fading whiter on belly

Dark brown above with white wing patch; pale or white rump above black tail

Stonechat

13 cm 14-17 g

Sparrow

Juvenile can show pale throat, hint of pale line above eye, but not so much as on whinchat

Frequent call is a loud, hard 'weet-tak-tak' or 'tak' – like two stones being knocked together, from which it gets its name

Stonechats are like whinchats but a little rounder and a little more extravagant in the way they scold people who go too close to a nest. They are likely to be in wilder places with more rocks and thick gorse bushes. Whinchats go to Africa in the winter but stonechats stay in Western and Southern Europe. In colder areas, such as Britain, they are more or less restricted to the coast, where winters are less severe.

Stonechats are found over much of Europe, Asia and Africa; some from the far north and east migrate west to Western Europe in autumn: they are long-distance travellers. Those that breed in the west never move far from home.

The five or six eggs, in a nest on the ground, hatch in 14 to 15 days, and the young fly after 12 to 13 days.

 Smaller than a sparrow; upright, dumpy, large-headed. Slim, short bill. Short, square tail. Often on top of bush, rock, post or on wire. Hops on ground. Nervous, agitated, calling often. Male sometimes sings in short flight high into the air.

WHERE AND WHEN Eastern, Central and Western Europe, not Scandinavia; all year in west.

PLACES IT PREFERS Rocky slopes with bushes, heaths, clifftop grassland.

LOOKALIKES

Whinchat, page 262, paler, with pale stripe over eye, paler throat, pale patches on tail.

Wheatear

Oenanthe oenanthe

Spring male clean pale grey above, bright yellow-buff below, with black mask and very dark wings

Some northern males look browner above, more orange-buff below than birds further south

Female browner than male, wings less contrasted, face less marked

Brilliant white rump at all ages; tail has black centre and tip in T shape

In flight, dark wings contrast with pale back, but white rump still catches the eye

Autumn birds much browner above, bright buff below, with dark brown wing feathers all broadly edged with buff

Wheatear

14 cm 20-30 g

Sparrow

Short black bill; black legs

Calls 'heet' and 'chak'

Of all the spring migrants returning to Europe from Africa, the wheatear is one of the earliest and most handsome. Clean, spring males look immaculate and bring a welcome touch of colour and life after the long winter. They may appear almost anywhere, on the coast or on a playing field, on a ploughed field or the grassy shore of a reservoir. Autumn migrants can often be found in unlikely places. In summer they prefer remote spots, often on hills where people are few and far between. Birds that breed in Greenland pass through Europe in spring, but most go direct across the sea to Africa in autumn: one of the most remarkable migrations of any small bird.

Six eggs are laid in a hole in the ground: they hatch 14 days later and the chicks fly at 15 days old.

 Sparrow-sized; boldly marked. Upright or dumpy. Short bill; strong legs. Long wing tips extend to sides of tail. Often tilts forward and flicks wing and tail. Hops, makes quick shuffling runs. Perches on rocks, walls, wires. Sings in flight.

WHERE AND WHEN Whole of Europe, March to October.

PLACES IT PREFERS Stony places with grassy slopes, golf courses, dunes, rocky hillsides.

LOOKALIKES

Whinchat, page 262, smaller, spends less time on ground.
   Stonechat, page 264, has dark throat.

Blackbird

Turdus merula

Male all black except for yellow ring around eye and vivid yellow bill

In flight wing tips show paler against dark background

Female brown, dark above, blacker on wings and tail, but throat dull whitish, streaked dark; bill dark brown or yellow

Juvenile redder brown with rusty or ginger spots above and below

Hops, runs forward, tilts to pick up food; throws dead leaves aside with its bill in noisy rustling

Young male in winter/spring has browner wings, dull bill

Flies up with loud clatter of alarm; repeated, noisy 'pink pink'; softer 'tuk' and long, thin 'srree'

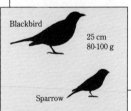

Blackbird
25 cm
80-100 g

Sparrow

While nightingales capture the hearts of poets and composers, the blackbird is the favourite of most people who listen to birds from their garden. All spring and summer it is the blackbird that produces the most wonderful chorus at dawn and dusk, with the richest, most musical of songs. Its varied phrases and frequent changes in pattern are no more than a way of saying 'this is my patch of ground: keep off.'

Blackbirds are widespread and common, and in winter many from the north and east migrate to Southern and Western Europe to join the residents in fields and gardens everywhere.

The four to five eggs, in a nest in a bush or hedge, hatch after 13 to 14 days; the young fly when 13 to 14 days old but leave the nest a day or two earlier.

Bigger than a starling, smaller than a dove. Stout, short bill; strong legs. Rather rounded, with long, full tail often raised and half-spread. Flies up in alarm with loud rattle; settles with tail raised above back and slowly lowered. Hops on ground.

WHERE AND WHEN Throughout Europe, all year except in far north, where only in summer.

PLACES IT PREFERS Woods, fields with hedgerows, gardens, parks.

LOOKALIKES

Ring ouzel, page 379, has a white breast band, paler wings.

Song thrush, page 272, paler with more obvious spotting below.

Starling, page 334, short-tailed, noisy, more sociable.

Fieldfare

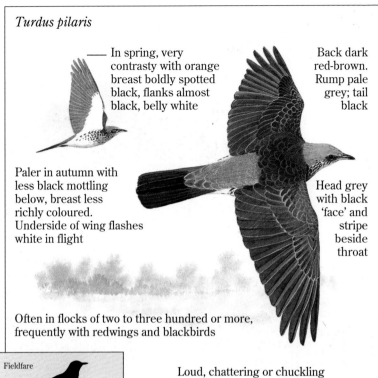

Turdus pilaris

In spring, very contrasty with orange breast boldly spotted black, flanks almost black, belly white

Back dark red-brown. Rump pale grey; tail black

Paler in autumn with less black mottling below, breast less richly coloured. Underside of wing flashes white in flight

Head grey with black 'face' and stripe beside throat

Often in flocks of two to three hundred or more, frequently with redwings and blackbirds

Fieldfare

25 cm
80-130 g

Sparrow

Loud, chattering or chuckling calls; a nasal 'wheeip' in flight and a deeper, chuckling 'chak chak chak'

Fieldfares are familiar and popular winter visitors in Western European countries, such as Britain, France and Spain. The birds arrive in large numbers in the autumn, often in wild weather, and settle in the hedges until the berries have gone. Then they move on west and feed on worms in the fields. If disturbed, they fly up to a tall tree or hedgerow until the danger has passed, then swoop back into the field again to carry on feeding. All the time they keep up a cheery, rattling chatter, a familiar winter sound. Sometimes large flocks are seen on the move after snow. In summer they nest in Central Europe, in parks and tall pine woods; in the far north they even breed in open, barren tundra. The four eggs hatch in two weeks and the young fly at 14 to 16 days old.

 Blackbird-sized. Stout; broad-tailed. Short, broad, pointed wings. Hops; perches in trees and hedgerows. Feeds in flocks, in fields and in bushes with berries or apples. Flight strong, undulating, in large flocks in winter. Breeds in small groups.

WHERE AND WHEN Northern and Central Europe, April to September; Central and Western Europe, September to May.

PLACES IT PREFERS Farmland, woodland edge, heaths.

LOOKALIKES

Mistle thrush, page 274, has white under wing but is paler, larger, with pale tail.

Song thrush, page 272, smaller, browner, without white under wing.

Song thrush

Turdus philomelos

Bill short, brown; legs pale pinkish

Underside creamy-buff, whiter on belly, with round blackish spots in lines along chin and throat, more blurred, browner V shapes on sides

Juvenile

In flight, underwing looks pale orange-golden

Warm, soft brown above. Head rather plain, with large, dark, gentle eye, pale stripe from eye to bill

Adult

Song thrush

22 cm   70-90 g

Sparrow

Short, sharp 'stit'; loud, varied song repeats each phrase two or three times

This is the familiar spotted thrush, the one that feeds on lawns and hammers snails to pieces against bits of stone or on the edge of the patio. It is also one of Europe's finest songbirds: its song doesn't have the flowing grace of the blackbird's, but it makes up for this in power and brilliance. Some of the phrases sound really loud and excited, and every short phrase is repeated two or three times in succession.

Hot summers and frosty winters, both making the ground hard and worms hard to get, have meant a decline in song thrush numbers. Slug pellets and pesticides may have had an effect, too: in places these birds are much scarcer than they were.

The four or five eggs, laid in a nest low down in a bush, hatch within 14 days and the youngsters fly after 13 to 14 days.

 Smaller than a blackbird. Short rounded wings; broad tail. Usually quiet, inconspicuous, living on ground or in thickets. Hops and runs on open ground, flits into shrubbery or wood if alarmed. Stands with head tilted, searching for worms.

WHERE AND WHEN All of Europe, but in north and east only in summer, in Spain only in winter.

PLACES IT PREFERS Gardens, parks, woods, farmland with hedges.

LOOKALIKES

Redwing, page 274, darker, with striped face.

 Mistle thrush, page 274, bigger, paler, rounder spots underneath, with white under wing.

Mistle thrush & redwing

Redwing
Turdus iliacus

Redwing small, dark. Face striped dark brown and cream; bright stripe over eye

Underside of redwing silvery with spots in long, dark grey stripes

— Redwing's underwing reddish; can just be seen on side of perched bird

Mistle thrush
Turdus viscivorus

Mistle thrush's — wings have pale feather edges

Mistle thrush large, greyish or yellowish brown

Juvenile mistle thrush has pale spots over back

Mistle thrush's underwing white

Tail of mistle thrush long, square, with whitish sides

Redwing   Mistle thrush

21 cm 60-70 g

26 cm 110-140 g

Sparrow

Mistle has dry rattle, loud, wild song; redwing calls high, thin 'seeee'

Underside of mistle thrush all cream-yellow with many round or broad black spots

Mistle thrushes are not as well known as they deserve to be: they are not rare, but they are not as familiar as song thrushes and not seen so much in gardens. They like to stay in big parks and farmland, often in treetops, but feeding on the ground. In the autumn there may be ten or 20 together. Their four eggs hatch after 14 days and the young fly in 14 to 16 days.

Redwings are more sociable, going around in flocks from autumn to spring, stripping hedgerows of their berries and then roaming the fields with other thrushes. They can be heard over much of Western Europe at night in October and November as they migrate westwards, calling with high, thin notes. In summer they favour birch woods in Scandinavia. Five or six eggs hatch in 13 days and the chicks fly 14 days later.

Mistle thrush
bigger than a blackbird, long-tailed; smallish, round head. Bounding hops on ground. Flight high, on long, pointed wings, in quick undulations. Noisy, aggressive; often on berries.

◁ *Mistle thrush*

Redwing
smaller than a song thrush, delicate; hops and shuffles. Flight lark-like but quick, often in flocks. Mixes with fieldfares in winter.

Redwing ▷

WHERE AND WHEN Throughout Europe, leaves north and east in winter.

Mistle thrush

PLACES IT PREFERS Parks, farmland.

WHERE AND WHEN In north during summer; moves to south and west in winter.

Redwing

PLACES IT PREFERS Remote woods, heaths, farmland.

Sedge warbler

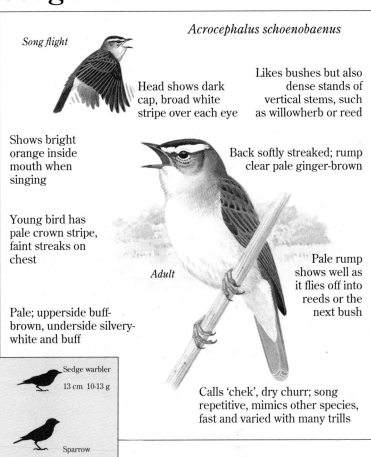

Acrocephalus schoenobaenus

Song flight

Head shows dark cap, broad white stripe over each eye

Likes bushes but also dense stands of vertical stems, such as willowherb or reed

Shows bright orange inside mouth when singing

Back softly streaked; rump clear pale ginger-brown

Young bird has pale crown stripe, faint streaks on chest

Pale rump shows well as it flies off into reeds or the next bush

Adult

Pale; upperside buff-brown, underside silvery-white and buff

Sedge warbler
13 cm 10-13 g

Sparrow

Calls 'chek', dry churr; song repetitive, mimics other species, fast and varied with many trills

The scolding, chattering song of a sedge warbler makes it a character in the marshes and nettlebeds where it loves to hide. In spring and, in fine weather, right through the summer, it pauses to sing from a bush top or a reed stem, or rises in a jerky song flight to show off and make itself heard all the better. It is a scratchy, too-fast, unmusical song, but some notes are clear and pure and it is, at least, a lively effort.

Although not as restricted to reeds as the reed warbler, sedge warblers do prefer damp places and are often found alongside other marshland birds. In autumn they put on huge amounts of fat – stored energy to carry them to Africa.

The five or six eggs hatch after 13 to 14 days, and the chicks fly when two weeks old.

Great-tit-sized. Slim; narrow head, slim bill, tapered tail. Perches upright when singing, but head hunched into shoulders. When feeding, slips through foliage in horizontal pose. Flight short, low, flitting. Song from perch or in flight.

WHERE AND WHEN Most of Europe north from central France; April to September.

PLACES IT PREFERS Rank growth in ditches, edges of marshes, reeds.

LOOKALIKES

Reed warbler, page 278, has plain head and back.

The rare **aquatic warbler** is more yellow-buff, striped black and cream.

Reed warbler

Acrocephalus scirpaceus

Flat forehead slopes into long bill to give dagger shape

Bill has pale orange base

Slight pale line from bill to above eye; dark line below this and thin whitish ring around eye

Whole upperside unmarked; rump often rustier

Pale, plain; soft brown above, creamy-buff below

Legs dark greyish to brown

Calls low, slow 'krrr', 'kech'. Song loud, rhythmic, repetitive churring with high whistles and harsh notes, but overall even, rolling effect

Reed warbler

13 cm 10-15 g

Sparrow

While Cetti's warbler (page 378) braves the winter in Europe, reed and sedge warblers migrate to Africa each autumn. Reed warblers are the most strongly associated with true reed-beds, swamps with a sea of tall, swaying reeds and little else, although they often move out to feed in willows at the edge. In the bigger reed-beds there may be scores, even hundreds, of pairs of reed warblers although the true numbers may be realized only if you go at dawn to listen to the remarkable chorus of song. These small, plain warblers live life in the strange world of thin, upright stems and even weave their nests around reeds above shallow water. They are often parasitised by cuckoos.

Four eggs hatch in 11 days and the young fly after 12 days.

 Size of great tit, but slim. Head flat, slopes into long, pointed bill. Tail rather round; feathers under tail are long, adding to tapered effect. Slips through stems of reed, bulrush and reed mace. Sings often from hidden perch, but not in flight.

WHERE AND WHEN Most of Europe, April to September; rare Ireland, Scotland, Scandinavia.

PLACES IT PREFERS Reed-beds, willow thickets near reeds, reed mace.

LOOKALIKES

Rare **marsh warbler,** page 378, and **Blyth's reed warbler,** exceedingly similar.

Sedge warbler, page 276, has stripe over eye.

Garden warbler, page 288, dumpier, short-billed.

Subalpine warbler

Sylvia cantillans

Female paler, with white moustache less contrasted; underside pale pink

Pale legs

Juvenile browner, moustache hardly visible; greyish on head and rump, dull grey-buff below, wings brown with bright buff edges to feathers

Spring male bluish-grey on head and back; wings browner than on back

White line under cheeks from bill

Underside deep rusty-pink, fading to white on belly

Subalpine warbler

12 cm 12-15 g

Sparrow

Call soft 'chek', 'cher', and typical *Sylvia* warbler 'tak'; song a fast, jumbled, scratchy chatter

Warblers are grouped into several broad types and the first word of their scientific names gives a clue to their nearest relatives. The *Acrocephalus* warblers are the reed and sedge types; *Phylloscopus* warblers are small, greenish leaf warblers; the *Sylvia* warblers are stouter, with short, slightly thicker bills, perky expressions and flicked tails, often edged with white. The subalpine warbler is one of these, typically lively and restless, flitting about on warm, stony slopes of Southern Europe.

Like many other warblers, it performs a song flight – the male will suddenly dart up into the air, fluttering his tiny wings and singing a chattering, unmusical song for all he is worth.

Four or five eggs hatch after ten to 11 days and the young fly 11 days later.

Blue-tit-sized, but long-tailed. Slim; short bill. Tail narrow, often held upwards or waved briskly. Short, round wings. Usually low to ground in bushes and hedges. Can be elusive in thick vegetation.

WHERE AND WHEN Spain, southern France, Italy; March to October.

PLACES IT PREFERS Scrubby slopes, bushes, thickets.

LOOKALIKES

Whitethroat, page 286, bigger, paler.

   Lesser whitethroat, page 284, has dark legs. Difficult to separate in autumn.

Icterine & melodious warblers

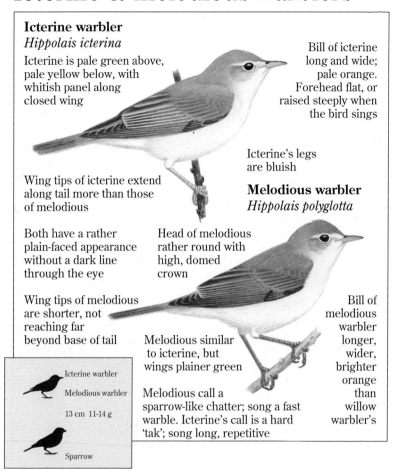

Icterine warbler
Hippolais icterina

Icterine is pale green above, pale yellow below, with whitish panel along closed wing

Bill of icterine long and wide; pale orange. Forehead flat, or raised steeply when the bird sings

Icterine's legs are bluish

Melodious warbler
Hippolais polyglotta

Wing tips of icterine extend along tail more than those of melodious

Both have a rather plain-faced appearance without a dark line through the eye

Head of melodious rather round with high, domed crown

Wing tips of melodious are shorter, not reaching far beyond base of tail

Bill of melodious warbler longer, wider, brighter orange than willow warbler's

Melodious similar to icterine, but wings plainer green

Melodious call a sparrow-like chatter; song a fast warble. Icterine's call is a hard 'tak'; song long, repetitive

Icterine warbler

Melodious warbler

13 cm 11-14 g

Sparrow

Although these two green-and-yellow warblers look very alike, they rarely cause an identification problem because they inhabit different parts of Europe. However, migrants on the coasts of the North Sea and English Channel in autumn could be of either species and are hard to tell apart.

They are both slightly larger than willow warblers, with longer, paler bills, bigger, broader heads and bulkier bodies. The icterine, especially, looks big and bulky for a warbler. Both have a habit of moving heavily through foliage and leaning over to grab berries, which they pull off with a twist of the head, more like blackcaps than willow warblers.

They lay four or five eggs which hatch within 13 days; the young fly at 13 to 14 days.

Rather bulky warblers, both larger than willow warbler, more like blackcap in build, willow warbler in colour. Round, broad head and spike-like, wide-based bill. Strong legs and feet allow ▶

◁ *Icterine warbler*

▶ *acrobatic but clumsy reaching for berries. Tend to crash heavily through foliage.*

Melodious warbler ▷

WHERE AND WHEN
Scandinavia south through Central Europe, northern and eastern of France eastwards; April to October.

Icterine warbler

PLACES IT PREFERS Hedges, orchards, bushy slopes.

WHERE AND WHEN
France and Iberia to Italy; April to September

Melodious warbler

PLACES IT PREFERS Woodland edges, bushy slopes, hedgerows.

Lesser whitethroat

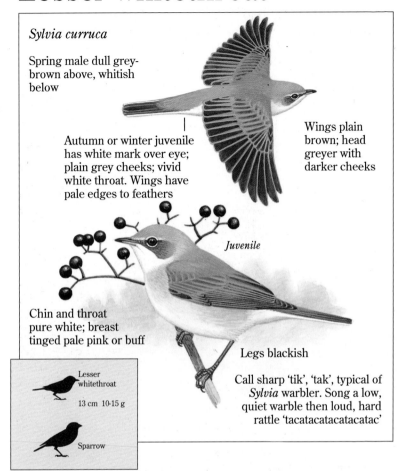

Sylvia curruca

Spring male dull grey-brown above, whitish below

Autumn or winter juvenile has white mark over eye; plain grey cheeks; vivid white throat. Wings have pale edges to feathers

Wings plain brown; head greyer with darker cheeks

Juvenile

Chin and throat pure white; breast tinged pale pink or buff

Legs blackish

Lesser whitethroat

13 cm 10-15 g

Sparrow

Call sharp 'tik', 'tak', typical of *Sylvia* warbler. Song a low, quiet warble then loud, hard rattle 'tacatacatacatacatac'

Lesser whitethroats like good, old-fashioned hedges, the sort that grow almost to the height of a short tree and as thick as a small barn. Here they can hide away in the depths of the foliage, slipping about out of sight, calling now and then and, several times each minute, giving the distinctive rattle that passes for a song. In the autumn, though, they cannot resist a fruiting elderberry or honeysuckle: if you wait patiently, quietly watching a bush full of succulent berries, you will often be rewarded by a number of lesser whitethroats and other warblers coming in to feed. They sometimes appear in gardens, but are unfamiliar to most people.

Four to six eggs hatch after ten to 11 days; the young fly when 11 days old.

Smaller than a great tit. Slim; tail narrow. Small head; neat, short, thin bill. Looks smart, rather grey. Keeps to dense vegetation unless feeding on berries in autumn. The loud, rattled song is a clue.

WHERE AND WHEN Most of Europe except Spain, Ireland; April to September.

PLACES IT PREFERS Dense hedgerows, blackthorn thickets, woods, parks.

LOOKALIKES

Whitethroat, page 286, paler, has rustier wings, pale legs.

Young **subalpine warbler,** page 280, has pale legs, greyer rump.

Whitethroat

Sylvia communis

Male warm brown with grey head

Song flight

Pale eye; cheeks plain grey, not dark. Puffy white chin and throat

Wing feathers edged bright rusty or ginger

Underside tinged pale pink

Legs pale pinkish

Tail dark, with white sides

Female browner, head pale grey-brown. White ring around eye

Whitethroat
14 cm 14-18 g

Sparrow

Juvenile browner still, pale, looks bright; wings edged ginger (see photo)

Calls low 'wit wit wit'; 'witchity witchity'; 'chair'; song a scratchy, quick chatter, from bush or wire, or in short upward flight

Whitethroats were once so common that they had many familiar, country names, such as Peggy whitethroat: they were everywhere, darting up out of hedges and thickets of bramble or wild rose to sing. Then a series of droughts in Africa caused them to decline suddenly and dramatically and their numbers all over Europe are still not what they were in the 1950s and 60s.

They like unkempt places, so modern parks, ornamental trees on smooth, short grass and flowerbeds around office blocks and shopping centres are no good for them: they need rough, thorny bushes and nettle patches.

Their four or five eggs hatch after 11 to 13 days; the young-sters fly when ten to 12 days old.

Robin-sized. Slim; tail rather long, narrow, a little rounded and often cocked or swung sideways. Perky head shape with raised crown. For a warbler, the bill is short and stout. Slides through dense vegetation, often looking rather horizontal.

WHERE AND WHEN Almost whole of Europe; April to September.

PLACES IT PREFERS Rough heaths, hedges, edges of woods.

LOOKALIKES

Lesser whitethroat, page 284, duller, darker-legged.
  Garden warbler, page 288, plain without white throat.

Garden warbler

Sylvia borin

Wing feathers have pale tips, especially in autumn

Only faint dark mark through eye and pale line above it. Pale eye ring

Dull, pale warbler. Basically pale olive-brown above, buffish below

Slight hint of grey on side of neck

Bill blunt, stubby

Chin and throat slightly paler, flanks slightly warmer buff

Garden warbler
14 cm 15-20 g

Sparrow

Call a hard 'chek' and softer 'tuk' or 'chuf'; song long, loud, rich warbling very like blackcap's, usually with less concentrated vigour

Garden warblers are nondescript 'little brown birds'; however, a close view reveals lovely subtleties and variations in shade. Like any small bird, they have a beauty and charm about them which repays close study. Above all, they can sing: garden warblers rate highly in the list of top European songsters although they lack some of the vitality of the nightingale and the larger thrushes. In spring, the song reveals their presence: otherwise they are hard to see in woods and shrubberies. In the autumn they may be easier to spot as they venture out to the edges of elder and honeysuckle, eager for berries which give them the 'fuel' – extra fat – for a long migration flight.

The four or five eggs hatch within 12 days and the chicks fly when ten days old.

Robin-sized. Rather a dumpy warbler, with tapered wing tips and tail. Short, thickish bill; round, gentle head. Dark eye set in rather plain face. Slips through foliage, hops fairly heavily through twigs. Flight usually short, low, quick.

WHERE AND WHEN Almost all Europe; April to October.

PLACES IT PREFERS Thickets, woodland with undergrowth, shrubs with berries.

LOOKALIKES

Spotted flycatcher, page 298, much more upright, softly streaked.

Reed warbler, page 278, more rusty, long-billed.

Lesser whitethroat, page 284, greyer, with white-edged tail.

Blackcap

Sylvia atricapilla

Juvenile has bright red-brown cap

Female browner than male, with small, smooth red-brown cap, often not very conspicuous

Often fairly sluggish, sitting still or hopping quite heavily through foliage

Grey-brown above with paler underside

Male has greyer back than female, pale grey breast and neat, small black cap

Loud, hard call, 'tak' sounds. Song loud, quickly rising to fast, furious warble, then fading away; usually a little shorter and brighter than garden warbler's, but often hard to tell apart

Blackcap

14 cm 15-20 g

Sparrow

Interestingly, blackcaps have recently changed their migration behaviour in some parts of Europe. In Britain all blackcaps used to disappear in winter. Now a few remain through the colder months and they appear to come in from Central Europe. These winter birds are often in gardens and survive on food put out on bird tables, as well as berries. However, the vast majority still arrive in Europe in spring and leave in autumn.

Blackcaps like woods and parks with tall trees. Like garden warblers, they are superb singers. You need practise to tell the two songs apart: see the caption in the artwork panel.

Five eggs hatch after ten to 11 days; the chicks fly ten to 13 days later.

Robin-sized, but slimmer. Quite long, slender tail. Slightly peaky crown exaggerated by colour of cap on male. Slips easily through foliage. Solitary. Reaches forward to pick berries in its bill. Usually seen after hearing call or song. Flight low, short, flitting.

WHERE AND WHEN All Europe except extreme north; mostly March to September, but a few all year in south and west.

PLACES IT PREFERS Woods, thickets, parks, large bushy gardens.

LOOKALIKES

Marsh and **willow tit,** page 306, have shorter bill and black bib.

Garden warbler, page 288, is like female blackcap but has plain head.

Wood warbler

Phylloscopus sibilatrix

Head green with broad yellow stripe over eye, yellow cheeks and throat

Rather a yellow warbler. Upperparts yellow-green, wings brown with yellower feather edges and dark patch on front edge

Underside silky white

Long wing tips, often held drooped, distinctive, especially if seen from below against sky

Call soft, sad 'tyoo'. Song of two kinds, one is 'tyoo tyoo tyoo'; but more often a thin, high note accelarating into a shrill, silvery trill, 'zip zip zip zipipiiiiiiii'

Wood warbler

12 cm 8-13 g

Sparrow

Bill mostly pale orange; legs pale pink-brown

Sometimes yellow–white contrast beneath is reduced, with paler yellow

Most warblers can be found in odd places around the coast, or inland where they don't nest, while migrating in spring and autumn. (For many people, this is the highlight of spring or autumn birdwatching).The wood warbler, however, is hardly ever encountered on the coast or in a bush by a lake: it seems to fly direct to its wood from Africa in spring, and straight out again in autumn. The best chance of glimpsing one is in early spring when the leaves are not fully out and the singing wood warbler can be tracked down and watched. Later, it becomes highly elusive in the dense woodland canopy and, by late summer, once it has stopped singing, it is hard to find.

Six or seven eggs, in a nest on the ground, hatch in 13 days; the young fly after 11 to 12 days.

Great-tit-sized, but slender. Long wings often droop below tail. Rather broad shoulders, wide tail. Usually looks clean and bright. Often on twigs in clear space below woodland canopy, flying from perch to perch, or feeding up in dense leaves.

WHERE AND WHEN Most of Europe except Iberia, Ireland; April to September.

PLACES IT PREFERS High woods with clear space beneath trees, especially beech and oak.

LOOKALIKES

Willow warbler, page 294, less white on belly, less yellow on edges of wing feathers.

Bonelli's less yellow on throat and over eye.

Chiffchaff & willow warbler

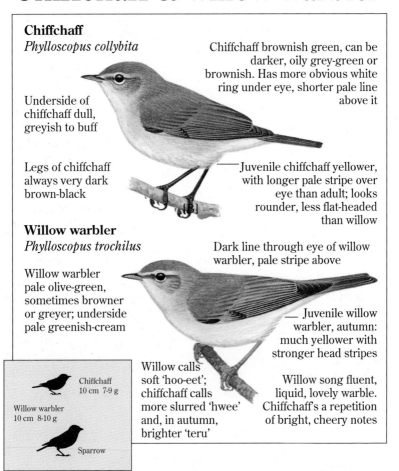

Chiffchaff
Phylloscopus collybita

Chiffchaff brownish green, can be darker, oily grey-green or brownish. Has more obvious white ring under eye, shorter pale line above it

Underside of chiffchaff dull, greyish to buff

Legs of chiffchaff always very dark brown-black

Juvenile chiffchaff yellower, with longer pale stripe over eye than adult; looks rounder, less flat-headed than willow

Willow warbler
Phylloscopus trochilus

Dark line through eye of willow warbler, pale stripe above

Willow warbler pale olive-green, sometimes browner or greyer; underside pale greenish-cream

Juvenile willow warbler, autumn: much yellower with stronger head stripes

Chiffchaff
10 cm 7-9 g

Willow warbler
10 cm 8-10 g

Sparrow

Willow calls soft 'hoo-eet'; chiffchaff calls more slurred 'hwee' and, in autumn, brighter 'teru'

Willow song fluent, liquid, lovely warble. Chiffchaff's a repetition of bright, cheery notes

These are two typical 'leaf' warblers, small, slim and greenish in colour. The chiffchaff is the earliest migrant to Northern Europe, arriving in March, and is an all-year resident in the far south of Europe. In late autumn many migrants from the far north-east can be seen around European coasts.

Willow warblers are more strictly summer visitors and look extremely similar to chiffchaffs, but are easily separated by their song. Both are insect-eaters, picking food from twigs and foliage rather than catching it in mid-air, so they are found in leafy bushes and places with plenty of insects and caterpillars: in spring, chiffchaffs especially like waterside willow bushes.

Both nest on or near the ground, laying six eggs which hatch after 13 days; the chicks fly within two weeks.

Small, slender; **chiffchaff** *fractionally rounder-headed, dumpier, shorter-winged than* **willow warbler***, also generally duller, but autumn juveniles are quite yellow* ▶

◁ *Chiffchaff*

▶ *below. Chiffchaff flicks wings and dips tail in regular down-up action. Best separated by calls and song, colour of legs.*

Willow warbler ▷

WHERE AND WHEN All Europe, mostly March to October. Some stay all winter in south and west.

Chiffchaff

Willow warbler

WHERE AND WHEN Most of Europe; April to September. In south, only April, or August to September.

PLACES IT PREFERS Thickets, woodland edges, gardens.

PLACES IT PREFERS Thickets, heaths, woodland edge

Goldcrest & firecrest

Goldcrest
Regulus regulus

Goldcrest rather subdued, dull; greenish, paler beneath

Face pale, plain, with slight 'grumpy' moustache; beady eye in pale cheek

Top of of goldcrest's head shows thin dark streak with yellow or orange centre. Spreads into broad orange patch in display

Wings have broad blackish and thin white bars

Juveniles of both species lack colour on crown; firecrests still have white over eye

Firecrest
Regulus ignicapillus

Bright, clean, whiter beneath than goldcrest

Calls thin, high, 'see see see'; firecrest also firmer 'pee' or 'zit'. Goldcrest song, high, thin with flourish – 'tidl-diee tidl-diee tidl-diee sisitueet'. Firecrest a simpler: 'si-zi-zizizizizit'

Firecrest's head has broader, blacker cap with thin orange centre. Broad white band above dark eye stripe is most striking feature

Side of firecrest's neck and chest has orange or bronze patch

Goldcrest
Firecrest

9 cm 5-7 g

Sparrow

These two are famous for being Europe's smallest birds, although both coal tit and wren run them close. They are tiny bundles of energy, round and fluffed-up in cold weather to keep warm under their feathers, but quite sleek and slim on warm summer days. Their calls often give them away, but getting a clear view of one or other in the top of a tall conifer can be difficult. They just look like tiny, dark shapes against the sky. In autumn and winter, especially, they may often be seen lower down in bushes when they may be remarkably indifferent to humans: not that they are tame – more that they simply ignore people altogether, often feeding just a metre or two away.

Both make tiny nests under branches; seven to ten eggs hatch after 14 to 16 days and the chicks fly up to 23 days later.

Both are tiny; smaller than blue and coal tits. Often rounded, puffy, with very thin tails, short wing tips slightly drooped. Thin bills; tiny, spindly legs. Shape and actions much ▶

◁ *Goldcrest*

▶ *alike; flit through leaves, hop about, twig to twig, hang upside down, hover.*

Firecrest ▷

WHERE AND WHEN
All over Europe.

WHERE AND WHEN
Mainly in south and west, rare in UK.

Goldcrest

Firecrest

PLACES IT PREFERS All kinds of woods, especially conifers; gardens, thickets.

PLACES IT PREFERS Mixed conifer woods, holly, willow thickets.

Spotted flycatcher

Muscicapa striata

Chest softly streaked

Pale greyish-brown, paler underneath

Belly and under tail almost white

Top of head has long darker lines, not very obvious

Wing feathers have obvious pale edges and thin wing bar

Black bill; short black legs often hidden when perched

Sits very upright on post, fence or twig. May be low down or high in tree

Young more obviously spotted, with buff and white on head and back

Quick, short calls: a thin, sharp 'tseet' or 'tseet-chup-chup'. Song poor, scratchy

Spotted flycatcher

14 cm 14-18 g

Sparrow

This sharp-eyed, quick little bird looks dull and inconspicuous: yet it flies to Africa and back each year just to be in Europe when there are flying insects about. It feeds almost entirely on insects caught in mid-air (warblers, by contrast, mostly pick food from stems and leaves). To do so it sits upright, watching intently, then flies out suddenly in an aerobatic flurry, catching the fly with a snap of its bill, and, more often than not returning to the same perch. It does exactly the same all winter in the forests and savannas of Africa: not such a dull bird after all. Spotted flycatchers are very late arrivals in summer; they may return year after year to the same spot, even the same nest. The four or five eggs hatch in 12 to 14 days and the chicks fly 12 to 13 days later.

Upright; flat-headed; very short-legged. Bill slim, but thicker than most warblers'. Sits still or flits to new perch, rarely hopping or slipping through leaves. Wings long, pointed, held along tail. Often flicks wings and bobs tail. Solitary.

WHERE AND WHEN All Europe, May to September.

PLACES IT PREFERS Openings in woods, gardens, parks, cemeteries, tennis courts.

LOOKALIKES

Garden warbler, page 288,more horizontal, different shape, plainer on wings.

Reed warbler, page 278, is hardly to be confused – it doesn't perch on open twigs.

Pied flycatcher

Ficedula hypoleuca

In autumn often has duller, darker head, brown outline to pale bib

Beady black eye. Short black bill and legs

Female similar but brown and white, lacks forehead spot

Male obviously black and white; white forehead spots and underside, white patches in wings

Tail edged white. Juveniles spotted pale on back

Pied flycatcher
13 cm 10-15 g
Sparrow

Usually in trees; very elusive after July, but later migrants on coasts turn up almost anywhere

Calls sharp 'hwit', 'hwit-tek'; song sweet, begins with unhurried, separate notes running into warble

Pied flycatchers are curiously localized. In many woods they are completely absent and always have been, yet the conditions do not look much different from the places where they breed. In Britain, they are not found in old oak woods of lowland England, but are common in the west where gnarled oaks grow on rocky slopes above rushing streams and there is plenty of space beneath the trees for the flycatchers to feed.

They sit quite quietly among the leaves, hard to see, (easier in spring, very difficult in late summer), fluttering out into clearings to catch flies, or dropping to the ground for a moment to snatch up a grub. They nest in holes and can be encouraged in suitable woods with nest boxes. The five to nine eggs hatch out after 12 to 13 days and the young fly 13 days later.

Robin sized. Slim; rather short tail, long wing tips often held drooped. Rounded head, short bill. Very short legs. Less upright than spotted flycatcher. Tail often raised and flicked. Solitary.

WHERE AND WHEN Northern and much of Western Europe (not south-east England, Ireland); April to October.

PLACES IT PREFERS Old woods with clearings, especially oak; riversides.

LOOKALIKES

Spotted flycatcher, page 298, more upright, tapered, longer-tailed, with buff not white in wing.

Female **chaffinch,** page 340, has thick bill, broad upper wing bar.

Bearded tit

Panurus biarmicus

Male has blue head, with narrow, peaky crown; vivid yellow eye and bill; pointed black 'beard' each side

Female has pale, dull head, grey on cheek; pale eye

Wings have black, rusty and white stripes

Black under base of tail

Bright ginger-brown or orange-brown, with long, pale brown tail edged white

Usually in tall, dense stems, clinging on with its feet. Almost parrot-like when feeding

Young male has plain head, darker eye, darker back

Bearded tit

17 cm 13-20 g

Sparrow

Calls loud, ringing 'tying', 'ping' or squeaky 'pink', often repeated from family group

Of Europe's small birds, few are as restricted to one kind of habitat as the bearded tit. It nests only in reeds, and lives the whole of its life in reeds if it can. Only if numbers are high and food is short do some have to move out and find food in unusual places, such as beds of reed mace or rushes. Usually they nest in dense leaf litter underneath standing reeds and feed on fallen reed seeds or in the flowering heads, often swaying about in the breeze. They can be hard to spot on a windy day when they stay near the bases of the reeds, but may also fly fast and low across the reed-bed. Usually their calls give them away: a variety of 'pinging' and 'kissing' sounds.

The five to seven eggs hatch in 12 to 13 days and the chicks fly nine to 12 days later.

Warbler-sized but with long, tapered tail. Short, triangular beak; short, strong legs. Males very colourful; females and young less striking. Clings to upright reed stems, or hops about on ground beneath, sometimes kicking away dead leaves.

WHERE AND WHEN Very scattered, in England, Denmark and the Low Countries, western and southern France, parts of Eastern Europe.

PLACES IT PREFERS Reed swamps.

LOOKALIKES

Penduline tit, page 379, in parts of Eastern Europe, is similar but short-tailed.

Long-tailed tit

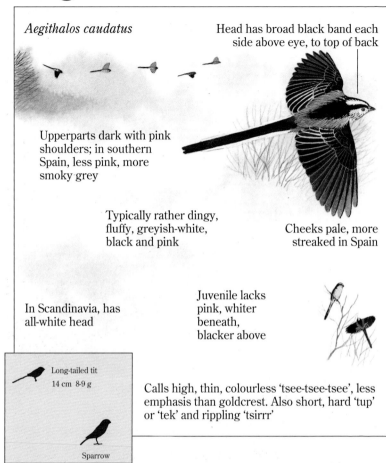

Aegithalos caudatus

Head has broad black band each side above eye, to top of back

Upperparts dark with pink shoulders; in southern Spain, less pink, more smoky grey

Typically rather dingy, fluffy, greyish-white, black and pink

Cheeks pale, more streaked in Spain

In Scandinavia, has all-white head

Juvenile lacks pink, whiter beneath, blacker above

Long-tailed tit
14 cm 8-9 g

Sparrow

Calls high, thin, colourless 'tsee-tsee-tsee', less emphasis than goldcrest. Also short, hard 'tup' or 'tek' and rippling 'tsirrr'

The long-tailed tit is not really a true tit, nor related to the other long-tailed 'tit', the bearded tit. It looks quite different and lives much more in family groups. It seems that several birds, rather than a single pair, may help out at a nest. These groups then roam around, often in willows and alders in swampy places or alongside streams, or move along hedgerows through open farmland, always calling to each other for comfort. They stay together, watch out for predators, warn each other of danger and have a better chance of finding something good to eat when several pairs of eyes are looking instead of one.

The eight to 12 eggs, in a domed nest of moss and lichen, hatch after 14 to 18 days, and the young fly 15 to 16 days later.

Extremely small except for long, slender tail. Tiny round head, very small bill. Looks like a round ball and stick. Acrobatic; often in groups of five to 20, following in line from bush to bush flying one or two at a time.

WHERE AND WHEN Virtually all of Europe, all year.

PLACES IT PREFERS Edges of woods, thick hedges, brambles, scrub.

LOOKALIKES
Nothing else is similar.

Marsh & willow tits

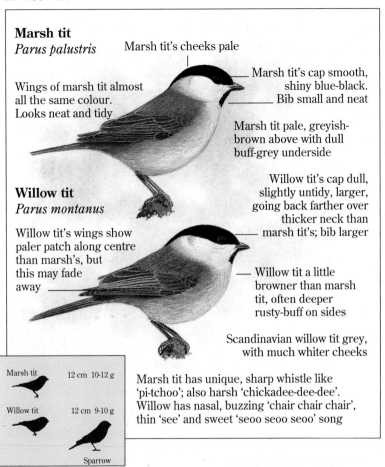

Marsh tit
Parus palustris

Marsh tit's cheeks pale

Marsh tit's cap smooth, shiny blue-black. Bib small and neat

Wings of marsh tit almost all the same colour. Looks neat and tidy

Marsh tit pale, greyish-brown above with dull buff-grey underside

Willow tit
Parus montanus

Willow tit's cap dull, slightly untidy, larger, going back farther over thicker neck than marsh tit's; bib larger

Willow tit's wings show paler patch along centre than marsh's, but this may fade away

Willow tit a little browner than marsh tit, often deeper rusty-buff on sides

Scandinavian willow tit grey, with much whiter cheeks

Marsh tit	12 cm	10-12 g
Willow tit	12 cm	9-10 g
	Sparrow	

Marsh tit has unique, sharp whistle like 'pi-tchoo'; also harsh 'chickadee-dee-dee'. Willow has nasal, buzzing 'chair chair chair', thin 'see' and sweet 'seoo seoo seoo' song

Few pairs of species are as closely similar as these; only perhaps the willow warbler and chiffchaff and common and Arctic terns are so difficult to tell apart. It was not until about 100 years ago that experts realized both of these small, black-capped tits lived in England. Their calls help to identify them, but habits and the places where they live give some clues, too. Even so, you can see both in the same wood, or visiting a bag of peanuts in the same garden. They both join in flocks of other tit species in autumn and winter, more so perhaps the marsh tit, but they are equally often seen in ones and twos, a little elusive and easily missed. Despite their dull colours they are worth a close look. Their eight or nine eggs hatch in 13 to 14 days and the young fly within 16 to 19 days.

Both are smaller than a great tit or a robin. No yellow, green or blue anywhere. **Marsh tit** *looks sleeker, paler, a little greyer than willow.*

◁ *Marsh tit*

Willow tit *looks thicker-necked, dumpier; has rougher plumage, a dull cap and larger bib.*

Willow tit ▷

WHERE AND WHEN
Most of Europe except Ireland, Spain, northern Scandinavia. All year.

Marsh tit

PLACES IT PREFERS Woods, thickets.

WHERE AND WHEN
Most of Europe except Ireland, west of France, Spain, Italy.

Willow tit

PLACES IT PREFERS Woods, thickets, scrub, hedges.

Crested tit

Parus cristatus

Top of head grey

Unique pointed crest of black and white

Upperside brown, underside pale greyish with buff sides

Face white except for black chin and throat, black line through eye and black edge to cheeks

Crested tit

12 cm 10-14 g

Sparrow

Call soft, almost purring trill, with quick rhythm, 'pit-rrr-r r rp', often repeated; also thin 'si si'

Crested tits rarely move far from where they were born, spending all their lives within one woodland area. They are restricted almost entirely to pines and other conifers, especially in Scotland, less so on mainland Europe, where they can be seen in mixed forest. Quite frequently, however, they move out to feed in smaller, young trees on the edges of moors or heaths. In places they come to bird tables in winter, but for most people they are rare and special birds. On the other hand, in some areas, such as the pines of Dutch heaths, the ancient forests of Scotland and the mountainside woods of the Pyrenees, they are quite common and easily found. However, it takes patience to get a close view – they are easily missed in dense foliage.

Five or six eggs hatch in 13 to 15 days; young fly at 17/18 days.

Blue-tit-sized. Dull, no yellow or blue. Spiky, pointed crest on back of head. Short, black bill. In action, a typical tit, hanging on tight while swinging from twigs or picking insects from bark. Flight quick, flitting. Call is best clue to where it is.

WHERE AND WHEN Most of Europe, but in UK only in northern Scotland. All year.

PLACES IT PREFERS Pine forest, forest edge with scattered trees, often in mountains.

LOOKALIKES

Coal tit, page 310, has white patch on back of head, no crest.
Marsh and **willow tits,** page 306, have solid black caps.

Coal tit

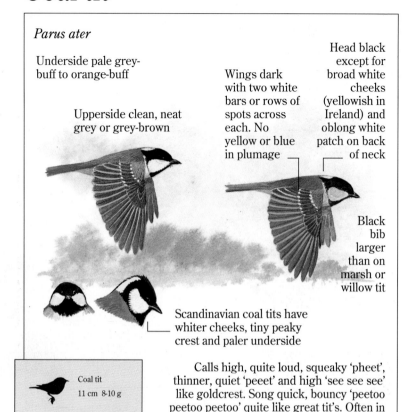

Parus ater

Underside pale grey-buff to orange-buff

Upperside clean, neat grey or grey-brown

Wings dark with two white bars or rows of spots across each. No yellow or blue in plumage

Head black except for broad white cheeks (yellowish in Ireland) and oblong white patch on back of neck

Black bib larger than on marsh or willow tit

Scandinavian coal tits have whiter cheeks, tiny peaky crest and paler underside

Coal tit
11 cm 8-10 g

Sparrow

Calls high, quite loud, squeaky 'pheet', thinner, quiet 'peeet' and high 'see see see' like goldcrest. Song quick, bouncy 'peetoo peetoo peetoo' quite like great tit's. Often in mixed parties of blue and long-tailed tits

This is one of Europe's tiniest birds: not much bigger than a goldcrest. It is a great acrobat, feeding just as well while hanging upside down at the very tip of the thinnest twig, as it does while pecking at a stout pine cone, or stealing a peanut from a basket. While most tits feed on a nut basket, coal tits take a nut and fly off with it, to eat it in peace nearby or to bury it, ready to eat later. This gives them a reserve for the winter, but most food they store in this way is pushed into the leaves and cones of pine trees and found again by accident when they search such places for food in the winter months.

Coal tits nest in holes, quite often old mouse burrows in the ground. The seven to 11 eggs hatch after 17 to 18 days and the chicks fly after 16 days.

 Slim, or rounded, depending on weather. Head looks big, can be fluffed out or sleek. Often in ones and twos, or in loose, scattered groups, moving slowly through treetops a few metres apart. Keeps in contact by constant sharp calls.

WHERE AND WHEN Almost all Europe, all year.

PLACES IT PREFERS Mixed woods and conifer forest, often in conifer, even among oak or beech woods or in a park.

LOOKALIKES

Marsh and **willow tit,** page 306, have no white on back of neck, no white on wings.

Blue tit

Parus caeruleus

Very small with distinctive square-bodied shape, steep forehead

Head largely white with black chin and edges of cheeks, pale blue cap

Tail vivid pale blue

Juvenile duller, yellower on head and greener on wings

Back green; wings blue, dull when worn but vivid blue in late winter and spring

Underside yellow with narrow, broken dark line in centre

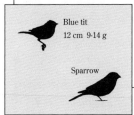

Blue tit
12 cm 9-14 g

Sparrow

Calls frequent, strident 'seee-si-si', 'pee-tsee-zay', thin 'see'. Song clear, bright with fast trill at end – 'psee-see t-r-rrrr'

Almost everyone knows the blue tit, one of the most familiar of all garden birds and perhaps the most frequent at a feeder filled with peanuts or scraps. It cannot really be confused with any other species, although sometimes people mistake it for the great tit. For every one or two blue tits seen together at a bird table, there might be ten or 20 which visit the garden during the course of a day.

Blue tits are great roamers, especially in winter, and flocks are large but loose, sometimes with other small species mixed in, covering quite a large area as they move steadily through woods and gardens. They keep in touch with constant calls.

Seven to 14 eggs hatch within 13 to 14 days and the chicks fly after 19 days.

 Tiny. Short, dumpy body, slim, square tail. Peaked head with very short bill. Strong legs allow it to cling acrobatically to twigs, undersides of branches, peanut baskets. Flight fast, whirring, with sudden stop at perch.

WHERE AND WHEN All but extreme north Europe, all year.

PLACES IT PREFERS Mixed woods, parks, gardens, reeds.

LOOKALIKES

Great tit, page 314, bigger, blacker on head with white cheeks, more black down front of chest.

Great tit

Parus major

Black head with white cheeks

Blue-black band continues down chest: broad on male, tapered on female

White edges to tail

Young ones have pale yellow cheeks and duller greenish cap

Great tit

14 cm 16-21 g

Sparrow

Vivid yellow underparts contrast with blue-grey wings and green back

Loud, strident 'tea-cher tea-cher' song in spring

Between a sparrow and blue tit in size, the great tit is a small, lightweight bird with the boldness and aggression of a bigger one. It dominates the nut feed unless chased off by a woodpecker or starlings.

In its ancestral woodland habitat, it lives in mature trees but often feeds around the base of the trunk and amongst dead leaves on the ground beneath. It is cleverer than a blue tit at picking up nuts and berries, wedging them into bark to split them open, but not so good at feeding at the tips of tiny twigs.

It nests in holes in trees or in nest boxes specially put out for small birds in woods and gardens.

In the wild the female great tit lays five to 14 eggs which hatch within 13 to 14 days, and the chicks fly after 19 days.

Small but well-built, with stout legs and a thick, blunt bill. Often taps loudly with bill. Explores dead leaves, old bark and foliage for caterpillars, spiders, berries and seeds. Loud calls very varid and often confusing.

WHERE AND WHEN All over Britain and Ireland, widespread throughout Europe; all year.

PLACES IT PREFERS Woods, gardens, parks, hedges, especially mature oaks and beeches, but also older conifer plantations.

LOOKALIKES

Blue tit, page 312, has blue top to whiter head, shorter, bluer tail and much thinner line down centre of breast.

Coal tit, page 310, smaller, no green and yellow; same white cheeks but also broad band down back of neck.

Nuthatch

Sitta europaea

Tail square, bluish, with white corners and black patch each side at base

Underside buff to white with brighter, more orange-brown sides

Blue-grey above, looks pale

Broad black line through eye ends at side of neck

Lively, bright, moves in quick hops and short flights from branch to branch

Nuthatch
14 cm 20-24 g

Sparrow

Scandinavian birds whiter underneath

Calls loud and clear, whistling 'peu peu peu', fast 'tswitwitwitwitwit', sharp 'hwit', thin 'seet'

The nuthatch is a stranger to many who could know it well: where it is common, it comes to gardens and establishes itself as a favourite at the peanut basket. It is full of character, a nervy, jerky feeder, hopping and sidling along, hanging on a basket for a few moments, then flying off low and fast.

Away from gardens, it is a woodland bird which forages low down among roots and fallen branches, or even on the ground, as well as high in the treetops.

It has a curious habit of plastering wet mud around the entrance hole to its nest cavity, probably to reduce the hole to a snug fit that will keep out larger birds and weasels.

There are six to 11 eggs which hatch after 14 to 15 days. The young leave the nest after 23 to 25 days.

 Great-tit-sized. Strange elongated shape; flat head, level with line of back; short, square tail. Strong feet allow it to cling to bark and move on or under branches. Often pecks, with loud taps, at food wedged in bark. Very noisy in spring.

WHERE AND WHEN All Europe except Ireland, Scotland, northern Scandinavia; all year.

PLACES IT PREFERS Mixed and broadleaved woodland, especially with oak and beech; parks.

LOOKALIKES

Nothing has similar shape or colour.

Treecreeper & short-toed

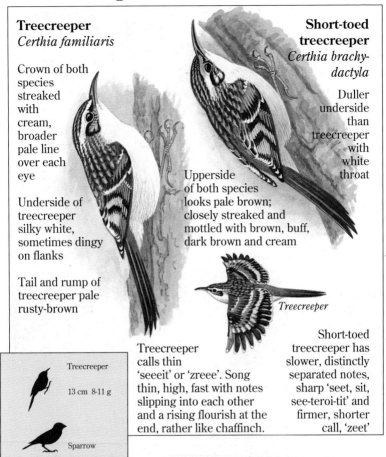

Treecreeper
Certhia familiaris

Crown of both species streaked with cream, broader pale line over each eye

Underside of treecreeper silky white, sometimes dingy on flanks

Tail and rump of treecreeper pale rusty-brown

Short-toed treecreeper
Certhia brachy-dactyla

Duller underside than treecreeper with white throat

Upperside of both species looks pale brown; closely streaked and mottled with brown, buff, dark brown and cream

Treecreeper

Treecreeper

13 cm 8-11 g

Sparrow

Treecreeper calls thin 'seeeit' or 'zreee'. Song thin, high, fast with notes slipping into each other and a rising flourish at the end, rather like chaffinch.

Short-toed treecreeper has slower, distinctly separated notes, sharp 'seet, sit, see-teroi-tit' and firmer, shorter call, 'zeet'

In Europe there is no greater test of identification skill than this pair. In fact, even experienced birdwatchers who trap them for ringing purposes cannot always tell them apart in the hand. Only when one sings can it really be identified with confidence.

Both have the same shuffling, mouse-like look as they clamber up the bark of a tree. Unlike a nuthatch, they rely on the support of the tail as well as the claws and find it hard to grip head-downwards, although they can hang from the underside of a branch. They are insect- and spider-eaters and never come to peanuts: if they visit gardens at all, they simply explore the bushes and old fruit trees.

Their six eggs, in a nest behind loose bark, hatch within 17 to 20 days, and the young fly 14 to 15 days later.

Both are slim and tapered, usually pressed against tree. Bills fine and curved; legs small but claws long and sharp; tails pointed or forked, used as a support. Often moves upwards on tree trunk, like shuffling ➤

◁　*Treecreeper*

➤ *mouse, spiralling round or hanging under branch; then flitting down to next tree, to work up again.*

Short-toed treecreeper ▷

WHERE AND WHEN Britain and Ireland, Pyrenees, eastern France to Eastern Europe and Scandinavia. All year.

Treecreeper

WHERE AND WHEN From Iberia to east Germany, south to Mediterranean. All year.

Short-toed treecreeper

PLACES IT PREFERS Mixed woods, conifers, tall hedges, parks.

PLACES IT PREFERS Mixed woods, conifers, parks.

Great grey & red-backed shrikes

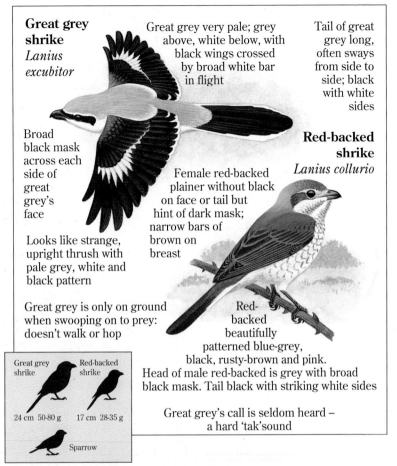

Great grey shrike
Lanius excubitor

Great grey very pale; grey above, white below, with black wings crossed by broad white bar in flight

Tail of great grey long, often sways from side to side; black with white sides

Broad black mask across each side of great grey's face

Red-backed shrike
Lanius collurio

Female red-backed plainer without black on face or tail but hint of dark mask; narrow bars of brown on breast

Looks like strange, upright thrush with pale grey, white and black pattern

Great grey is only on ground when swooping on to prey: doesn't walk or hop

Red-backed beautifully patterned blue-grey, black, rusty-brown and pink. Head of male red-backed is grey with broad black mask. Tail black with striking white sides

Great grey shrike

Red-backed shrike

24 cm 50-80 g

17 cm 28-35 g

Sparrow

Great grey's call is seldom heard – a hard 'tak' sound

Shrikes impale prey – beetles, lizards, small voles, even small birds – on thorns or barbed wire, so that they can tear off small pieces. Sometimes the prey is left on a thorn to be eaten later. They watch for their food, looking from perches such as bush tops or wires. Once a movement is spotted, down flies the shrike in a swift pounce. The prey is caught with the feet, but the hooked bill may be used to kill it before picking it to pieces. Shrikes are declining all over Europe and the red-backed has disappeared from Britain where it used to be quite common. It is not easy to see why, but changes in farming have probably made their large-insect and small-vole prey less abundant.

Five or six eggs hatch after 14 to 16 days and the young fly 15 days later.

Long, rather rounded tail. Bill quite stout, slightly hooked. Perch boldly on twigs, tall stems, tops of bushes, dead branches, but can be very secretive. **Great grey** *bigger, longer-tailed than* **red-backed**. *Flight* ▶

◁ *Great grey shrike*

▶ *low, swooping, with sudden rise to new perch.*

Red-backed shrike ▷

WHERE AND WHEN Most of Europe all year; northern birds move south and west in winter.

Great grey shrike

PLACES IT PREFERS Bushy heaths, woodland edge.

WHERE AND WHEN Most of Europe except UK, April to October.

Red-backed shrike

PLACES IT PREFERS Thorny hedges, heaths, scrub.

Jay

Garrulus glandarius

Pale, orange-buff to pinkish-brown, some much greyer

Crown whitish, streaked black (in parts of Europe, black)

In autumn, often flies with acorn in its bill

Broad black moustache below eye

Bend of wing has patch of vivid blue, not obvious except at close range

In flight, wide white band on middle of wing, big white rump patch above black tail

Wings rounded, fingered at tip, with jerky, downward fan-like action

Calls loud, harsh 'scrairk' and softer, mewing 'peeay'

Jay

34 cm   160 g

Sparrow

Perhaps oak woods would not have spread so widely across Europe without jays. Acorns cannot roll far, nor uphill, but jays carry thousands of them from woods into open countryside where they bury them. Many are remembered and eaten later, even the following spring when they provide nourishment for young jays, but many are forgotten and grow into oak seedlings.

Jays are persecuted in many places, but do little damage: they eat practically anything and a few eggs or chicks are swallowed eagerly, but overall they are not harmful to songbirds. They are so handsome and interesting that many people feel they deserve greater protection.

Five or six eggs, in a nest low in a bush, hatch within 16 days and the young leave after 20 days.

Bigger than thrush, smaller than crow. Looks pale, pinkish-brown with black-and-white patches in flight. Wings broad, blunt, giving floppy, unsteady flight. On ground, moves with long, bounding hops. Usually flies off before it is spotted, with harsh call.

WHERE AND WHEN Throughout Europe, all year.

PLACES IT PREFERS Old oak woods, mixed woods, farmland with old trees in tall hedges, parks.

LOOKALIKES

Hoopoe, page 214, has thin bill, barred wings without blue, barred tail, far less often in trees.

Magpie

Pica pica

Tail long, narrow, shiny green, purple and black

Young bird similar but duller and with short tail at first

Dull black on head, back, breast; shoulder patch and underside clean, white

Wings mostly black when closed, shining dark blue; show white lines at tip when spread

Magpie

45 cm 240 g

Sparrow

Call loud, hard, fast 'chak-ak-ak-ak'

Magpies are loved and hated in equal measure. They certainly rob nests and eat many eggs and small chicks but they always have. Where they have been persecuted, their numbers are greatly reduced. Recent increases are mostly a return to normal, and evidence of the easy life that magpies have around towns and suburbs where there is so much rubbish for them to eat. They are great characters. Often in groups of three or four, sometimes ten or 12, they roam around looking for trouble: but, more truthfully, usually looking for beetles, worms and leatherjackets. Their long, bouncy tails, loud calls and bold behaviour make them unmistakable.

Five to eight eggs, in a domed nest of thick sticks, hatch after 17 to 18 days; the young leave within 22 to 27 days.

Larger than a pigeon, with long, tapered tail. Short, rounded wings give floppy, weak appearance in flight – but it can swoop in and out of trees and hedges acrobatically. Bouncy hop on ground. Usually in twos and threes, sometimes flocks.

WHERE AND WHEN All of Europe, all year.

PLACES IT PREFERS Hedges, woods, woodland edges, gardens.

LOOKALIKES

Jay, page 322, less black and white.

Shrikes, page 320, much smaller.

Chough

Pyrrhocorax pyrrhocorax

Bill red; young bird has shorter, orange bill at first

Plumage all black, with shiny blue and purple

Legs vivid red

Square wings with upcurved fingers

Chough

40 cm 250 g

Sparrow

Calls loud, ringing, explosive 'charr', 'chow', 'chiar'

Choughs are wonderful birds. They are related to crows, and look all black, but eat only grubs, ants and other tiny insects and spiders. They dive and swoop through the air with abandon, for all the world as if they are doing it for fun. Pairs, family parties or winter flocks get together and play in the upcurrents around cliffs and spin round in the eddies above windswept gorges, calling all the time with excited, echoing sounds. They are not normally common, except in a few mountain areas in the south where numbers can reach hundreds when flocks move down to feed in fields during the winter months.

Nests are under ledges in caves or on cliffs; three to six eggs hatch in 17 to 18 days and the youngsters fly after 38 days.

A slender, long-winged crow. Bill slim, slightly curved. Wings look square across tip except for long, curved fingers. Tail square-tipped. On ground, flirts wings and bows forwards, probes with bill. In flight, zooms along with closed wings, soars, glides, dives.

WHERE AND WHEN Coasts of Ireland, Wales, France; most of Spain, Alps. All year.

PLACES IT PREFERS Cliffs, gorges; short grass near clifftops, along coast.

LOOKALIKES

Jackdaw, page 328, has rounder wings, longer tail, grey neck.

Alpine chough has yellow bill, round wing tips, longer, rounder tail.

Jackdaw & rook

Jackdaw
Corvus monedula

Rook all black, with shiny purple and blue reflections, except for bare whitish face on adult

Rook
Corvus frugilegus

Jackdaw greyer than rook, pale grey on neck; eyes gleam white

Rook's bill pointed; forehead steep, giving peaked crown

Jackdaw has black cap and chin

Tail of rook is rounded, sometimes almost like raven's (square on crow)

Rook has long wings, often slightly curved back, with fingered tips

Jackdaw flies fast, often with deep, smooth flaps; also glides, soars and dives in air currents

Jackdaw   33 cm 250 g

Rook   45 cm 490 g

Sparrow

Carrion crow very like rook, with thicker bill, flatter head, squarer wings and tail. Immature rook has all-black face

Rook calls loud, nasal 'kaaar'; jackdaw has squeaky, sharp 'chak'

Rooks and jackdaws are often found together and both are sociable, enjoying the company of maybe 50 or 100 others as they fly around the treetops where they nest, or seek food in the nearby fields. Rooks are big birds, part of the landscape in farmland areas where they are abundant. Jackdaws are smaller, often less numerous, but with a wider choice of habitat. They nest in holes and anything will do, from a cliff to a church tower or a big tree; parkland, farmland with isolated copses, towns and quarries or remote sea cliffs are all fine. Their four to six eggs hatch after 17 to 18 days. Rooks nest in colonies, or rookeries, building big, exposed nests of thick sticks which sway in the wind in the very tops of the tallest trees in a wood. Three to five eggs hatch in 16 to 18 days.

Jackdaw *is neater than rook, jaunty, bouncy; in flight shows rounder wings without fingered tips.*

◁ *Jackdaw*

Rook *bigger than a pigeon; jackdaw about pigeon-sized. Rook looks a little untidy, with long, pointed bill, steep forehead, loose feathering on thighs. In flight, has long, fingered wings.*

Rook ▷

WHERE AND WHEN All over Europe except far north, all year.

Jackdaw

PLACES IT PREFERS Farmland, woods, parks, cliffs and quarries.

WHERE AND WHEN Most of Europe except far north, all year; in Southern Europe, only in winter.

Rook

PLACES IT PREFERS Farmland, woods, parks.

Carrion crow/hooded crow

Corvus corone

Thick, heavy bill more abruptly curved near tip than on young rook

Carrion crow all black, much less blue than rook

In flight, looks square-tailed, wings a little broader, straighter than rook's

Hooded (which is a race, not a separate species) has grey body, often tinged pinkish or fawn. Some 'mixtures' on boundary have less grey than hooded, usually mostly on belly

Carrion crow / hooded crow

46 cm 570 g

Sparrow

Calls deep, hoarse, strong croak 'caw'

These are the same species. Over most of Europe, the all-black carrion crow is the usual bird. The grey-and-black hooded crow is the race found in Ireland, Scotland, Scandinavia, Italy and Eastern Europe. Nearly everyone is against the crow: yet it is admirable for its ability to survive despite persecution, and for its strong, handsome profile. True, it eats smaller birds' eggs and chicks, but much of the blame it gets is based on suspicion – people see them as black, 'evil' birds. If not molested, they become quite tame in parks, or around car parks.

Crows nest in tall trees, but in some northern parts where the land is bleak and windswept, they make do with the ground or a rock face. The four or five eggs hatch after 18 to 21 days and the young leave the big, stick nest in four or five weeks.

Bigger than a pigeon. Hefty; broad-shouldered, solid build. Thick, tapered bill. Tightly feathered body. Long, fingered wings, square tail. Often solitary, but usually in pairs and sometimes much bigger flocks.

WHERE AND WHEN Throughout Europe, all year; some hooded crows move west in winter.

PLACES IT PREFERS Bushy heaths, moors, farmland, seashore.

LOOKALIKES

Rook, page 328, has thinner bill, peaky head, loose thigh feathers.
　Raven, page 332, bigger, with wedge-shaped tail, longer, narrower wings.

Raven

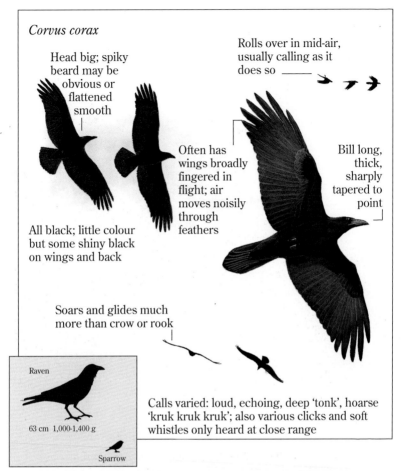

Corvus corax

Rolls over in mid-air, usually calling as it does so

Head big; spiky beard may be obvious or flattened smooth

Often has wings broadly fingered in flight; air moves noisily through feathers

Bill long, thick, sharply tapered to point

All black; little colour but some shiny black on wings and back

Soars and glides much more than crow or rook

Raven

63 cm 1,000-1,400 g

Sparrow

Calls varied: loud, echoing, deep 'tonk', hoarse 'kruk kruk kruk'; also various clicks and soft whistles only heard at close range

This is the biggest of all the world's crows, but at a distance it is not always obvious that it is bigger than a carrion crow or rook. Once it is seen beside another bird or at close range, its size and giant bill become obvious. Ravens are usually seen in pairs, but young birds which have not got mates or territories gather into flocks and now and then quite large numbers may be seen together. Usually these find a cliff with a strong updraught of air and perform all kinds of aerobatics together. Part of the raven's display is a roll over in mid-air, turning on to its back then rolling back again.

Ravens build strong, stick nests on cliff ledges, often under overhangs, or in tall trees. The four to six eggs hatch after 20 to 21 days but the young are in the nest for five or six weeks.

Strongly built, broad head exaggerated by spiky 'beard' feathers; can be raised (even in flight). Wings long, often feathers missing in moult give angled effect. Fingered wing tips can be swept back to a point. Tail large, broad, diamond-shaped.

WHERE AND WHEN Most of Europe except lowlands of France, Low Countries; all year.

PLACES IT PREFERS Moors, cliffs, coasts, quarries, mountainsides.

LOOKALIKES

Carrion crow, page 330, has square tail.

   Rook, page 328, has rounder tail, bare face, thinner bill.

Starling & spotless starling

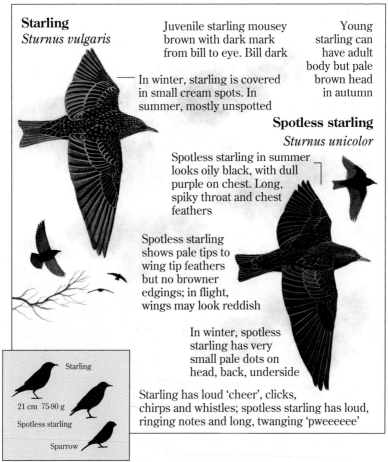

Starling
Sturnus vulgaris

Juvenile starling mousey brown with dark mark from bill to eye. Bill dark

Young starling can have adult body but pale brown head in autumn

In winter, starling is covered in small cream spots. In summer, mostly unspotted

Spotless starling
Sturnus unicolor

Spotless starling in summer looks oily black, with dull purple on chest. Long, spiky throat and chest feathers

Spotless starling shows pale tips to wing tip feathers but no browner edgings; in flight, wings may look reddish

In winter, spotless starling has very small pale dots on head, back, underside

Starling has loud 'cheer', clicks, chirps and whistles; spotless starling has loud, ringing notes and long, twanging 'pweeeeee'

Starling

21 cm 75-90 g

Spotless starling

Sparrow

Starlings are familiar, popular, bustling birds, always in a hurry and always in a group. Sometimes flocks of hundreds or thousands are encountered and roosts, often on city buildings, may number hundreds of thousands. Spotless starlings are found only in Iberia, some Mediterranean islands and in parts of North Africa, replacing the starling there in summer – although some starlings reach these places in winter.

Although often closely linked with people – both species nest in roofs and towers and feed in gardens or around villages – they are also as likely to be found well away from people and are quite at home in a wild environment.

Five to seven eggs hatch after 12 to 13 days and the young leave the nest 20 to 22 days later.

Both smaller than blackbird. Quick, shuffling walk with jerky head. Often probe in grass with bills but do not stop to listen like a blackbird. In flight, wings pointed, tail short. both fly straight, fast, but flocks have up and down, rolling effect.

◁ *Starling*

Spotless starling ▷

WHERE AND WHEN From Pyrenees and Italy north; in north and east only in summer; reaches Spain in winter.

Starling

WHERE AND WHEN Only in Iberia, Sardinia, Corsica, Sicily.

Spotless starling

PLACES IT PREFERS Woods, moors, heaths, farmland, villages, parks, gardens.

PLACES IT PREFERS Old villages, farms, open fields.

Waxwing

Bombycilla garrulus

Mostly dull pink-brown; deeper red patch under tail

Foxy-red face, silky black bib

Rump greyer, tail black with broad yellow tip

Wings have fine lines of white and yellow; close views reveal red spots in middle of closed wing

Waxwing

18 cm 60-80 g

Sparrow

Crest often flattened, but can be raised almost vertically

Call a distinctive, high, metallic, ringing trill

Waxwings are engaging and beautiful creatures, the more so because they are often so tame that they can be watched from a few metres away as they feed greedily on fresh red berries. In most winters they are rare in Western Europe, but when numbers are very high in the far north, and berries are few, they must move south and west to find food. Then flocks reach the Low Countries, Britain and France, even Ireland, and isolated birds or small groups are frequently seen in gardens. They feed aerobatically, almost like tiny parrots.

In summer they like dense, tall spruce trees mixed with birch, where long, straggly lichens clothe branches. They make a nest of grass and moss; five to six eggs are incubated for 14 to 15 days and the young fly when two weeks old.

Starling-sized, large-headed, crested and short-tailed bird, with stout bill, very short legs. Colourful in strong light, but can look dark or greyish in dull conditions. High trilling calls draw attention.

WHERE AND WHEN Extreme north of Scandinavia in summer; farther south and west in winter, usually scarce, sometimes common.

PLACES IT PREFERS Dense woods; in winter, parks, gardens, shrubberies and hedges with berries.

LOOKALIKES

Starling, page 334, similar in size and shape but more pointed head and wings. In flight, shorter rump and tail; blacker; no crest. Starling flocks are more erratic and often settle on the ground – waxwings usually in bushes.

House & tree sparrows

House sparrow
Passer domesticus

Male house sparrow: grey centre to top of head, red-brown each side; black chin

Undersides of house sparrow unmarked pale grey; back streaked red-brown, black and cream

In summer, house sparrow has enlarged black bib

Tree sparrow's bib smaller. Rump buff, less grey; streaks under tail

Female house sparrow has yellow-brown look, with unmarked paler underside. Broad pale stripe over eye

Tree sparrow
Passer montanus

Tree sparrow like male house sparrow, but whole of cap rich red-brown; whiter ring around sides of neck; big black patch on white cheek

Juvenile

House sparrow
14 cm   25-30 g

Tree sparrow
13 cm   20-25 g

House sparrow calls are loud cheeps and chirrups, noisy; tree sparrow has distinctive hard 'tek' as well as chirrupy song

The starling and tree sparrow are happy to live near people, but can also live in places where humans are rarely to be seen; the house sparrow seems to be almost always in places where there are people. It follows them to the most remote spots, so long as there are a few houses to perch on and nest in, and some scraps to eat. It forms flocks in the fields in autumn and winter, feeding on weeds or spilt grain, but it is most familiar as a garden bird.

Tree sparrows have gone up and down in numbers for hundreds of years: recently they have declined drastically. They frequently mix with finches in winter. Both species lay three to six eggs which hatch after 12 to 14 days; the young fly after 12 to 15 days.

*Head slightly flat on **house sparrow**. Wings and tail short on both. Noisy, quarrelsome, often in flocks. Male and female house sparrow different. House sparrow always near human habitation.*

◁ *House sparrow*

Tree sparrow *also in farmland, woods, cliffs. Stout, triangular bills. Short legs. Head rounder on tree sparrow, male and female tree sparrow identical.*

Tree sparrow ▷

WHERE AND WHEN Almost everywhere in Europe, all year.

House sparrow

WHERE AND WHEN Most of Europe except southern Spain, northern Scandinavia.

Tree sparrow

PLACES IT PREFERS Villages, town squares and parks, gardens, farmland.

PLACES IT PREFERS Villages, gardens, woodland, farmland with trees.

Chaffinch

Fringilla coelebs

In flight both wing bars show up, as well as white sides to dark tail

Underside unmarked, like female sparrow's

Spring male has blue-grey top to head, pale red-pink or orange-pink face and breast

Male

Winter male has duller head with browner tinge, paler breast

Shows white bar across closed wing; larger, broader band higher up wing may be hidden

Female pale, greyish or pinkish-olive, with greyer sides to neck and pale line above eye

Chaffinch

15 cm   19-23 g

Sparrow

Song loud, bright trill with up-and-down flourish at end; same phrase repeated several times each minute. Calls 'chink' and, in flight, softer 'chup chup'

Although never such a hanger-on to human beings as the house sparrow, the chaffinch often seems to be more confident, coming up to people to beg for a crumb wherever there are car parks and picnic places in woodland or farmland with plenty of trees and hedges. Chaffinches look prettier than sparrows, and have a cheery, bright song which they begin as soon as winter is coming to an end: they are popular birds.

In winter they form flocks, sometimes with males in groups of their own. They flit from hedge to field and back again but don't dash around together in tight bunches like some of the smaller finches and the house sparrow.

Their four to five eggs hatch in 11 to 13 days and the chicks fly when 14 days old.

 Sparrow-sized. Male bright; female and young duller. Thick bill. Long, with slim, notched tail. In flight reveals striking pattern of white lines. In flocks during winter but pairs in breeding territories. Often at bird tables, but not nut-basket feeders.

WHERE AND WHEN All of Europe, all year in centre and south, summer only in north.

PLACES IT PREFERS Woods of all kinds, hedges, parks, gardens.

LOOKALIKES

Brambling, page 342, very similar, but has whiter belly, white rump.

Brambling

Fringilla montifringilla

Female duller, paler, but still shows hint of dark marks on back of head, grey band behind cheeks

Underside orange on chest, white on belly

Back brownish, wings dull, with orange bar; underside shows paler orange chest

In winter, head mottled dark and pale buff; often a double dark stripe down back of neck

Spring male has black head and back

Both sexes show white centre to rump, best seen in flight

Song deep, drawn-out 'schrreee'; calls nasal, twangy 'swairnk' and hard 'chut' in flight

Broad orange upper wing bar; narrow lower one paler, orange to white

Male

Brambling

15 cm 22-30 g

Sparrow

Bramblings are quite exciting winter visitors in Britain, sometimes in good numbers but in many years quite rare. They are usually found with chaffinches, especially under beeches where they feed on the seeds. Because of this they turn up year after year in traditional places. In much of mainland Europe, however, they are much more abundant in winter and some huge flocks, running into millions, have been seen. Their numbers tend to rise and fall with the abundance of their food, especially the beech and hornbeam seed crop. They are closely related to chaffinches and, in basic shape and outline, look much the same: only their colours are different.

Their six or seven eggs hatch after 12 days and the young fly within two weeks.

Sparrow-sized. Shape like chaffinch. Hops and shuffles on ground beneath trees or in weedy fields. Also feeds in birch and other trees in spring and summer, when quiet, acrobatic and elusive. Visits gardens and bird tables mostly in very cold weather.

WHERE AND WHEN In summer in far north-eastern Europe; in winter moves south to whole of Southern and Western Europe.

PLACES IT PREFERS Birch and beech woods, farmland, parks.

LOOKALIKES
Chaffinch, page 340, has whiter wing bars, green rump.

Serin

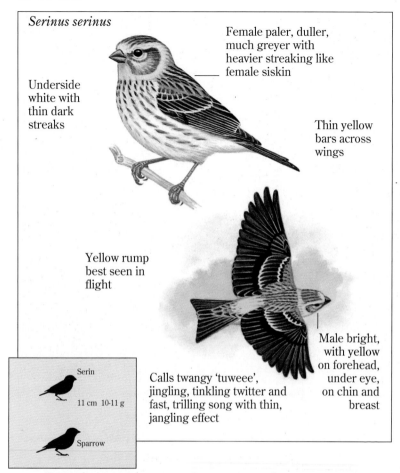

Serinus serinus

Female paler, duller, much greyer with heavier streaking like female siskin

Underside white with thin dark streaks

Thin yellow bars across wings

Yellow rump best seen in flight

Male bright, with yellow on forehead, under eye, on chin and breast

Serin

11 cm 10-11 g

Sparrow

Calls twangy 'tuweee', jingling, tinkling twitter and fast, trilling song with thin, jangling effect

Serins are unmistakeable birds, characteristic of Mediterranean countries, where their frequent twittering calls and songs, sounding like splintered glass, seem to go well with the hot sunshine and bright colours. Farther north they are summer visitors which have spread a little in recent years, but nesting in Britain is rare. Of all the finches, they are the smallest and daintiest, with a slightly stumpy, flat-headed look. They love leafy trees, such as cherries and small oaks, as well as conifers, and they can often be found in the middle of villages or around farms. Parts of the serin's song is similar to a canary's – and in fact it is a close relation of the cage bird.

Their three or four eggs hatch in just 12 days and the young fly 13 to 14 days later.

344

Blue-tit sized. Tiny triangular bill; thick neck. Tapered body, short, notched tail. Very short legs. Often perches on top of tree, singing, before going off in song flight with slowly waved wings, like a big butterfly. Often feeds on ground, not easy to see.

WHERE AND WHEN All year in Spain, Italy, southern France; in Central Europe in summer.

PLACES IT PREFERS Orchards, gardens, avenues in villages.

LOOKALIKES

Greenfinch, page 346, bigger, less streaked.

Siskin, page 350, has dark chin, more yellow on wings and tail but less on head.

Greenfinch

Carduelis chloris

Spring male bright apple-green with grey wings; duller in winter

Broad yellow streak on outer (front) edge of wing, a wide band across wing in flight

Yellow patch each side of tail

Female like winter male, or duller, with a little less yellow

Triangular bill very pale; dark mask

Juvenile more olive-brown, very softly streaked on top

Calls nasal, rising 'tuweee', fast, trilling 'chichichichichi'. Song a rich warbling trill and deep, buzzy 'djeeee'

Hops on ground or in bushes, but unable to cling to thin stems of weeds; often hangs on peanut baskets

Greenfinch

14 cm 25-30 g

Sparrow

Numbers of greenfinches across Europe have declined as farming methods leave fewer seeds in winter and fewer insects and larvae in summer. Modern methods of sowing and harvesting grain and wiping out pests are not good for finches. In the past, large flocks would feed in a rough field, swooping in a sudden rush to the nearest hedge if scared by a dog, or a hawk, before trickling back to the ground when the danger had passed. Now this is seen less often. Greenfinches are still, however, common in gardens where they have quickly learned to feed from baskets of nuts and other food, often driving away the smaller blue and great tits.

Their four to six eggs hatch in 13 days; the chicks fly when 13 to 16 days old.

 Sparrow-sized. Thick, heavy bill and 'angry' expression. Wings quite long, pointed; tail short and deeply notched. Legs very short. Hops. Song flight distinctive with wings spread wide, flapped slowly. Flocks in winter move fast when disturbed.

WHERE AND WHEN Almost all Europe except far north, all year.

PLACES IT PREFERS Parks, gardens with berries, conifers; woodland, fields.

LOOKALIKES

Female **chaffinch,** page 340, has paler wing bars instead of yellow streak.

Female **house sparrow,** page 338, more streaked on back.

Goldfinch

Carduelis carduelis

Body pale fawn-brown to sandy coloured, with white belly

Adult unique with red, white and black face

Young bird: duller wings but still large yellow bands; head greyish, no red and black

Buff or white tips to wing and tail feathers, most obvious in autumn and bigger, duller on young bird

Feeds in tall alders, birches and on all kinds of tall, strong weeds such as teasels, thistles, sowthistles

Wings dull black with broad band of yellow all the way along

Goldfinch

12 cm 14-17 g

Sparrow

Calls lisping, liquid 'swit-wit-wit'; harsh 'jee'; song-like calls but longer, more a twittering warble

Nothing has quite the charm of a group of goldfinches moving from clump to clump of thistles or teasels, clinging to the old seedheads to extract tiny seeds with their long, tweezer-like bills. They twitter sweetly as they go, and each time they fly they show off the broad yellow bands across their wings.

They are quite at home in northern areas, even in winter, yet seem particularly suited, with their colour and lively action, to the south. There the biggest flocks are found, sometimes scores or hundreds at a time. They prefer leafy trees to nest in, the kind that are often planted as ornamental trees around towns and houses, but they are not really garden birds.

The five or six eggs hatch after 12 to 13 days, and the chicks fly at 13 to 14 days old.

 Short legs. Deeply notched tail; quite long wing tips. Flight very buoyant, bouncing up and down with final flourish of wings as it lands. Usually feeds on tall stems or in trees, less often on ground. Normally in small flocks or family groups.

WHERE AND WHEN Most of Europe except Scandinavia, all year.

PLACES IT PREFERS Orchards, waste ground, woodland edge, parks, farmland.

LOOKALIKES

Nothing has the same black and yellow wings.
   Greenfinch, page 346, less contrasted.

Siskin

Carduelis spinus

Wings of female blackish with sharp palebars

Male colourful with yellow-green breast, black wings crossed with yellow bars

Female greyer than male, whiter underneath, with longer, fine, dark streaks

Belly pure white. Flanks streaked black

Cap and chin black

Yellow-green rump; the deeply forked tail has a yellow patch each side

Siskin

12 cm 12-17 g

Sparrow

Not much bigger than blue tit

Loud 'tsy-ee' and fast chatter from flocks

A red mesh bag full of peanuts attracts siskins like bees to a honey pot. Perhaps it looks like a giant pine cone, whose seed is the siskin's natural food. Siskins come to gardens mainly in late winter, when natural food is short and the peanuts no doubt keep many alive at one of the hardest times of year.

Normally, siskins are woodland birds, in winter wandering to strips of alders, larches and birch in search of seed. They are often in flocks, moving in tight bunches. Almost as acrobatic as tits, they feed on the thinnest twigs, hanging upside down and probing with their finely-tipped bills. In summer, they prefer more extensive conifer forests.

Their three to five eggs hatch in 11 to 12 days and the youngsters fly after 15 days.

 Tiny: smaller than a sparrow. Lightly built, with long, pointed wings. Very short legs; thin triangular bill. Flat head and rather rounded body. In flight, quick, dashing, with fast bounds and glides with closed wings. Loud, clear, squeaky flight calls.

WHERE AND WHEN Mostly in Northern Europe and mountains; lower levels and farther south in winter.

PLACES IT PREFERS Conifer forest; in winter mixed woods, shelter belts, wooded parks and gardens.

LOOKALIKES

Greenfinch, page 346, bigger, less acrobatic; has soft grey and green wings with yellow streak, not cross-bars on black.

Linnet

In spring, male has blue-grey head with red forehead, bright red breast _____

Carduelis cannabina

In flight, white shows as streaky panel in wing

Pale tawny-brown finch with white streaks in wings and sides of tail. Wings and tail black and white

Back plain pale orange-brown

Female greyer _____ than male, more streaked with fine dark lines on back and breast

Wings and tail like male's

Male has greyer head, unmarked underside

Linnet
14 cm 14-20 g

Sparrow

Loud, rapid, light twitter, especially from flocks; liquid warbling song

Linnets were once common farmland birds over Western Europe, but changes in agriculture have caused a widespread decline. On heaths and the edges of moorland they remain frequent, often perching on top of bushes or fence wires to twitter musically to themselves.

Linnets are sociable even in summer, gathering to feed wherever there are weed seeds. In autumn and winter there may be large flocks, which feed quietly out of sight until disturbed, then fly up and dash round, sweeping up and down as they go, before swirling back to the ground or into a hedge at a safe distance. They mix with larger finches and sparrows.

The four to six eggs hatch in ten to 12 days and the young fly in 11 to 12 days.

Smaller than a sparrow; slim, with long body, long forked tail. Round head; short, stubby bill. Very short legs; not acrobatic, feeds mostly on ground. Perches in trees but does not feed there. Often in flocks, flying together in whirring groups.

WHERE AND WHEN Most of Europe, summer in north, moving south and west in winter.

PLACES IT PREFERS Bushy farmland, hedges, gorse-grown heaths, moors.

LOOKALIKES

Twite, page 380, more streaked, has orange throat.

Redpoll, page 354, more streaked, has black chin.

Sparrows, page 338, bigger, unmarked beneath.

Redpoll

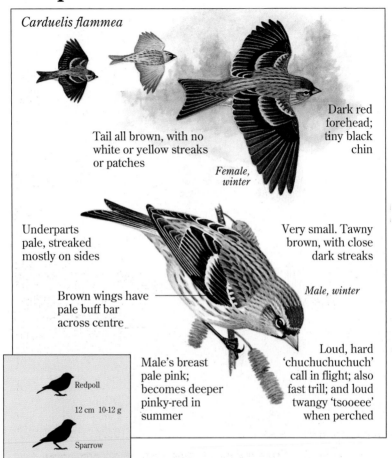

Carduelis flammea

Tail all brown, with no white or yellow streaks or patches

Female, winter

Dark red forehead; tiny black chin

Underparts pale, streaked mostly on sides

Very small. Tawny brown, with close dark streaks

Male, winter

Brown wings have pale buff bar across centre

Redpoll

12 cm 10-12 g

Sparrow

Male's breast pale pink; becomes deeper pinky-red in summer

Loud, hard 'chuchuchuchuch' call in flight; also fast trill; and loud twangy 'tsooeee' when perched

While linnets are ground birds, redpolls are mostly seen in trees. They do, though, feed on the ground with other finches in weedy fields or on fallen seeds beneath birch and larch trees. Usually, however, redpolls are seen flying over their nesting area with bouncy flight and loud, tinny trills; or in the highest twigs of trees such as birch, alder and various conifers where they can find an abundance of seeds. In winter they are frequently mixed with siskins.

They have, in places, become birds of the suburbs, nesting in large gardens and parks, although only a few decades ago they were restricted to edges of upland woods and bushy slopes. Their four or five eggs hatch after ten to 11 days and the young fly within two weeks.

Smaller than sparrow; neat, slim, long-winged finch. Very small, triangular bill. Long wing tips and slender forked tail. Quite acrobatic in thin twigs or on tall weed stems.

WHERE AND WHEN Northern Europe, northern Britain; moves south and west in winter to northern and eastern France, Italy.

PLACES IT PREFERS Young conifers, mixed, open woods, moorland edges; in winter, alder and birch thickets.

LOOKALIKES

Twite, page 380, has no red on head or black on chin, and has white streaks in wing.

Linnet, page 352, bigger, less streaked, less often in trees.

Crossbill

Loxia curvirostra

Crossed bill unique except for Scottish crossbill (only in northern Scotland) and parrot crossbill (Scandinavia)

Juvenile pale, greenish with close, thin, dark streaks

Female greenish with brown wings, yellow rump

Old male red with browner wings and tail

Crossbill

17 cm 35-50 g

Sparrow

Younger male browner, or greenish with redder patches; bright, pale red rump

Calls loud, echoing, sudden 'chip chip chip' or 'glip glip glip'. Varied song

Crossbills live almost entirely on the seeds of conifers. In most places what you see is the common crossbill, eating seeds of various pines, spruce and larch. But where bigger, tougher pine cones grow in Scotland and Scandinavia, bigger species have formed, with even bigger bills. In fact each area with crossbills – the Alps, the Pyrenees, the Balearic Islands – tends to have its own distinctive form.

All crossbills tend to be quiet when feeding, moving like mice through the upper branches of trees and dropping bits of pine cone, or whole cones. Then they burst out with loud calls, or move to the very tops of the trees for a while before flying off.

The four eggs hatch within 12 to 13 days but the young do not fly until 17 to 25 days old.

Big, heavy finch. Head rounded, even domed, or with flatter crown. Stumpy body but long wing tips; forked tail. Very short legs. Bill thick, looks hooked; in fact tips of mandibles are crossed. Acrobatic, even almost parrot-like when feeding.

WHEN AND WHERE All year in north, parts of UK, Alps, parts of Iberia; scattered widely in late summer, autumn.

PLACES IT PREFERS Conifer forest; shelter belts of pine, spruce and larch.

LOOKALIKES

Bullfinch, page 358, different colour pink and pale grey.

Scarlet rosefinch, page 380, smaller, bill rounded.

Greenfinch, page 346, most like female crossbill, but has yellow in wings and tail.

Bullfinch

Pyrrhula pyrrhula

Male pale blue-grey on top; vivid pink underneath

Bill, chin, neat skull cap all inky black

Large, clean white rump patch above blue-black tail

Female soft brown-grey above, dull fawn or pinkish-brown beneath

Black wings have broad greyish and white band

Bullfinch

15 cm   20-25 g

Sparrow

Juvenile is like female, but without black cap

Single, piping 'tsew' or 'sooo' call

The round, broad bill of a bullfinch is ideal for nibbling the layers off the outside of soft buds, or for working into the insides of soft seeds such as ash and sycamore keys. Bullfinches love fruit buds especially, but spend much of their time in hedgerows and like a treat, occasionally, of shrivelled blackberries with their tiny brown seeds.

While feeding, usually two or three at a time, they keep in touch by calling with simple, soft, low whistles. In spring the males have hardly any song except for a few whistles together with strange creaky sounds. Even where they are common, bullfinches are usually quite secretive and easy to miss.

Their four or five eggs hatch out in 12 to 14 days and the chicks fly after 12 to 16 days.

Sparrow-sized; dumpy, rather upright, finch, with broad, flat head, thick bill and square tail. Very short legs; can swivel around twigs to reach food; usually in shrubbery rather than treetops. Flies off low and straight, showing white rump.

WHERE AND WHEN Most of Europe except extreme north and most of Spain. All year.

PLACES IT PREFERS Thick hedges, shrubberies, overgrown ditches, parks, orchards.

LOOKALIKES

Male **chaffinch,** page 340, less red, with no white on rump.
   Brambling, page 342, has smaller white rump patch, much more orange and brown.

Hawfinch

Coccothraustes coccothraustes

Pale grey side to neck contrasts a little with orange cheeks and dull brown back

In flight, shows broad white bands across wings and obvious white tip to short, square tail

Thick-necked, large-headed, top-heavy look, with large, triangular bill

Black bib and mark through eye

Flat crown; long wing tips but short tail

Looks dark on top, paler underneath, with diagonal pale band across wing

Hawfinch
18 cm 25-30 g
Sparrow

Often in small parties under trees or sitting bolt upright high in treetop

Calls like robin, sharp unmusical 'tik'

The hawfinch is known as a secretive bird, difficult to see, but sometimes it allows a close approach: although they keep quiet and well hidden, once you see one, you could well get a clear view. Usually there are several together, either a family in summer or a little flock in winter, gathered to feed on certain tree seeds or fruits. The big, sharp-edged bill is for cracking open fruit stones and peeling tough seeds.

In Northern and Western Europe this is a bird of open woodland and tall shrubs, but in the Mediterranean region it is often found in olive groves and orchards, sometimes mixing with chaffinches to feast on the fruits.

The four to six eggs take nine to ten days to hatch and the young fly after just ten to 11 days.

Thickset, heavy-headed, short-tailed. Sits upright in treetops, or feeds quietly in lower twigs or on ground. Flies with 'tik' call, to perch high up or fly off over wood out of sight. Has traditional areas; rare away from regular haunts.

WHERE AND WHEN Central Europe, UK, all year; summer only in east, winter in most of Spain, Portugal.

PLACES IT PREFERS Orchards, olive groves, woods with hornbeam, beech, cherry.

LOOKALIKES

Chaffinch, page 340, is much smaller-billed, with a smaller head, and a different pattern in wings and tail.

Snow bunting

Plectrophenax nivalis

A ground bird, never in trees but sometimes perches on buildings

Female and juvenile have less white in wing than male ___

Short black legs; in winter, bill yellow

___ Male has white head and underparts in summer. In winter back warm brown, head marked with orange-brown or chestnut-red

Wings white with black tips

Snow bunting

17 cm 30-35 g

Sparrow

Birds in winter flocks are mostly warm brown with red-brown on head and sides of chest; dull white beneath

Calls twittering, liquid, rippling 'tililililip' and loud, full 'tsew'

In summer, snow buntings are found only along the peaks of Scandinavia and Scotland and a few places in Iceland. They nest amongst boulders and feed alongside beds of permanent snow. In winter they move south, to the coasts of Britain and the Low Countries, where they feed along strand lines of sea-weed and assorted flotsam on sandy or pebbly beaches. They seem almost to disappear when they settle to feed, suddenly flying up and away, flickering white as they fly.

Only in summer are male snow buntings really black and white. Most people see their winter plumage, with rusty marks on their heads and only a little white showing on the wings.

The four to six eggs hatch within 12 to 14 days and the chicks fly ten to 12 days later.

Bigger than a sparrow. Stocky, long-bodied, short-legged. Runs along ground, looking low, horizontal; flies in light, airy bounds. Often in small flocks, sometimes scores. Feeds busily, nibbling among seed heads and fallen stems, or on the tideline.

WHERE AND WHEN Northern Scotland, Scandinavia in summer; in winter also east coast of UK, Denmark to northern France.

PLACES IT PREFERS Mountains; high moorland plateaux, sandy beaches, salt marsh.

LOOKALIKES

Lapland bunting has less white.
  Finches with white in wing usually perch in bushes or trees, unlike snow bunting.

Yellowhammer

Emberiza citrinella

Female's tail and rump same as male's

Female duller than male; pale, less yellow, with blurred streaks on breast, pale lemon-yellow belly

Upperparts rich orange-brown, streaked black

Male bright, with mainly yellow head and breast

Rump red-brown; tail black with white sides

Head yellow with greenish-black bands, blue-grey bill

Yellowhammer
16 cm 25-30 g

Sparrow

Calls sharp, metallic 'tswick'; song lazy, sharp, monotonous ticking sound with piping note at end, 'ti-ti-ti-ti-ti-ti-titeeee'

The thin repetitive song of the yellowhammer really is a sound of summer: it sings all through the hottest months and the middle of the day when many other birds are silent. The male, sitting on top of a gorse bush or hawthorn hedge, singing with little variation over and over again, is a lovely sight, one of the brightest yellow birds in Europe.

In winter, groups of yellowhammers roam the fields and also the edges of salt marshes, even beaches, where weeds and seeds are washed up. Here they feed on the ground, inconspicuous until disturbed, when they fly off low, flicking their tails, like buntings rather than the more compact, dashing finches.

Their three to six eggs hatch after 12 to 14 days and the chicks fly when 12 to 13 days old.

Slim, with sharp face, flat crown, long forked tail. Often sits upright on bush or fence. Flocks in winter, usually scattered, sometimes mixed with sparrows and finches. Often flies up in loose group to perch in hedge, then back to ground one by one.

WHERE AND WHEN All Europe except Spain and Portugal in summer; moves south in winter.

PLACES IT PREFERS Farmland with hedges, open slopes with bushes, high Alpine meadows.

LOOKALIKES

Female **cirl bunting,** page 366, very like female yellowhammer, but has duller rump, less yellow below.

Cirl bunting

Emberiza cirlus

Male red-brown on back, paler below. Pattern of reddish, green and yellow on chest not always obvious

Black chin and throat usually best feature to note. Yellow stripes beneath throat, below and above eye

Compared with female yellowhammer, head shows slightly firmer dark bands across cheek and below eye, and more uniform dark cap contrasting with stripe over eye

Black stripe through eye

Female like yellowhammer, but rump dull, back with redder marks, breast with thinner, blacker streaks

Cirl bunting

16 cm 25 g

Sparrow

Call almost always the same simple, sharp 'sip'. Song loud, flat, hard rattle or faster, tinnier trill

This is a bird of warm, sunny, often rocky slopes with scattered bushes and close-cropped grass. In Britain it likes hedges and open fields on south-facing slopes above the coast. It looks a little like a yellowhammer (the female is very similar) but in Southern Europe is found lower down, in hotter places, or on more scrubby, stony slopes rather than lush farmland or high plateaux where the yellowhammers live.

In Britain, winter stubble fields are important to the cirl bunting; here it finds plenty of spilt grain and tiny weed seeds. Small flocks spend the cold months on stubble fields before spreading out on to their nesting territories in spring. The three to four eggs hatch in 12 to 14 days, and the chicks fly when 11 to 13 days old.

Sparrow-sized; slim, with long, forked tail. Neat, triangular bill; slightly peaky rear crown. Looks more compact than yellowhammer. Often in pairs; usually on or near the ground but sings from sides of trees or treetops. Sometimes in flocks in winter.

WHERE AND WHEN Southern Europe north to northern France, south-western England, all year.

PLACES IT PREFERS Bushy slopes, hedges, farmland, edges of poplar plantations.

LOOKALIKES

Yellowhammer, page 364, brighter yellow (male) with rusty rump.

Ortolan bunting, page 379, has yellow throat, orange belly.

Reed bunting

Emberiza schoeniclus

Head has dark crown, cheeks and stripe from base of bill; and creamy stripe beneath cheek

Male looks yellowish- or reddish-brown, with black streaks on back and a broad white collar

Female's tail like male's

Winter: blurred and brown

Female heavily streaked; often two broad cream lines down back

Breast dull white with black streaks

Tail black with broad white sides

Call loud, full 'tseu' and sharp, very high 'tsi'

Reed bunting

16 cm 16-20 g

Sparrow

Song short, un-musical, monotonous: slightly jangling, same phrase repeated over and over

Head black in summer with white 'moustache'

Reed buntings are waterside birds that have spread, in places, to drier habitats such as winter fields and even gardens. Some now breed in the damp rushes and bracken at the foot of moorland slopes and boggy valleys, but most are still found in true lowland – watersides with swamps and stands of reeds.

Here they are easily spotted: the males often sing in spring and summer, with a typically unmusical bunting sound, yet still very pleasant on a warm summer's day. In spring, they join migrant wagtails and pipits and feed on short grass beside lakes and reservoirs; in winter they roam the fields with finch flocks or flit about on their own in waterside willow thickets.

Four or five eggs hatch in 13 to 14 days; the chicks fly at ten to 13 days old.

Sparrow-sized, with longer tail. Rather thick, short bill. Head slightly peaked. Loose-looking tail often flicked out sideways and jerked in flight. Perches upright on bush top or tall, upright stem; feeds on ground or in waterside vegetation.

WHERE AND WHEN All Europe, except most of Iberia in summer; in winter leaves Northern and Eastern Europe, some move to Spain.

PLACES IT PREFERS Waterside swamps, ditches, reeds; damp patches on moors; stubble fields.

LOOKALIKES

Female **sparrow,** page 338, plain underneath.

Female **yellowhammer,** page 364, less reddish or buff, more yellow, with chestnut rump.

Corn bunting

Miliaria calandra

Pale brown with fine streaks. Head sometimes shows bolder pattern with dark cap and lower edge to cheek

Bill noticeably large, pale, looks slightly tilted forward

Tail plain pale brown, no black or white

Large, like skylark, but perches upright – lark stands horizontally on wall or fence but not in trees or upright on wires

Perches on twig, wire or mound of earth, singing with dry, shaking jingle, like rattled keys

Corn bunting
18 cm 40-50 g

Sparrow

Call short, hard 'plip' or 'tik', thicker, less metallic than yellowhammer's spidery call

This is the heavyweight among the finches and buntings, looking almost as big as a starling. It is a rather plain bird, dull brown and streaky, yet has a fascinating lifestyle. Males sometimes pair up with several females and they defend territories by singing over and over again from prominent perches or, if need be, from the ground.

Their numbers have declined in many areas as farming methods have reduced the number of insects in summer and weed seeds in winter: the corn bunting has vanished from many traditional haunts. It has become, with the skylark, a barometer of the health of the 'common' farmland bird.

The three to five eggs hatch in 12 to 13 days and the young fly within just nine to 12 days.

Round head; large, triangular bill. Long, square tail. Pale; close views show narrow streaks but no bright colours. Often in small flocks outside breeding season; in flight overhead looks big and chunky and has distinctive abrupt calls.

WHERE AND WHEN Most of Europe except Scandinavia; all year.

PLACES IT PREFERS Warm slopes, farmland, cereal fields; also wilder coastal districts in north and west.

LOOKALIKES
Sparrows, page 338, not streaked on breast.
Smaller buntings have white in tail.
Skylark, page 228, has white in tail, walks on ground.

Rare, localized, difficult to see

The birds in this back section are one (or more) of these types:
- Scarce over the whole of the book's range
- Absent over most of the book's range, but locally common

Great northern diver
Gavia immer
80 cm 1,600-4,000 g

Black-throated diver
Gavia arctica
70 cm 1,300-3,400 g

Rare in summer, more frequent from autumn to spring. **Identification** Black head, chequered back in summer; dark brown in winter with white breast, back of head blacker than back. **Character** Heavy, cormorant-sized diving bird with dagger-bill. Flies with drooped head, wings long and slim. **Where and when** Breeds in Iceland; coasts of Scandinavia, North Sea, Channel, Ireland in winter.

Found on remote northern lakes in summer, moving south around European coasts in winter. **Identification** Grey head, chequered back, dagger-bill in summer; in winter almost black and white, back of head greyer than back. **Character** Sleek diving bird, never on land. Flies with head and feet extended, wings long and slim. **Where and when** Scandinavia, Scotland; coasts in winter.

Red-throated diver
Gavia stellata
60 cm 1,000-1,600 g

Slavonian grebe
Podiceps auritus
35 cm 375-470 g

Breeds on small pools, usually feeds in the sea. Scarce, inhabits remote areas. **Identification** Sleek diving bird; in summer, grey head, dark throat (actually red), brown back. In winter, back brown, speckled with white, face largely white. **Character** Slender, with tapered bill held tilted up at a slight angle. **Where and when** Scandinavia, Scotland; in winter on coasts farther south.

A rare northern bird found on wild moorland lakes. **Identification** Reddish neck and flanks, black head with straight golden ear tufts in summer; in winter black and white with clean-cut black cap, white face. **Character** Can look dumpy or long-necked; short tailed, buoyant. **Where and when** Breeds Scotland, Scandinavia. Rare but widespread on north-western European coasts in winter.

- Restricted to a rare or specialized habitat
- Hard to see
- Require a special journey

Black-necked grebe
Podiceps nigricollis
30 cm 250-400 g

Mainly Eastern Europe, widely scattered; always rare in west. **Identification** In spring, black neck, peaked head with golden, drooped ear tufts; in winter black with white breast, smudged grey face below black cap. **Character** Light, dumpy diving bird with slightly up-tilted bill. **Where and when** Denmark, Germany; rare in UK and France in summer; UK, French and North Sea coasts in winter.

Storm petrel
Hydrobates pelagicus
15 cm 20-30 g

Large numbers breed on islands, but rarely seen from land. Visits nest at night. **Identification** Blackish, with square white rump, white line under wing. **Character** A tiny seabird, flying with fluttery wing beats and swallow-like swoops low over the sea. **Where and when** Islands off north-western Europe, western Mediterranean and open sea; April to October.

Purple heron
Ardea purpurea
85 cm 600-1,200 g

A secretive heron of marshes, rarely seen in the open. **Identification** A dark heron, neck striped orange and black; wine-red patch on front of wing. **Character** Tall, slender; snake-like head and bill stretched forward or upwards; stalks through reeds; flies like grey heron but neck more angular. **Where and when** Scattered south from Netherlands; April to October.

Bittern
Botaurus stellaris
80 cm 850-1,900 g

A rarely seen bird of reed-beds, entirely restricted to this special habitat. **Identification** Almost grey heron-sized, bright tawny-brown with complex bars and streaks. **Character** Long, thick neck, dagger-bill. Secretive, stretches upright in reeds when alert; flies with arched wings like heron. **Where and when** Very sparse; absent from most of Scandinavia; all year.

Rare, localized, difficult to see

Black stork
Ciconia nigra
100 cm 205-3 kg

A stately, upstanding woodland stork, rare in Western Europe. **Identification** Bigger than a heron, with red, dagger-like bill, long red legs; all black except for white belly and 'armpits'. **Character** A slender stork; flies on long, fingered, flat wings, head outstretched. Soars and glides magnificently. **Where and when** Rare, Spain, Belgium; rare migrant elsewhere. April to September.

Goshawk
Accipiter gentilis
50-60 cm 600-1,500 g

A generally rare, fierce forest predator; females bigger than males.
Identification Grey-brown above, grey-white below. In flight, head longer and rounder, wings longer than sparrow-hawk's. Tail longer and underwing plainer than buzzard's. **Character** Hard to see unless dashing out over open ground. **Where and when** All year, all of Europe, but rare in many areas.

Ruddy duck
Oxyura jamaicensis
40 cm 550-750 g

Introduced by accident, from North America. Rare except in UK.
Identification Spring male reddish, with black cap, white face, blue bill. In winter, dull with white face; dumpier than female smew, with plain wings. Female dark, with dark line crossing pale cheeks. **Character** Small, dumpy, round-bodied duck, often in flocks. **Where and when** UK all year; may spread elsewhere.

Ptarmigan
Lagopus mutus
35 cm 250-550 g

Restricted to high peaks and bleak, cold northern moors. **Identification** Grey, peppered darker in spring; browner with buff speckles in summer; white in winter, male with black near bill. Tail always black, wings always white. **Character** Tame, small chicken-like bird, creeping over rocks and gravel. **Where and when** Rare, Pyrenees, Alps; peaks of Scotland; Scandinavia, Iceland. All year.

Black grouse
Tetrao tetrix
40-55 cm 950-1,500 g

A declining bird of heaths and moor where trees are mixed with heather. **Identification** Blue-black male with curved tail; white wing bars and 'powder puff' under tail unique; female like round-tailed hen pheasant. **Character** Large, chicken-like bird; flies fast, straight and quite high. **Where and when** Northern Britain, Scandinavia; scarce in Alps, Central Europe. All year.

Capercaillie
Tetrao urogallus
60-87 cm 1,800-4,500 g

Giant turkey-like bird, confined to northern conifer forests. Female is smaller and different in colour from male.
Identification Male blackish with pale bill, 'beard', white wing spots, huge round tail; female barred brown with orange chest.
Character Secretive and shy, but males crash out of trees or heather if disturbed.
Where and when Scandinavia; rare in Scotland, Pyrenees, Alps. All year.

Corncrake
Crex crex
30 cm 120-200 g

A rare and declining bird of hayfields and iris beds. **Identification** Call harsh, repeated 'crek crek'; hard to see; warm brown, streaked dark, wings orange-red. **Character** Creeps through dense crops, rarely in the open; stops to call, head stretched up, tossed back with each 'crake'. **Where and when** Rare in Ireland, Hebrides, France; more in Eastern Europe. April to September.

Dotterel
Charadrius morinellus
20 cm 100-120 g

A scarce bird of northern hills, and a rare migrant in the south. **Identification** Black cap with white stripes meeting as V at rear. In summer, pale breast band, black belly; in autumn buff-brown, mottled on back, hint of breast band. **Character** Stop-start running action like ringed plover's; dumpy at rest, slender if alert. **Where and when** Scotland, Scandinavia. April to September.

Rare, localized, difficult to see

Temminck's stint
Calidris temminckii
13 cm   20-30 g

Little stint
Calidris minuta
13 cm   20-30 g

A rare northern wader, always scarce, even on migration. **Identification** Legs greenish or yellow-ochre. Dull, grey-brown above, white below with dusky chest like tiny common sandpiper. White on sides of tail shows in flight. **Character** Slim, sluggish bird of wet grass, sticky mud by fresh water. **Where and when** Rare breeder in Scandinavia; scarce migrant, mostly in Southern Europe.

Small wading bird, often with dunlins, but usually small numbers. **Identification** White underparts, black legs, short black bill. Mostly seen in autumn: breast pale buff, red-brown with dark spots above, pale V high on back. **Character** Sparrow-sized; tiny, quick wader, smaller than sanderling. **Where and when** Migrant in spring, more in early autumn; muddy coasts, fresh water.

Black guillemot
Cepphus grylle
30 cm   350-450 g

Little auk
Alle alle
18 cm   140-170 g

A lovely northern seabird, which rarely moves south. **Identification** In summer, smoky-black except for white wing patch, red legs, red inside mouth. In winter, mottled black and white with same white wing patch. **Character** Buoyant swimmer, dives frequently. Whirring flight low over the sea. **Where and when** Scandinavia, Iceland, Scotland and Ireland, all year.

Breeds in the north but some years moves south over North Sea. **Identification** Black and white; black head in summer, throat and breast white in winter. Tiny black bill, black cap; white streaks on shoulders. **Character** Tiny, bouncy seabird, swims like a cork, flight fast, whirring. Often sick and dejected but fit birds lively. **Where and when** Off coasts in autumn and winter gales.

Woodlark
Lullula arborea
15 cm 25-35 g

A beautiful singer, sparse or rare on bushy heaths and woodland clearings. **Identification** Bright, streaky; long cream stripe above eye, rufous cheeks, black and white patch at edge of wing. **Character** Elusive; creeps low to ground; in flight, very short tail and broad, floppy wings. Repetitive fluty song. **Where and when** Most of Europe, rare Scandinavia and UK, all year.

Water pipit
Anthus spinoletta
17 cm 19-25 g

In summer, only on Alpine meadows; in winter, moves down to coasts and fresh water. **Identification** Dark-legged pipit; white stripe over eye. In summer, head grey, breast pink or buff. In winter, plain brown above with two white wing bars, white below, streaked dark. **Character** Shy and elusive in winter. **Where and when** Alps, Pyrenees; winter, Iberia, France, rare UK.

Shore lark
Eremophila alpestris
16 cm 30-45 g

A rare northern lark most often seen when it appears on sandy shores and salt marshes in winter. **Identification** Grey-brown, white beneath, with dark breast band (crisp black in summer). Pale yellow face with black mask, less clear in winter. **Character** Long, low, short-legged lark, easily missed. **Where and when** Breeds on Scandinavian fells; in winter on North Sea coasts.

Tawny pipit
Anthus campestris
16 cm 20-25 g

A sparse, wagtail-like bird of dry heath and bushy slopes. **Identification** Pale brown with white-edged dark tail; row of dark spots along front of closed wing. Long pinkish legs. **Character** Runs, stops in rather upright pose; long tail obvious in flight. Song flight undulating, with repeated 'chu-veee' calls. **Where and when** April to September; most of Europe except Scandinavia, UK.

Rare, localized, difficult to see

Grasshopper warbler
Locustella naevia
13 cm 11-15 g

Marsh warbler
Acrocephalus palustris
12 cm 10-18 g

Hard to see, easier to hear: prolonged high, unmusical, fast, trilling song like freewheeling bicycle. **Identification** Dull, brown, with soft dark streaks, white on chin. **Character** Slim, with rounded tail; creeps like mouse in long grass and low bushes; sits on bush to sing. **Where and when** Most of Europe except southern Spain, northern Scandinavia; April to September.

One of several almost identical 'reed' warblers. **Identification** Dull, plain olive-brown, pale beneath. Rather rounded tail, spiky bill. Song richer, much more fluent than reed warbler's, full of imitations. **Character** Elusive, slipping through reeds, nettles, bushes. **Where and when** Mostly from northern France and Netherlands eastwards across Europe; rare Scandinavia and UK.

Cetti's warbler
Cettia cetti
14 cm 10-18 g

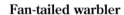

Fan-tailed warbler
Cisticola juncidis
10 cm 8-12 g

Not uncommon in Mediterranean countries, rarer farther north. Always hard to spot. **Identification** Dark, red-brown with pale underside; rounded dark reddish tail. Pale grey line over eye. **Character** Skulks low in bushes or ditches; sudden outburst of very loud, bright song distinctive. **Where and when** France, Iberia, Italy; rare in Low Countries, southern UK. All year.

The only European *Cisticola*, a common group in Africa. **Identification** Tiny, pale sandy-brown with dark streaks on back; cocked or twisted tail shows white spots beneath tip. **Character** Flits through tall grasses. Song flight in long, high and jerky arcs with a short, sharp, buzzing 'dzit' with each undulation. **Where and when** Southern and western France, Iberia, Italy, all year. Rare elsewhere.

Bluethroat
Luscinia svecica
14 cm 15-25 g

Often skulks in bushes near reed-beds, but a fine singer. Restricted distribution. **Identification** Dull brown on top, white below, with white stripe over eye and bright reddish sides to tail. Male has blue on breast, female marked with black and buff. **Character** robin-like, tail often cocked. **Where and when** Scattered from Scandinavia to Spain; rare migrant in UK. April to October.

Ring ouzel
Turdus torquatus
24 cm 100-125 g

Mostly restricted to uplands, more widespread (but scarce) on migration. **Identification** Male black with paler wings and white crescent on breast; female dull with scaly underparts, dull chest band. **Character** Slender, long-tailed thrush, shy and wary. Loud, wild song. **Where and when** Mountains, cliffs, moors; Alps, Scandinavia, UK uplands, Pyrenees. March to September.

Penduline tit
Remiz pendulinus
11 cm 9-12 g

Mainly a reed-bed bird, rare in Western Europe, also found in damp poplar belts near fields and rivers. **Identification** Pale, with reddish back, grey head with black mask (except on young birds). **Character** Tiny; usually in reeds in winter but high in leafy trees in summer; long, high, sharp call like 'tseeee.' **Where and when** Eastern Europe, slowly spreading to the west; all year.

Ortolan bunting
Emberiza hortulana
16 cm 18-30 g

A rather scarce, declining bird of upland farms and bushy slopes. **Identification** Pink bill, pale ring round eye. Male has grey-green head, pale yellow chin, orange breast. Female duller with hint of same pattern. **Character** Shy, easily overlooked, shuffling on ground or perching in bush tops. **Where and when** Northern Spain, southern France, Central Europe, Sweden. April to September.

Rare, localized, difficult to see

Twite
Carduelis flavirostris
14 cm 13-19 g

Restricted to north; an equivalent of the linnet around upland and coastal farms and moors. **Identification** Warm buff-brown; throat bright tawny-buff. Streaked, with wing bar, like redpoll, but also white in wings and tail like linnet. **Character** Usually in small groups; bouncy flight, settling to feed on ground or in low shrubs. Buzzing 'twaa-eet' call. **Where and when** Northern UK, Scandinavia; Baltic and North Sea coasts in winter.

Scarlet rosefinch
Carpodacus erythrinus
14 cm 19-25 g

A rare migrant in Western Europe. Oldest spring males bright strawberry-red, others dull and far less obvious. **Identification** Sparrow-like, with stubby bill. Brown above; two pale wing bars, no white in tail. Female shows beady eye in plain face; head of male orange or red. **Character** Hops on ground near willows, rather shy. **Where and when** Eastern Scandinavia, Eastern Europe; rare migrant in west. April to October.

Nutcracker
Nucifraga caryocatactes
32 cm 110-190 g

Unique crow-like bird, quite common but confined to conifer forests; diet of pine seeds. **Identification** Dark except for white around base of tail. Deep brown cap, black wings and tail; body brown with rows of white spots; bigger than starling. **Character** Bouncy, joyful actions, bounding flight; sits on treetops. **Where and when** All year, southern Scandinavia, Alps; flocks occasionally move west.

Golden oriole
Oriolus oriolus
24 cm 60-80 g

Glorious, but difficult to see. **Identification** Loud, brief, fluty song like 'wheedl-whew', from depths of wood or poplar plantation; male elusive but vivid yellow and black. Female green with yellow rump like green woodpecker but streaks underneath, short pink bill. **Character** Thrush-like but long, slender. **Where and when** Most of Europe except Scandinavia, rare UK. April to August.

INDEX

Index

Index

Editorial Director Andrew Duncan
Art Director Mel Petersen
Editorial assistants Sarah Barlow and Nicola Davies
Designers Beverley Stewart and Christopher Foley
Maps Christopher Foley
All artwork is by **Peter Hayman** except for pages:
100-112, 164-172, 214-218, 222-224, 242-246, 250-264, 272-296, 316-320, 338-344,
348-356, 364-368 and pages 372-380, which are the work of **Richard Allen**

Photographs by
Alan Williams 183 **A.T. Moffett** 97, 101, 111, 115, 195, 219, 239, 243, 247, 263, 265, 267, 275, 287, 299, 313, 323, 325, 329, 331, 333, 335, 339, 341, 347, 365, 371 **Bob Glover** 9, 25, 33, 35, 41, 43, 47, 49, 51, 53, 55, 57, 61, 63, 67, 69, 79, 93, 105, 113, 125, 127, 129, 133, 139, 141, 143, 151, 153, 155, 169, 181, 193, 197, 215, 217, 223, 229, 231, 233, 235, 285, 305, 311, 355 **David Cottridge** 159, 165, 337 **David Kjaer** 261 **Gordon Langsbury** 15, 17, 19, 21, 23, 31, 89, 95, 99, 103, 109, 111, 117, 121, 123, 131, 145, 161, 171, 173, 175, 187, 199, 201, 205, 211, 213, 227, 241, 251, 255, 269, 271, 273, 275, 281, 291, 303, 315, 343, 345, 349, 351, 357, 363, 369 **Mark Hamblin** 27, 37, 71, 301
Robin Chittenden 257, 335 **Roger Wilmshurst** 59, 107, 221, 293, 367
FLPA: B. Borrell 319 David Hosking 207 **E. & D. Hosking** 113 Eric Hosking 283 **F. Merlet** 297
M.B. Withers 91, 153 **M. Gore** 283 Roger Tidman 145 Silvestris 209
Other sources: Andrew Hay 191 Carlos Sanchez 83, 119, 353 Chris Gomersall 85, 157, 163, 179, 189, 259
Colin Carver 327 David Kjaer 157 **E. Woods** 193 Frank Blackburn 289 George McCarthy 45, 65, 149, 167, 185, 203 Gerald Downey 97, 149, 225, 237, 307, 319 Gordon Langsbury 137 Jan Sevcik 171
M.K. Walker 277, 307, 317 Malcolm Hunt 295, 297 Mark Hamblin 75, 89, 135, 239, 249, 253, 309, 359
Michael Gore 321 Michael W. Richards **177**, 279 Mike Lane 11, 37, 45 P. Doherty 29, 81 **P.R. Perfect** 39
Philip J. Newman 203 Richard Brooks 243, 247 361 Richard Revels 71, 191, 245
Roger Tidman 321 Roger Wilmshurst 77, 163, 185, 329 **S.C. Porter** 147 Steve Knell 13, 87, 127, 179, 295
Tony Hamblin 257 W.S. Paton 73, 83